FROM THE OLD COUNTRY

An Oral History of European Migration to America

BRUCE M. STAVE   JOHN F. SUTHERLAND
with ALDO SALERNO

FROM THE OLD COUNTRY

An Oral History of
European Migration to America

UNIVERSITY PRESS OF NEW ENGLAND
Hanover and London

University Press of New England, Hanover, NH 03755
© 1994 by Twayne Publishers
All rights reserved

Originally published in cloth by Twayne Publishers in 1994.
University Press of New England paperback edition published in 1999,
by arrangement with Macmillan Publishing.

Printed in the United States of America   5   4   3   2   1
CIP data appear at the end of the book

To the Memory of
Linda Collett Sutherland, 1940–1995
and for
Stephanie Ray Sutherland and
Sondra Astor and Channing M-L Stave
and for
the memory of the great-grandparents and grandparents
of Bruce M. Stave and John F. Sutherland,
who migrated to America

Contents

Acknowledgments		*ix*
Introduction		*xi*
1	The Homeland	1
2	Crossing and Arrival	25
3	At Work in America	51
4	Family and Community	93
5	Women and Men, Love and Marriage	139
6	Immigrants United and Divided	175
Conclusion		*235*
Notes and References		*257*
Bibliography		*271*
Index		*277*

Illustrations follow page 138

Acknowledgments

The immigrant voices heard in this volume resonate from the true authors of this book. We thank the many individuals who were interviewed for our own oral history projects and by the WPA Ethnic Group Survey more than half a century ago. An oral history interview is a partnership between an interviewee and an interviewer, and we acknowledge with gratitude the interviewers, both past and present, who captured these echoes of the European migration.

Our academic institutions have supported this effort. We thank the University of Connecticut Research Foundation and its director, Thomas G. Giolas, for the grant that assisted our research and writing. President Jonathan Daube and Dean Luene Corwin of Manchester Community-Technical College and William Dowd and Mary Ann Handley, chairs of the Social Science Department, consistently supported the Institute of Local History, which is the source of some of the interviews found here. Similarly, the University of Connecticut has encouraged the Center for Oral History, whose projects produced many of the narratives in this volume. The sabbatical leave granted to Bruce Stave during the fall of 1991 helped bring this effort to a conclusion. We appreciate the inspiration of William V. D'Antonio who initiated the Peoples of Connecticut Project two decades ago while a University of Connecticut Sociologist. Both of us acknowledge the friendship and support of our departmental colleagues.

Randall Jimerson, director of the University of Connecticut Homer Babbidge Library Division of Historical Manuscripts and Archives, provided generous access to the WPA collections and made us feel welcome even when our demands upon his time and staff were inconvenient. Lisa Ferriere, Dee Gosline, and Roberta Lusa of the UConn Department of History staff assisted greatly with the preparation of the manuscript. Michele Palmer, manager of Tapescribe of the Center for Oral History, and Martha McCormick, an expert transcriber, brought to type the conversation that appears as the final chapter of this book.

The photographs for this volume could not have been selected without the assistance of several dedicated archivists; especially helpful were: Barry Moreno of the Ellis Island Immigration Museum; Mary Witkowski, Diane Kurtz, and Roseanne Mansfield of Historical Collections, Bridgeport Public Library; Theodore Wohlsen of the Connecticut State Library; Stephen Rice of the Connecticut Historical Society; and Herbert Bengston of the Manchester (Connecticut) Historical Society. Sylvian Ofiara, Photographer Emeritus of Manchester Community-Technical College, assisted in photographic reproduction with his usual artistry.

The General Editor of this series, Donald A. Ritchie, encouraged our progress throughout this venture and shared his many insights about oral history. Mark Zadrozny, Lesley Poliner, Katherine Ness, and the editorial staff at Twayne Publishers worked to improve the manuscript. John Sutherland acknowledges a long-standing debt to Allen F. Davis, Herbert J. Bass, and John W. Hakola, who had nothing to do with this book but everything to do with the fact that Sutherland became a historian.

Aldo Salerno began his work on this book as a research assistant and proved so indispensable to its successful completion that he has become a coauthor. He thanks his wife, Leah, for her love and support. We thank him for his outstanding effort. Our families, Sondra Astor Stave and Channing M-L Stave and Linda and Stephanie Ray Sutherland, although busy pursuing their own careers and education, understood and encouraged their husbands' and fathers' need to recapture the echoes of the past.

BRUCE M. STAVE
Coventry, Connecticut
JOHN F. SUTHERLAND
Vernon, Connecticut

Introduction

Almost a quarter century ago, the popular writer Studs Terkel began his oral history of the Great Depression, *Hard Times*, by noting that it was a "memory book, rather than one of hard fact or precise statistic."[1] Ours, too, is a "memory book," bringing together many individual recollections regarding the immigrant and ethnic experience. We recognize that no one immigrant is every immigrant and that memory has many filters. Nevertheless, we hope the reminiscences collected in this volume will add to the general understanding of immigration in American life.

The immigrants we deal with are those who came from Europe during the great migrations of the nineteenth and early twentieth centuries. We also include interviews with their children and in some instances with their grandchildren.

Between approximately 1820 and 1914, 30 million Europeans came to the United States; 5 million were German, 4.5 million each came from Ireland and Italy, more than 2.5 million each were English or Polish, and 2 million Jews arrived. The origins of these immigrants shifted as the nineteenth century progressed into the early twentieth. This is clearly demonstrated by an examination of the two peak years of European immigration. In 1882, 87 percent came from northern and western Europe; in 1907, on the other hand, 80.7 percent originated in southern and eastern Europe. The impact of this European migration upon both the United States and the countries of origin was dramatic.[2]

Most of these immigrants came seeking the work that was being generated by America's industrial transformation in the late nineteenth and early twentieth centuries, when industrial capitalism in the United States rapidly outpaced economic change in Europe. Capitalists mechanized the means of production and brought large numbers of workers into factories to tend the machines that were mass-producing manufactured goods. Immigrants filled many of these jobs. Some, but not all, were of rural origins and required time to adjust to urban industrial life. Others had already experienced industrial routine in their homelands and brought skills with them, although for some these skills had been rendered obsolete by technological innovation. Adjustment to life in the new land required adapting Old World modes of behavior to the culture of the New World.[3]

Each group brought its own culture and traditions, which were transplanted to, and modified in, the American environment. Similarities and differences appeared within and between groups, and many experiences were shared by all. While it would be a mistake to contend that there was one immigrant experience, while it would be an error to erase the importance of individual decisions that affected the immigrants' experiences, certain commonalities were shared. The decision to pick up and move thousands of miles from one's original home, the crossing from one continent to another, the search for the first job, the initial days at school—all are experiences etched in immigrant memory. Such activity may be mediated by family and community, by a relative who works in the factory, by a teacher who is friendly and speaks your native language or one who makes your day miserable. With this in mind, with an understanding that the universal and the particular are at work simultaneously, we suggest that the interviews found in this volume may be relevant to America's most recent newcomers.

Our concentration on European immigrants does not mean that we are blind to those coming to America today or that we think that the process of immigration ended during the 1920s, when the first major restriction laws went into effect. The fact that the nation at the end of the twentieth century is witness to a new and powerful wave of immigration from other parts of the world makes the European story all the more important. Clearly the origins of today's immigrants have changed. In 1991 the largest numbers came from the former Soviet Union, the Philippines, Vietnam, Mexico, mainland China, India, the Dominican Republic, Korea, Jamaica, and Iran, in that order—a very different mix of national origins from those who came earlier in the century. Such backgrounds add to the nation's cultural diversity just as the Europeans we study here did a hundred or so years ago. Our emphasis on the migration from Europe reflects the time period with which we deal and the sources available.[4]

These sources can be found among the collections of oral histories that we have accumulated during the past two decades at The University of Connecticut Center for Oral History and the Institute of Local History at Manchester (Connecticut) Community-Technical College. These collections range from a continuing study of workers in the Manchester Cheney silk mills to projects that involved Holocaust survivors, women political activists, workers and technological change, left-wing politicians, and, essential for this volume, an oral history study of Connecticut's ethnic groups, undertaken during the 1970s, which emphasized the Irish, Italians, Poles, and Jews. All of these projects involved tape-recorded interviews, which followed standard oral history practice. With the exception of some of the Manchester material, the interviews were transcribed. We have included excerpts from only those interviews for which we received written permission to use the material. Minor changes in language and format have been made for the purpose of clarity.

We began with the intention to build this book primarily around these, our own oral histories. However, we quickly identified another source that became central to our efforts. The WPA (Works Progress Administration) Ethnic Group Survey undertaken during the late 1930s in Connecticut, as well as in other states, included a series of interviews with immigrants and their children that proved so rich in information, description, and memory that it became the core of this work. Since the interviews were conducted from 1938 through 1940, they permit us to push the frontiers of memory back into the second half of the nineteenth century. Linked to our own material, these sources cover at least a century of recollections about the immigrant experience. Again, for purposes of clarity, we have made minor editorial changes.[5]

The WPA interviews enhance this book in several ways. The thrust backward in time to the turn of the century and beyond is certainly valuable, since that era obviously is now lost to living human memory. Moreover, the people interviewed by the WPA generally were closer to the immigrant experience than were those we interviewed during the 1970s and 1980s. Often (but not always) their memory portraits are clearer and more graphic. But there also is considerable value simply in possessing interviews conducted during the 1930s. Those were desperate years, when the Great Depression was challenging fundamental assumptions about the viability of American industrial capitalism. Many of these first- and second-generation immigrants saw their hopes and dreams disintegrate during these years. Their recollections have a sharp and sometimes bitter edge; they differ qualitatively from the reminiscences of the subjects of the 1970s and 1980s. Their voices resonate with the timbre of the Great Depression.

Then, too, we are reminded by the WPA interviews that some Americans' attitudes toward their neighbors were not generous and were more directly expressed than is common nowadays. These years found the quota restrictions of the 1920s very much in force. Old-stock Americans who had been here for many generations viewed the new immigrants from southern and eastern Europe with suspicion. Prejudices that have long since mellowed were quite real then, particularly in the down-and-out years of the Depression. For example, in 1939 a public opinion poll revealed that 50 percent of the respondents believed Italian-Americans to be the worst citizens of all immigrants. Those prejudices are amply displayed in this book. It is not the antipathy toward southern and eastern Europeans, Jews and African-Americans, that jars our sensibilities, as despicable as such attitudes may be. After all, the diatribes and nastiness are being expressed at a time, regrettably, when blacks were still routinely lynched in the American South and when Hitler was on the rise in Europe. Rather it is the willingness with which such attitudes are expressed to a representative of a government agency that we find shocking today. These interviews remind us that Americans have been divided as often as they have been united.[6]

The WPA interviews present other challenges as well. We are not informed as to all of the procedures followed by the interviewers. Some interviews read as though the interviewers had produced reasonably accurate transcriptions of their conversations. Others consist of interviewer narrative with long interviewee quotations woven throughout. Still others sound suspiciously like edited manuscripts prepared for deposition. Eighty-year-old Mr. H., an Irish immigrant from the Waterford area who lived on State Street in Bridgeport, sounds as if he had read a history book before the interview:

> I came to America in my twentieth year. I came over on one of the old sail vessels. It was a long, dangerous journey. I came for religious and personal freedom to escape English rule. As I think back now, economic conditions were the main reason for my coming. We were very poor.[7]

Whether such a statement represents the actual statement by Mr. H. or the interviewer's attempt to synthesize his notes is difficult to determine. Often the write-up did not come until the next day, if that early. On occasion it was quoted in dialect, sometimes in what appears to be a condescending tone. From lists included in the administrative files of the Connecticut WPA, we were able to identify and contact one of the interviewers. He related how when studying the Poles of New Britain, he received instructions from the head of the project, Dr. Samuel Koenig, who told him and fellow interviewers to do their work as thoroughly as possible: "The doctor told us what he wanted. He told us to get all we can. I wrote it up often the next day, not in a week or two." The former WPA questioner claimed he wasn't sure that he knew the purpose of the material he was collecting, "although it might have been for a history." In those pre–tape recorder days, clearly, his memory of the interview served as a filter for what actually was stated.[8]

Sometimes interviewing occurred in a very informal atmosphere. For example, William J. Becker spoke to a chain-smoking Irish-American in a tavern and was invited "at least half a dozen times to have a drink which was thankfully declined." On other occasions, conversations occurred under an aura of suspicion. Leo Armstrong asked WPA representative P. K. Russo:

> Are you a reporter for one of the Bridgeport newspapers? You're working on the Writers Project? Say, how is that outfit working, still holding out? What's that, a racket? I suppose you have to have pull to get on it. You know, I tried for a couple of years to get on WPA and I was eligible, too. I didn't have a cent, and I needed a job, but all I got was the runaround.[9]

We have few examples of the actual questions asked by WPA workers during an interview. In at least one instance in which we do, the results are disconcerting. The following excerpt reveals naïveté and a tendency toward leading questions on the part of the interviewer, while the interviewee demonstrates considerable common sense:

INTERVIEWER

Evidently, Mr. Califi, you have socialistic ideas. By that I mean that a worker should be paid according to production.

INTERVIEWEE

No, God dam no. I'm no socialist. I was all time strong and work like hell. I work more like four people together, and that's the reason I want get more money. You 'stand now what I mean? Alright, look here. I work for you and I give you lots work for day. Alright, you put me day work, you no give me piece work. Why you do that way, tell me? If I make work for four people, why you no pay me for two people anyway? I know some people work easy and take it easy and no give much profit. That's alright, too. This kind people you give day work, but no give me the same because I make more work for you.

INTERVIEWER

Well, Mr. Califi, that's what we could call share the profit or profit sharing.

INTERVIEWEE

I no care what you call it. Give me my money and I no care for anything you want to call it.[10]

And what are we to make of this exchange?

INTERVIEWEE

Well, you like to know too much. I like to tell you, too, but you get paid to listen to my story, but me get hell. Anyhow, you good friend the family, and I tell you everything. If someone else com'n my house, I chase'm out, see.

INTERVIEWER

Thank you, Mr. Califi, you shan't regret it, for some day I may do you a good turn.[11]

In actuality Samuel Koenig, the sociologist who directed the WPA project, did provide specific guidelines for his field-workers. Koenig required them to read heavily in the background of the nationality groups under study. His instructions called for each field-worker to write a personal life history before interviewing others. He warned them against stereotypical bias, and above all told them to learn from their interviewees all they could about the culture of the ethnic group and the immigrant experience. They were provided with a sample questionnaire that went into great detail concerning the homeland, family life, attitudes and values, religion, diet, recreation, reasons for emigration, first impressions of America, adjustment, and work. While Koenig instructed his workers to prepare questions in advance, he warned them against continually consulting them during the interview. He warned his staff to "be careful not to believe everything that is told them by the persons being interviewed." Above all, Koenig was seeking an in-depth understanding of the nationality groups he was investigating, and that is what gives his project value today.[12]

We begin this book where the immigrants began—at home in Europe. In chapter 1, immigrants describe their homelands. Many of them were farmers, and uniformly they expressed their discontent with the drudgery of agrarian life. While we recognize that not all European immigrants had such backgrounds, this experience was widespread. The interviews reveal that immigration was a conscious choice for each of them. For some, departure from the cohesive family unit was heart-wrenching; others departed with a good deal of youthful enthusiasm. All make clear that their ambitions could not have been fulfilled within the confinement of their European homes.

Chapter 2 describes the transatlantic crossing and arrival in the United States. Those who speak do not lend credence to the myth of the alienated, uprooted sojourners cast adrift, rootless, without connection to their common past. Most of them had some economic assistance for their journey, from either family at home or relatives in the United States. They usually describe being met upon arrival by family or friends who helped ease their adjustment. Nevertheless the experience was, if not traumatic, certainly adventurous. They encountered shipboard accommodations that were far from luxurious, and most of them gaped in amazement at the tumult and hurly-burly of early-twentieth-century New York City. Little time existed for sightseeing; they had to find jobs.

In chapter 3 the immigrants contend with the all-important task of securing employment. And again they were not alone. Kin and ethnic compatriots actively assisted the job search. Some intervened with their employers; others were valuable simply because they spoke English. Even those who moved from place to place seemed to have friends or at least to have known in what part of town their countrymen lived.[13] Although most lacked skills, some had acquired an introduction to factory routine in Europe. For them the new job held less mystery. While the American work experience differed from that in Europe, immigrants understood that their survival required maintaining the family as an economic unit. In those early years, many labored for their families rather than for themselves.

Family, however, can be overly romanticized as a unifying force. Chapter 4 reveals both cohesion and conflict within the home. While this varied according to ethnic group, generational differences emerged to separate parents and children. Formal education held out hope for advancement, but also blame for distancing the young from their elders. Neighborhoods developed institutions that brought people together but also allowed them to live apart from others unlike themselves. Politics offered recognition to ethnic groups but also intensified ethnic conflict. Family, neighborhood, and community witnessed both unity and division.

Nowhere were the tensions more salient than in the relations between men and women. Chapter 5 reveals the prevailing attitude, particularly during the 1930s, that a woman's place was in the home. That view, of course, reflected the male perspective, although some women accepted it as truth. Again, ethnic differences colored the relations between the sexes. Even where the woman did stay at home, she often controlled the decision-making while frequently deferring to her mate, giving him a false sense of authority. Regardless of such deference, some relationships reflected wife and child abuse exacerbated by alcohol and unemployment. One woman complained of living with an "animal that was no man." Some women, however, moved from the private to the public arena through political activism and into a world quite different from that of their abused sisters.

The tensions revealed in the preceding chapters explode in chapter 6. Practically all of the immigrants confronted prejudice and discrimination from old-stock Americans. That division intensified as a consequence of interethnic rivalry. While examples exist of unity among immigrant groups, frequently they battled each other for the limited resources that society had to offer, particularly during the Great Depression. Fifty years later it is still sobering and embarrassing to read the blatant anti-Semitic remarks made in America on the eve of the Holocaust, often by immigrants who themselves were targets of bigotry. It is no more comfortable to learn of the racism that was expressed then and later. Even in more prosperous times, cultural divisions did not disappear.

Just as we have heard the voices from the old country, in the concluding chapter we hear the voices of the authors as we talk to each other. Through a tape-recorded interview, we employ the oral history technique to convey our purpose in writing this book and what we have learned in doing so. In the final analysis, however, the value of this collection of immigrant interviews rests with the voices of those who spoke to us during the past 20 years and to WPA interviewers 50 years ago.

FROM THE OLD COUNTRY

An Oral History of European Migration to America

I

THE HOMELAND

A stereotypical view of the life left behind by most European immigrants is that of a timeless, unchanging medieval environment. Historian Victor R. Greene's description of a late-nineteenth-century Polish village is eloquent in its simplicity:

. . . small huts grouped along a dirt road and surrounded by mud, filth, and a few stray dogs, some chickens, and perhaps a duck. The interior [of the hut] confirmed the exterior destitution. A hall separated two dark rooms, living quarters on the left and a combined tool shed and barn on the right.

The living area was dominated by a large brick stove, which served for cooking as well as a bed for the family in cold weather. Straw mats covered part of the earthen floor. A bench stood at one side, and the only other furniture was a table and a chest. A crucifix hanging over the doorway and perhaps a gilded picture of the Virgin above the chest provided the only interior decoration.[1]

Such descriptions are indeed similar to some contained in the interviews examined for this book. An example is the portrait given in 1980 by Lucy Richardson of Manchester, Connecticut, of her little native village of hand-loom weavers in Bann Foot, Northern Ireland, in the early twentieth century:

There was a little street with 10 houses on each side. That was in the middle of the countryside. There was a pump right in the middle of that street, right beside my home, and the public house was right there. I was born right beside the public house, and that was away at the end of the world as I thought as a child. Living there with the Bann River on one side, it seemed that I was surrounded. I was away from everything, and that was the end of the world for me. I remember this anyway.[2]

. But such images conceal the fact that many European communities were undergoing considerable change in the nineteenth century, and almost all were enduring, directly or indirectly, the effects of the enormous economic tumult that was upending traditional society throughout most of the world. Commercial and industrial capitalism extended its reach into all European countries, causing changes in the economic and social environment—changes that often created the conditions that encouraged emigration. Except in Ireland and France, population increases throughout Europe dimmed the hopes of millions of would-be landowners. At the same time, from Ireland to the disintegrating Austro-Hungarian Empire, farm consolidation in favor of commercial, rather than subsistence, agriculture forced, or "freed," peasants from the land. Foreign tariff policies had a negative impact upon home industries such as tin-plating in Wales and wine-making in Italy. And the importation of cheap mass-produced factory goods severely restricted the competitive abilities of local craftsmen. All nations, regardless of the progress of their own industrialization, were affected by the industrial transformation of much of the Western world throughout the late nineteenth and early twentieth centuries. Even the tiniest villages could not insulate themselves from the economic changes that were transforming the United States and Europe.[3]

The migration that followed should not be portrayed as an evacuation of Europe's "wretched" poor and "teeming masses." This flight-from-poverty thesis dominates popular immigration imagery. Most research has indicated, however, that the immigrants, while certainly not well-to-do, were generally not among the very poorest, but were from what historian John Bodnar characterizes as "the middle and lower-middle levels of their social structures."[4] Even in the late nineteenth century, when a higher proportion of day laborers and farm laborers emigrated, they had to pay for the journey, and to satisfy inspectors that they would not become public wards in the United States, they had to possess a small amount of money when they arrived. Fares often were provided by remittances sent back by earlier emigrants.[5]

The immigrants, regardless of their points of origin, shared a sense of dissatisfaction with their homelands. Those who worked on farms, whether as landowners or as tenants, complained of long hours, drudgery, and little reward. They had enough to eat, but their recollections are of unrelenting dreariness. In 1978 Ignazio Ottone of Manchester, Connecticut, described the work on his father's farm in Cicarro Monferrato, in Italy. The fact that he was not a tenant was of no comfort.

We start to work on the farm from 3:00 in the morning, milk the cow, to plough, and then work till sundown. That's why I left and come to this country. . . . Because I don't like to work on the farm. It was too hard over there. . . .

I liked it but it was too much, too many hours, for nothing. You worked for 10¢, 15¢ a day. I worked 20 hours a day. . . . I worked for my father. Once in a while we had time off; we'd go help somebody else, you know. . . . My father died in an accident in 1907, and I had to take over the farm myself. My brother, he went to California; then I wrote him a letter and he came right back. And then I didn't like it over there and I came over here [in 1907].[6]

Similarly, Nathan Nussenbaum, an Austrian Jew, emigrated from his father's farm in 1896. When interviewed for the WPA in 1940, he recalled:

I first saw the light of day in a small town in Austria, a town named Zwiael. It was so small that we did not have any public schools. I lived on a farm with my parents and I never had the chance to enjoy the many activities that a boy should have. The other boys in the town were as hard hit that way as I was. I did not complain; I just made the most of conditions.

Both my father and mother were born in Zwiael and they were married there. My father was always a farmer. He raised enough produce to keep us in "eats" but we did not have much money. I wanted to go to school, but the only kind of school in our town was a private one and my father sent me to it for a while.

I had five sisters and four brothers. I was the third oldest. We all lived on the farm while growing up and we helped with the chores. You may not believe it, but I used to milk cows, feed the chickens, hitch the horse to the wagon and did other things I was asked to do. I never liked farm life and made up my mind I would get away from it as soon as I could. My parents were good to me; in fact, they were good to my sisters and brothers but I had a hankering to come to the United States and that longing never got out of my system.[7]

"I Was Born a Farmer's Son; I Would Have Died a Farmer."

The family emerges from these interviews as the most significant unit in the European social order, regardless of country. The family was the collective economic unit before which most individual desires had to be subordinated in the cause of survival. All family members, including schoolchildren, were expected to work on the farm, whether tenant or family-owned.[8] It is that aspect of their childhood which most interviewees, regardless of nationality or generation, recall most vividly. Anthony Tapogna emigrated from Italy with his family at the age of 10 in 1920. He went on to become a successful attorney. When interviewed in 1975, he was under no illusions concerning his fate had he remained in Italy:

But the fact of the matter is that the economic setup of Italy was such that maybe 5 percent of the people owned maybe 95 percent of the wealth. So that you had the very, very, very rich and the very, very poor, with a broad, broad base of the poor. And that's why my father and his brother and a lot of others like him had to find a way of getting out of this stranglehold. . . .

Like his father was a farmer. And he owned some land where he would grow the necessities of life for his family and maybe have something left over to sell. So that if he sold something he was able to buy some cloth so they could make clothing for themselves. They lived in a modest sort of place, and it was nothing that you could aspire to beyond what you were born to do—farming. And I would have been a farmer if I had remained there. There would have been no opportunity for me to go beyond the few grades of school like my father did—the same experience my father had. . . .

[After his father came to America], he was able to get a little bit [of money] not only to sustain himself but to send some money back to Italy, so that my mother would take those few dollars and accumulate them. And my mother would make sure that she wouldn't even touch that money. Not that she wasn't allowed to, but that she would preserve that money for some day when my father would come back and find the occasion for all of us to come back to America. My mother worked in the fields in Italy just like all others did—to make a few dollars to keep us going, the three children that were then there. She raised chickens and she would have eggs to sell, and from the eggs that she would sell she was able to buy us some clothing and that sort of thing. It was just a meagre existence. We had no conception of what we went through there, and when we came here, it was just a little bit better. Just a little bit better, not much. At least the opportunity was here to develop, to enlarge, to have available an opportunity somewhere in the distance—still out of reach, but maybe we could reach it, as was my good fortune. By hard work to be able to reach an opportunity that I never would have had in Italy. I was born a farmer's son; I would have died a farmer. Like the rest of us. There wouldn't have been a chance to go to school, or an occasion to go into a profession. It was only my friend, who is a doctor there now, whose father was the padrone; he was the owner of that town and of wealth and that's why he's a doctor today. I wouldn't have had that opportunity. No, indeed.[9]

Thirty-five years earlier a Mr. Michaelewski and a Nicholas V. were interviewed by the WPA. Both had emigrated from Poland at the turn of the century and discussed their sense of hopelessness at being landless peasants.[10] Stressing the importance of letters from those who already had migrated to America, as well as the admonition of those left behind to send back money, Michaelewski explained:

Where I come from they have farms, farms all over the place, and that's all the people do—take care of the farms all the time. My father, mother, they always work for the farm, and the children they have to do the same things, too. Over that place there was nothing else to do, because in Poland everything was farms. That place, my people, they could make no living because they don't own the property themselves. There they have one big boss that owns lots of property and these people they have to pay the rent just like we pay for the house. We learn no trade there because there is no place to learn and there is no schools for the children. Only in the big cities they have the school'n and the high school like they got in this country. That time, before I come to this country we hear talk all the time about how they make the money in this country, and lots of people they want to come here to make the money just the same. My people they say that they are too old, that they live all the time in Poland, so they don't want to come. Before this time some people they come to America, United States, and they say that they are work, so they write the letters, too. I see this, I tell'm to my father this and they say, "Alright you could go but you take care to send the money! Because we need it on the farm."

Country life there no good for nothing, all the time have to stretch everything, no clothes, no nothing—all the time have to livin' like the same.

Work all the time. Work in the morning to the night, doing nothing, only sleep and eat all the time.

Morning have to be takin' the cows out in the fields, then have to take care of work, then have milk'n the cows, all these things all the time.

Sometimes we have holiday. That's only time that we do something; then we drink and have good times, and maybe when we have the weddings we have celebration for all week. All the people they come, and some they have to sleep in the barns and on the floors and they drink and they eat all the time. This is the way they have in Poland, but not in this country.[11]

In some ways, Nicholas V.'s situation was more desperate, because his parents were former landowners who were now tenants. As he explained, they "had been used to the better life and to be so low like they were on this farm was like dropping in a new world."

I was born near Warsaw and my people were farm-owners. When I got a little older my people lost all the property that they had. All this time my people were taking care of the lands and they used to plant and sell. When they lost the property they had to work like all the rest of the people in that part of the country.

There it was all farms, the people used to all think the same way, and if anybody wanted to be something else instead of a farmer the people were thinking that they were crazy, because they were brought up that way.

My people were always farmers and they thought that we should be farmers. My brothers were following the same way of my father and mother, and when I was coming home from school I had to work out in the fields to help the family.

If we see the way that the American people are brought up it is different than in Europe because there the children work in the fields and they know that they have to do something. In this country the children grow old and they don't know what to do for a living.

I went to the elementary school there; and there the law don't say that you have to go to school. Because this is true all the people don't even think of school, because it is just the different nature with the Polish people. I was a little bit different. I wanted to stay away from the farm because when I was a boy and I had to work on the farm and go to school at the same time I was hating it all the time. There all the people follow, like I said, the farm life. It was different with me; instead I wanted to learn something in mechanics. There all the people worked in agriculture because more than 80 percent did that kind of life all the time. Some of the people learned blacksmith trade and carpenter work. When I had these ideas my people said that I would waste time if I learned the mechanic trade—so I went by what they said—but still I was hoping that some day I would do what I liked.

After I got out of the elementary school, I went to another school and then I went to the gymnasium that was in the city. I stay there for almost two years and then I had to stop because my people could not make money on the farm. They lost all that they had. They went to work for a big landlord that had properties in all parts of that province [Gobernia]. On this farm they had more than 80 families that were working and living on it. Life was poor and all the people lived like serfs that you read about. No matter how you had you would have to see it in true life to believe it. My people had been used to the better life and to be so low like they were on this farm was like dropping in a new world. When this happened we have to work, all of us.

I don't stay a long time in Poland after this. I was hearing that the steamship companies in the city were making propaganda for the people to go to America—because in America there was lots of money. That time it was hard to get the passports from the officials in the city, and lots of people had to leave the border [frontier] almost secret.

I wanted to go to America because I was feeling that I could not stay in farm life all the time. I was feeling that there was never any money if I stayed there. I had different political ideas and religious ideas that lots of people had different. When I was in the home of my people they were very religious and I don't care for that. Some of the people in Poland, in some of the provinces were under the influence of the czar, and in the other parts of Poland they were under the influence of Germany. All the priests were the servants of these aristocrats and they kept the people in ignorance. They wanted that the people be this way for their own use. There was the suppression of the Polish language and the people didn't care for this. That why I learned the Russian language. In Poland the teachers could only show the Polish writing in a book, but they could not make the pupils write for themselves. When Pilsudski [Joseph Pilsudski (1867–1935), Polish leader during the 1920s] come to Poland he made the things just as bad because he gave to the Polish people their own language, but at the same time he made all the minorities have the Polish language which they don't care for.[12]

The story of a family's economic descent is not an unusual one. In Sweden, John E. Heyke's father lost his business, a disruption that may well have led to his parents' divorce, an acceptable practice in Sweden that would have been unthinkable throughout much of Europe. Even so, the extended family saw to his upbringing before he emigrated in 1888. Heyke was interviewed in 1938.

I was born in 1868 in the town of Folkarana in the parish of Dolorna. I was the oldest of four children. I had two brothers and one sister. My father was a master mechanic. When I was two years old my father lost his business and all his money. We went to live with my Uncle Andres. We were very poor so we worked on different farms after school and during our summer vacations. At first whatever money we received went to our father and our uncle. When we grew older we worked in the forest cutting down timber. I do not remember how much pay we received. If the weather was bad we would work in our father's machine shop making tools and fixing over furniture for our home. The road to the forest was very bad and we walked six miles twice a day.

Our house was a log cabin of four rooms. Two upstairs and two down. Of course there were no modern conveniences of any kind. We had a grand open fireplace in one room and a cook stove in the kitchen in which we burned wood that we had cut ourselves. Our beds were folded against the walls in the daytime and at night they were let down. We slept on straw mattresses and straw pillows. Our coverings were made of sheepskins to keep us warm. Outside we had two wells, one for the house and one for the animals. My uncle had the horses and chickens and a cow.

Our town consisted of about 15 families and each family was composed of from 8 to 10 people. We had one general store in our town that sold everything from food to clothes, farm implements, and it also was the post office. Our food was very simple—it mostly consisted of salt meat, American pork, potatoes, cabbage, bread and coffee. At Christmastime we could have rice pudding but that was the only change. Our clothes were bought and they were just working suits of denim or overalls. On Sunday we would dress up in a regular suit. We only bought new suits when our old ones wore out.

My mother and father had public school education. After my father grew up he would study algebra at home by himself. I had a public school education. My parents wanted all of us to have an education but it was very hard because we were so poor. At the age of 13, I started to study the clarinet and the bassoon. I was very fond of music and would practice for hours when I had the time. I also used to go to the library about once every two weeks for books on history, essays, and fiction. I soon learned to like to read Schoepenhauer and Nietzsche. The sayings of Socrates and Plato have helped me in many ways through my life. We had newspapers in our home regularly. We all were very fond of music and we would sing a lot of songs. We very much enjoyed the folk dancing.

Our vacations were only about once a year when about 100 of us would charter a boat and go to visit some historical place in Sweden. These trips would only be for a day. My uncle belonged to a Cooperative Society.

When I was about seven years old my father divorced my mother and we children were separated. I lived with my uncle and was really brought up by my grandmother. I have described the town in the first part of my story. Of course we believed in divorce. I do not know the circumstances of my parents' separation as I was too young at the time. In school we were taught to be very patriotic to Sweden and so we were not very favorable to the Danes or the Norwegians. The other nationalities didn't matter to us at all. In school we were taught that Sweden was always on the right side when we had our wars with Russia. If we won, the papers would be loud in their praises, but if we lost there would be very little said at all. We had two hours of religion in school every day. We were not a very religious family, but we children went to church through compulsion. When I was 13 years old I began to doubt what they told me and ever since I have not been religious. I believe in the truth in everything, but have found it is very hard to find the truth in anything.

When I was 13 years old I served three months in the army. I did this until I was 20 years old. At this time I wanted to go out and see the world, so I decided I would like to go to America. My father had been in America twice and when he would come back to Sweden he would tell me so much about the opportunities there, so I wanted to go. My father had the rheumatism so badly in America, he had to return to Sweden. I did not care how hard I worked so long as I could go to America.[13]

Quite similar in tone are the recollections of another Swede, Nils G. Sahlin, who emigrated in 1921, 33 years after John Heyke. Again, the family was less cohesive and there was opportunity for intellectual enrichment at home:

I was born on the island of Oland in the Baltic Sea. I lived on this island until I was 16 years old. My father was an unskilled worker and my mother just stayed at home. Neither of my parents had very much education.

My father died when I was two years old. My mother had to go out to work, so I was brought up by a foster mother whom I lived with until I came to America. My foster father was an engineer on a Swedish steamboat. I remember very little of him because he was very seldom at home and he did not help my foster mother very much financially. My foster mother used to do housework in the village. I had no brothers or sisters. At the age of seven years I started to work on a farm for 12 hours a day. I received 5¢ a day and my food. I have no idea how much money was brought in by the family. We were very poor in every way. We lived in a rented frame wood house. We did not own our home until 1917, when I bought it for my foster mother.

Our house had three rooms which were furnished very sparingly. A kitchen, living room, and a bedroom. In the winter we often slept in the kitchen because it was warmer. In the living room we had a stove made of tiled brick which had pipes running up and down inside the stove to throw out heat. In the kitchen we had a regular kitchen range in which we burned wood that we gathered from the woods. We built a woodshed next to our house where we piled the wood in the summertime. We had a brick oven in the kitchen beside the stove in which we burned wood, then we removed the wood ashes and put in our bread. This bread would keep fresh for a long time. We had no conveniences at all in our house. A well stood just outside the kitchen door where we got our water. We had a few trees around our house but not any interesting scenery. We were about 20 minutes walk from the Baltic Sea.

Our food was very simple. The only food we raised was potatoes. Our food was very limited. We had fish, potatoes, dried meat, salted pork, oatmeal, bread, carrots, cabbage, apples, pears, cherries, and plums. On Christmas and holidays we would have rice pudding and cutfish. We were so poor we just had enough to keep us going. Life was very hard for my foster mother and myself. I was very shy as a child and in some ways I have never outgrown my shyness. Our clothes were very plain. A tailor would come around about once a year and make what we needed. A seamstress also would come about once a year and make dresses for my mother. The local shoemaker would make our shoes whenever we needed them.

I was quite a problem as a child because I did not want to play with the other farmers' children. I went to school until I was 11 years old, finishing about the sixth grade. My foster mother and father had about five years of public school education. My parents were very favorable to my having an education, especially my foster mother. I went into the Swedish navy when I was 17 years old and stayed there for three and a half years. This was during the World War. I went into the medical department. I was a pacifist and did not believe in war so I thought if I went into the medical department I would not have to kill people but could help the wounded. I hated war in every way. I wanted to be a doctor. I finished my training as a noncommissioned officer.

I really outgrew my parents and surroundings when I was about 12 years old. I associated mostly with my teachers and the minister and his family. When I was 15 years old I had read most of the classics of different nations. When I first started to read I was mostly interested in fiction. These I procured from friends and the public library where I went about once a week. We had a newspaper which came about twice a week. My foster mother and I read most of the papers. There were a few magazines in our home. Once in a while a friend would give us one. I had to walk nearly two miles to school every day so I had very little leisure time. When I did have any extra time I spent it in farming. I educated myself a great deal by studying and reading. I studied German, botany, mathematics, Swedish, and many other subjects. I read the works of Dante, Goethe, Strindberg, and all the Swedish writers of note. I enjoyed Mark Twain and Jack London very much. I also read Boccaccio. I was unable to study music for lack of money, but my son studies the violin. I enjoy music very much. I became interested in the works of Selma Lagerlöf and I think I have the finest collection of her works in America today. When I was 12 I outgrew my foster mother's influence.

We did not belong to any cultural organizations. I went to church fairly regularly but I have never been real religious. The only way we entertained was with coffee parties and cheese-making parties. I belonged to the IOGT, which was a temperance organization. It was mostly social and we read and discussed current books on fiction and travel. We never had any vacations.

My foster father was very seldom at home so my mother ran everything. We worked out our problems together.

My religion allowed divorce. I outgrew my parents' influence at 12 years old, so of course I was allowed to do as I pleased in the choice of a mate. I was on my own in many ways from this time on.

The town of Oland was a small island in the Baltic Sea. They raised grain, beets, and cattle. They also produced cement. The island is of limestone. The roads were of dirt and very dusty. About five miles away there was a general store and a railroad station. The countryside was not very picturesque, mostly fog. I was not very interested in the people as they were mostly farmers.

I was very strongly attached to my foster mother for all she had done for me. When I grew up and earned my own living I bought her a home in Stockholm and took care of her until she died.

I was very patriotic toward my country. No hate and very few prejudices to anyone. I was a great reader of history, travel, and fiction. I was influenced by my teachers and my minister. I was not very religious. I was really too tired from work to attend church regularly. I admired and respected the minister very much. I was interested in Germany, France, and England and their histories and culture. America appealed to me from an economical standpoint. My foster mother attended church, but not every Sunday.[14]

"We Had Few Comforts and Many Hardships"

In Lithuania, John Lukasavicius's, family was both cohesive and authoritarian. He followed his father to Pennsylvania in 1923 and recalled hard work with his brother and sister on his no-nonsense mother's farm. He was interviewed in 1939.

We owned a small tract of land of about five acres in the village and the whole family—my mother, elder brother, and younger sister—all worked the land. My father left for America when I was four years old and used to send us money once in a while so that we managed to get along. He was working in a mine in Pennsylvania.

Until we children grew up so that we were able to help on the land, our mother did most of the farm work with the help of neighbors. When I was about six years old, I started to help by herding the few pigs and other animals we had. Our house was like the rest of those in the village, a log cabin with a thatched roof, dirt floor, one room with a clay stove built in one corner. My brother and I used to sleep outdoors or in the barn when the weather was warm. We only slept in the house in the winter. All summer we worked hard, from dawn to dusk, raising food for ourselves and the animals. With my father sending money occasionally we were able to use that to pay taxes with and were able to keep our food instead of selling part of it in the market.

Most of our meals were black rye bread, soup from vegetables we raised, and milk and cheese. On holidays we had better meals, roast goose or duck, vegetables with sour cream, and perhaps a loaf of wheat bread bought from a baker in the neighboring town. Our clothes were almost all homemade, though my father sent us some from America. He sent me a woolen overcoat, my brother a suit and shoes, and my mother and sister each a velvet dress. We only wore those clothes to church on Sundays and holidays.

In the early years of my life, I learned reading and writing in Lithuanian from the traveling teachers who stopped at our village. They used to stay at each house where there were children and hold classes for all the children in the village. None of them stayed at our house because we couldn't afford to feed them. I used to go to neighbors' houses when the teacher was there. Another lesson I learned besides reading and writing was distrust of some of the people in the village. If a suspect person came to the house while a class was in session, the teacher would hide all his books in a prearranged place and tell us children to start playing games. He also told us not to tell what we had been doing. It was a great secret with us and if those people had children we would not play with them or let them know our secret. Afterwards I learned that these people would tell the Russians about our classes and teacher so that the Russians would grant them favors. If a teacher was caught, no one ever found out what happened to him. When I grew older, I went to a Russian school for five winters with my brother. There we learned to read and write in Russian.

We had no books or papers in the house except a prayer book. Once my father sent a newspaper from America but the postmaster wouldn't give it to us. When we went to the Russian school they gave us some books written in Russian. My godfather, an old man who lived in our village, told us not to read them so we burned them in the stove.

My mother was the boss in our house and we all obeyed her orders. If we disobeyed she would give us a good beating. As we grew older my brother and I worked the land and she helped with my sister, when they weren't busy in the house. The only time we did anything different from working and sleeping was when there was a dance at one of the neighbors' houses or a wedding. I never paid much attention to my sister, and my brother was a moody fellow so we didn't do many things together outside of our work. At present my brother is a watchmaker and general village mechanic in Lithuania. I remember how he learned the business. One of the people in our village who had returned from America had one of those cheap dollar watches. When one of the wheels inside of it broke, he gave it to my brother, who had always wanted it.

My brother tried to fix it but only made it worse. He traveled to a town 20 miles away, where there was a watchmaker, and had him fix it. While the man was repairing the watch, my brother stayed there and watched his every move. Coming home again with the watch, he took it apart to see if he could put it together, but when the mainspring flew out of the case he didn't know what to do. Again he went to the watchmaker and watched closely as the man put it together. The watchmaker worked too fast for my brother to get an idea on how he fixed the watch, so when he got home, he opened the case and threw sand in the watch. Then he took it back again to have the man clean it. After that trip, my brother was able to take the watch apart and put it together anytime he wanted to. From that time he began to buy broken-down clocks and repaired them. When they were fixed, he sold them and developed a business of his own.[15]

The following unidentified Lithuanian also was interviewed in 1939. His family was just as cohesive and authoritarian, and in this instance it served to drive this ambitious young man away.

I don't know just what classification you could give my father since he was the postmaster of the town of Jacobstadt. Perhaps here in America it could be called a "profession." I don't believe I know what the Waterbury postmaster has been called. However it was a responsible position even though the wages weren't very high. We had a rather large family, consisting of two sisters and my brother and of course my parents. When my sisters were eight years old they went to work for the wife of the town's sheriff. The hours were long and the work was quite hard since the house was large and they were required to keep it spotless. The sheriff's wife was a very cross woman but she was also very generous. They were paid the equivalent of about $1 in American money each week but they were given food and the discarded clothes of her daughter.

My brother and I went to work for the sheriff at about the same age, tending to his garden and poultry. We had to be at work at five in the morning and worked until around eight at night. We were paid the same wages as my sisters, but I did not mind the work so much since I was allowed to read the sheriff's books and he had a great many. Oh, they were books about the stars and the sea, fairy tales, and a great book written in Latin and illustrated with beautiful colored pictures. Nobody could read it but the parish priest, so one night I took the book over to him and asked him if he would read it to me. He very willingly translated the book, which proved to be a complete study of mythology. I guess it was the greatest moment of my life when he suggested that I write down the myths as he read them; it took a long time but I always felt that it was worth it.

It was quite necessary for all the family to work since the earnings of the entire family amounted to about $8 or $9, American money. We lived in our own house. The house was low with a thatched roof and four rooms; it had windows that opened like doors and were set in deep recessions. My mother always managed to have some kinds of flowers on the wide windowsills. The house set back about 50 feet from the dirt road and the rest of the acre of land was left for cultivation of vegetables and flax and for the raising of a few chickens, sheep, and pigs. The house had four rooms with three bedrooms and the kitchen, living room, and dining room all in one. The rooms were quite small with the exception of the kitchen, which was the length of the entire width of the house in front. The kitchen was furnished with a large fireplace which heated the whole house, so you see heat really was a luxury; it had a large trestle-style table and six chairs; a large cupboard housed the dishes and other utensils; the floor was of hard packed earth and very cold to step on. The ceilings throughout the houses were raftered and in the kitchen the bundles of herbs and other vegetation of the same kind hung from these rafters. You see my mother, having no medical aid near at hand, relied upon her own concoctions to keep the health of her family in good stead. The pungent odor of these herbs brewing was very pleasant if you could forget their taste. Each bedroom was furnished about the same. It had a bed, a chest, and a chair. There was a small mirror in the girls' room. While we were considered a well-to-do family with a fine home there, we were pretty poor according to American standards. We had few comforts and many hardships.

Our food was sufficient but had no variety. It was hardy (sic) food. Usually we had potatoes, bread and cheese, and coffee; sometimes we had fish or meat. On holidays we had a number of hard cookies that we soaked in wine, in very much the same way that doughnuts are dunked here. We also had a dish made at Christmas of oatmeal and salt allowed to ferment and then used. In a farming country the food luxuries of the city are always scarce but we used to get pastries once a year when my father went to Vilna. His return was always a great day!

We were adequately dressed, but not what you would call well dressed. My mother made all our clothes and made over the clothes my sisters' employer gave them. We had new clothes every winter. As far as clothes were concerned we never suffered but we never set any styles either.

We all went through the school in town. We were taught reading, writing, and figures but the teacher was so strict that it was hard to learn. When I finished, or that is when I thought I couldn't learn any more there, I pestered my father to let me go to school in Vilna. Through the aid of the village priest I got to Vilna. The priest's brother owned a cheese factory there and he let me work for him and live in his house.

My benefactor and his wife were fine people and really gave me my start in life. When I went to live with them the man told me that he usually paid the boy who did my job the equivalent of about 85¢ American money a week, but since he was furnishing me with room and board I would not be paid. I agreed with this plan and thus my school career really began. Four years after, when my schooling was completed, he secured a teaching position for me, and the day I left he gave me a package and told me not to open it until I was near my own home. When I finally opened it I lost my senses for it contained about $108 American money, payment for every week that I had worked for him for four years. When I finally got over my surprise I decided to hide it and add to it when I started teaching. I considered myself to be quite a wealthy man.

My parents favored education for men but not for women; they believed that too much education for anyone was bad and especially was this so in regards to women. The only books in the house were the prayer book and a few school books that I brought back with me. I was about the only one who read them because in that country to make ends meet it was necessary to live on an all-work-and-no-play basis.

There was no library in the town and the only newspaper we had came from Vilna for my father once a month. It was devoted almost entirely to political issues and of little interest to anyone but my father. The only language spoken was the native tongue and the little Latin I knew was used only to translate. The family had little leisure and this was spent in dancing and singing with the other villages or in calling all the villages together while I read to them. At this gathering my mother and sisters, bursting with pride, usually served coffee and some little cakes made of oatmeal. The regular holidays were spent in participating in folk festivals which took in singing and dancing and at these times I was always called upon to read. The villagers were a simple peaceful people and delighted in hearing the old myths and the battles of Caesar and the rest. There were no vacations and nobody traveled just to see the countryside. The family did no entertaining except when they gathered the townspeople together to hear me read. There were no organizations or societies in my village and nearly everybody belonged to the choir. The choir planned for the festivals and everyone joined in wholeheartedly.

In the old country the father is the man of the house and no decisions are made without first consulting him. His word was law and that was a law it was not wise to break. My mother or her children had no voice in any matter outside the home; that is, she could not sell any produce unless my father gave her permission to. Despite the fact that my mother had no education, she was far more intelligent than my father, who had a failed education. She could get a shrewd bargain, where he would practically give the things away. He depended more on my mother than he cared to admit.

We were allowed a good deal of freedom, but the girls were not. Their freedom didn't exactly depend upon the strictness of our parents as much as it did on the amount of leisure time that they had. We didn't quite fear our parents but we were a little in awe of them; we would not be allowed to enjoy the wonderful sense of companionship that American children enjoy with their parents. As a result of this awe the children of our family did not have a close bond of affection for one another.

Our religion does not allow divorce and it is held in our family to be as great a crime as murder. In our country the old custom of selecting a suitable mate for a girl is sometimes employed and at other times the young people are given a free rein in choosing their own mates. There was little love between my parents or for that matter between any members of the family. I remember not being very anxious at all when my father was very ill. The only thing I thought of was his job and who would get it if he died. The old country has no time for much love because living is too hard.

I know that there are many romances written about old country people, but not many are written about Lithuania and her sister countries. Have you ever read one? No, I didn't think you had. Romance comes from leisure and peace and knowledge that your life doesn't depend on a rainstorm. While I came from a pleasant peaceful village where life flowed on from one day to another and year after year passed uneventfully, still there is always the hidden worry and fear of not knowing just how the crops will turn out.

After I had taught school about three years I decided to go to some big city and study English. One morning I announced to the family that I was going away for a while to study. That statement was the declaration of open war between every member of my family and most of the villagers. They had resented my education for a long time, feeling that I was superior to them, and they welcomed an opportunity to show it. My father was in rather poor health, and they declared that I should remain at home and help him instead of always sticking my nose in a book and thinking of running away to some other city. They shouted insults after me and laughed at me. Finally they went to the village priest and begged him to make me stay home. His reply came the following day in the form of a scorching sermon wherein he told them point-blank to mind their own business. This upbraiding only made matters worse. My family was worst of all; it seemed that they screamed at me all day long.

Finally the day came to start and just before daybreak I left the village, and except for an overnight visit when my father was dead, I never returned. I wandered around for a month or so and finally ended up in Petrograd. I found work teaching in a small private school. I stayed there about two years and was quite content when I met with a crossroad in my life.

One day in the spring I found a letter from the village priest awaiting me at my room. He stated that my father was gravely ill and in all appearances death seemed near. I left that night with all the money I possessed, about $500, and a few days later I arrived at my home. I got there about an hour before the funeral. Everyone glared at me and my family openly cut me. I was told not to join the funeral procession, but to get out of the village as quickly as I could for my people hated me intensely. I went into the church alone and sat by myself. After the burying I cornered my mother and told her that I wanted her to come and live with me. She abused me heartily and told me that I was responsible for my father's death. The thread of tension that held a not very affectionate family together suddenly snapped, and I discovered that I didn't care what happened to them. I was free and I intended to make use of this freedom. Still, all the way back I seethed with indignation. Of all the abuse, my mother's hurt the most.

It was while I was in this mood that I met an American over on a holiday. I could speak English well by then and we fell into a close friendship. About a week before he was to sail for America, he suggested that I return with him as a tutor for his son. By that time I could speak French and German well and a little Italian and Spanish. That night when I went back to my room I took stock of myself. Cast off from my family, I discovered that I had nothing in common with them, that for that matter I never had. I shared none of their beliefs or ideas; I believed that every man had a right to live his own life and it wasn't necessary that he live up to the dictates of his neighbor. Finally I decided to go. I wrote to the village priest telling of my good fortune, but I had no inclination to see or hear from my family. My affairs in order, I sailed for America with my friends.

As the boat pulled away, I stood looking over the city. Strangely enough, I felt no pangs of homesickness or loneliness. I felt as if I was sailing toward the pot of gold at the end of the rainbow. America loomed before me. Great big America, where fortunes were made overnight and opportunities beckoned at every corner. I was a free man with no encumbrances, and I had a position and a home when the boat sailed into port. The voyage was pleasant and with over $500 in my pockets, I could afford to enjoy it. Family could affect a person's future through inheritance.[16]

In Lithuania the practice of primogeniture meant that Michael Daunis would see the family farm go to his older brother. Of course division of land, or partible inheritance, brought its hardships as well, because often the equally divided plots were not large enough to sustain a family.

The village I was born in had about 30 houses. My father owned a small farm of about 20 American acres. There were 10 people in my family, 3 boys and 5 girls besides my parents. Everybody in the family went to work on the land as soon as they were able to do something. We had to because our farm was small for such a large family. Most of the year we worked from dawn until dark. In winter we were not so busy because all the crops were harvested.

Our house was like the rest of them in the village. It was a log cabin with a thatched roof, two rooms and only one of them had a wooden floor. Our furniture was homemade and for light we had a kerosene lamp. Like the rest of the houses we had a clay stove in one corner of the kitchen. The floor was hard-packed dirt. My mother used to clean it by sweeping and then covering the dirt with white sand.

We raised everything we ate and wore. Most of the time we ate black rye bread and soup. Three times a week we had a little fat pork for meat. On holidays of course we ate a little better. Those were the only times that we had a goose or chicken for our own table. Any other time we killed animals it was for market, because the only time we had any money was when we sold some of the things we raised. Our clothes were made from cloth that my mother and sisters weaved from wool or flax we raised on the farm. I never wore any other clothes until I came to this country.

I never had much education. I learned to read and write Lithuanian from some of the traveling teachers who came to our village and taught us a little, but I never went to a regular school. Nobody in my family did because none of us could be spared and the nearest school was too far away for us to walk. The only books we had in the house were prayer books and once in a while an almanac printed in Lithuanian. The almanacs were against the law because they were printed in Lithuanian, so my father kept them hid in the hay in the barn.

We didn't have much spare time. Once in a while there was a dance or a wedding in the village so we went. Most of the time we played cards or visited someone nearby. On holidays we went to church in the morning, and outside of having something a little special to eat we did the same things that we did all the other days. I never heard of vacations at that time.

When we had visitors at our house, the women used to sit and talk about different things and the men would play cards. Later on they would have a little of something to eat and drink. We children played around outside or in the barn. When the priest came to visit us once a year, we had to sit quiet while he talked with my father. There were no organizations of any kind in the village, so we didn't belong to any. One time I think my father joined a socialist group and went to their secret meetings somewhere in the woods, but he never spoke about it to anyone. I know it was something secret because he used to go out late at night and come home just in time to wake everybody up to go to work. My mother was frightened because I heard her argue with him to stop going out. He did after a few months. My father was the boss of the family. He told everybody what to do. My mother took care of the small children, made sure we went to church when we were supposed to, and did all the work in the house. Cooking, weaving, and even feeding the small chickens and other animals we raised. We children were all afraid of our father, but my mother used to get mad at him once in a while and made him go out of the house to get away from her scolding.

Before I came to this country I never heard of a divorce. Now I know the Catholic religion says it is a mortal sin. When a young fellow in the part I came from wanted to marry, if he picked a girl for himself he told his father and he would make arrangements with the girl's father for a suitable dowry. If his father could not agree with her's, there was no marriage. Another way the fellows would marry was through an agent. This agent would have a list of girls with the amount of dowry each would have. If a fellow and his father were satisfied with the amount, arrangements would be made through the agent for them to marry. Sometimes the couple would not see or know each other until the day of the wedding. I know one fellow who made that arrangement and when he saw what his bride looked like, he ran away to America to get out of marrying her. I know of some cases where fellows picked girls with big dowries and married them so that they could use the money to come to this country because they did not have any of their own. Girls sometimes picked their own husbands by having their father make arrangements with the fellow's father.

I don't think I was very attached to my family and home, because after I left I didn't write very much, though I did send money once in a while. While I was home all I did was work and I never had much chance to do things by myself. I always had to do as my father said, and if I earned some money for myself I always had to give it to him.

I didn't know anything about other countries and their people, though we all hated the Russians because they controlled the country. I guess I hated them because my parents did, because I didn't know much about the history of Lithuania.

Our family and all the families in the village went to church every time we were supposed to. We all were taught to honor the priest and obey his orders.

A year before I came to this country, a cousin of mine had come here. He wrote once in a while and told of how he was earning a lot of money and how everybody in America lived like princes. Other people in the village had relatives here, too, and they used to talk over the letters that were sent. All the letters said how big wages were paid for easy work and how wonderful it was in America. I wrote my cousin and begged him to send me a ticket to America. I thought that I could come and work hard and get enough money to buy a big farm in Lithuania for myself. I didn't want to stay on my father's farm because I knew that when he died my older brother would own the farm and I would have to depend on his good will to make a living.

When my cousin sent me a ticket, everybody was happy at my good fortune. I left home two days after it came. I crossed the border with six other fellows who came from nearby villages and started my journey to America. I expected that when I came back in a few years I would be able to own the biggest farm in the village.[17]

"I Didn't Have to Work"

Of course there were also emigrants who were quite well off by their fellow countrymen's standards. But some of them nevertheless felt the urge to seek greater opportunity. Consider the case of W. S., an American-born son of Ukrainian parents who returned to Galicia with him while he was an infant. In 1937, at age 20, he returned to the United States. Two years later he was interviewed by the WPA.

My sister and I were well taken care of because we had property and money. We ate well and had good clothes. We had three or four cows and two horses. I didn't have to work. The village we lived in consisted of 550 families. Of these, 120 families were Polish, 3 Jewish, and the rest Ukrainian. The Poles and the Ukrainians had separate churches. Before the war there was a school in the village, but during the war the school was destroyed. Later people rented a house where two classes were held. At one time both Polish and Ukrainian were taught, but when the Poles took over the section, only Polish was taught.

Father and Mother knew how to read and write. I went to the village school and then to Zbaroz to a gymnasium. I wanted to study to be a dentist, but I couldn't get into the school because they wouldn't take any Ukrainians unless you could bribe them with a couple of thousand dollars. Before Polish people took the section over, in Galicia there were 3,000 schools. Now there are only 30 schools in all Galicia. Before we prayed in Ukrainian; then we had to pray, as well as speak, Polish. However, I had a few Ukrainian books, as well as Polish. I had history, geography, poetry, and others. I also owned a radio.

People in Galicia wanted to give their children an education, but high schools cost a lot of money. It cost me about 10,000 zloti, or about $2,000, and sometimes it cost even more. We had a library in school. Then in the city there was a lending library, but it cost money to borrow books there.

My sister had seven years of schooling and then she went one year to the seminary. My uncle knew how to read, but my aunt didn't. My uncle was a leader in the village, and he was well liked and respected. I read Polish newspapers. In high school we were examined three times a week on the news in the papers. We read magazines also. I knew German, Latin, Ukrainian, and Polish. I also can read Russian.

I don't remember anything about my father and mother, but my aunt and uncle got along very nicely.

The man was the head of the family. That's how it always was at home. But since the woman took care of the house, she had more to say in the running of the home than the man. My uncle couldn't very well boss her, because he didn't know what was going on in the house. The children in the village started working early. When they were 10, they had to work in the pastures watching the livestock; at 14, they started working in the fields. Girls had freedom until they were old enough to get married. In the village they didn't have much choice as to whom they married. In the city it was just like here.

We had religious education in high school for one hour each week. Since our religion doesn't allow divorce, it didn't teach us anything about divorce. It was very hard to get a divorce in Poland.

I lived with a Ukrainian family while I was attending high school. The father was a well driller. This is a very skilled and highly paid work. I felt very much at home with the family.

The school I went to was of course Polish, but I didn't like Polish. I felt very bad when they were abusing Ukrainians and arresting them. The Poles tried to make everything Polish, but we studied Ukrainian history at home, and that made us dislike the Poles. At home we heard the Ukrainian language and about Ukraine.

I wasn't allowed to belong to any organization while I was going to high school. The girl in the house where I lived finished at a private Ukrainian gymnasium. She told me about Ukraine. She knew many students and they would get together and talk to me. They used to go to different villages and stage plays.

I had to go to church every Sunday, and I wanted to go. I did know some people, though, who were irreligious. I knew one man who was a lawyer and another one who was a teacher. The teacher was a Communist. He never got a chance to teach because he was Ukrainian. I didn't like these people because they were radicals, and I was a nationalist. Most of the students were nationalistic. We were against all Polish people. We didn't like Jewish people because we thought Jewish people tried to gyp us, since some of them were businessmen. In universities, however, when the students voted, the Ukrainian and Jewish students would vote together against the Polish students. The Ukrainian and Jewish students fought the Polish students. In Vilno, after such a fight, a student was killed and every year after that there was a pogrom against the Jews in Vilno.

I decided to come to America at the time I finished gymnasium. I was angry because I wasn't called to take a regular examination. Our school priest had a grudge against me because he didn't like the family I lived with, and I refused to move away from them because I liked them. He was influential in not having me called for final examination. Then, also, I had some financial difficulties with him. I had no trouble in getting to America since I was an American citizen.[18]

Similarly, Walter Mrozowski's parents owned a profitable farm in Poland, but after seeing action in the Russo-Japanese war, Mrozowski realized that farming held no interest for him.

I was born in Poland on a farm near Ludz. It was about like Fairfield and Bridgeport, four or five miles apart. My parents had eight children, five boys and three daughters. I was the fifth child. There were two kinds of people in Poland, poor people and rich people. My parents happened to be what you would call "rich." My father had a good business and made money. He had farms and raised vegetables which he sold in the markets of the city. He was also a butcher and he ran a restaurant. He used to make trips into Russia to buy wild horses. He would bring them back to his farm and train them and then sell them.

All children in the family got good educations. My father could afford it. Public schools were few and some of them were miles away from the farms. I did not go to a public school. My parents decided I should go to a private school and I did. I had to live at the school, but went home on holidays. Also the professor used to take us on trips and show us the fields and forests and tell us how they grew.

I liked to go on those trips. I learned a lot that helped me later on when I left home. The professor was kind to every child. My parents were glad when I got through with school. I went right back to the farms and helped out along with the other children. When I left school I had not made up my mind what I would like to do. But I knew I did not want to stay on the farms all of my life. I wanted to see the world.

I stayed on the farms about two years. Then I made up my mind to leave. I went to Germany. I was 16 years old at the time. I was only a boy. I had some luck when I got to Germany, more than I looked for. I met a man who was a major in the army. He asked me what I was doing and I told him I had just come from Poland. He took a liking to me. He asked me if I knew anything about forests and I told him I did. We had a long talk and it wound up with him hiring me.

He sent me to his farm and told me I was to have charge of 13 persons, 7 girls and 6 boys. I thought I was pretty young for such a job, but I was out to make a living and took it. We were to plant a forest. The man agreed to pay me one penny for every section we planted. I paid each of the workers one-half a penny each. They were satisfied and I made some money. The work for me was not hard. I used a string and measured the distance from one hole to another, where shrubs should be planted. I liked the work and remained in the farm about two and one-half years. That experience proved I could make money, good money, if I tried hard.

Russia went to war with Japan and I got an idea I would like to fight, so I joined the Russian army. I went as a volunteer and I was with the army for more than a year. Then I got out. It was the kind of work I did not like. I felt when I joined it would be good fun, but I did not have much fun while I carried a gun and wore a uniform. I got all I wanted of war. I don't know how many Japs I shot. All I know was I kept shooting and never got shot myself.

After I got out of the Russian army I went back to Germany. I went to the man for whom I had worked before the war and asked him for a job. He liked my work when I was with him before, so he hired me again. I was glad to get back to the forests and away from gunfire. I worked for the man about a year. I was 21 years old at the time, still a young man. After leaving the job I went back to my father's farm and stayed there for about two years. But I had lost interest in farm life and wanted to get away from it. The longer I stayed on the farm, the more I wanted to get away. And I did. I decided I would go to America.[19]

Whatever their status, they came not only with luggage but with cultural baggage as well. That baggage would not be discarded when they boarded ship and embarked on the crossing.

2

CROSSING AND ARRIVAL

The popular image of transatlantic immigrant crossings during this period has been indelibly etched onto the American consciousness by Emma Lazarus's famous poem for the Statue of Liberty, "The New Colossus." Words such as "tired," "poor," "huddled masses," and "wretched refuse" conjure up depictions of uprooted passive people figuratively tossed into New York's harbor by the ocean's waves. Two somewhat contradictory images also emerge: One is the close-knit, poverty-ridden family, huddled together on the ship's deck with all of its meager possessions on the father's back or in bundles at their feet. The other is the lone young immigrant, without family or friends, confronting an uncertain and fearful future. Some of the individuals who speak in this chapter indeed were friendless and without family. But often the immigrant experience was more complex.

Most late-nineteenth-century immigrants did not come over as entire families; they could not afford it. But family and kinship groups held enormous significance in immigration. Families might raise the money to send one member over, with the understanding that he or she would send money back for the others as soon as possible. Or someone already here sent money or a prepaid ticket so that a relative could come. Most immigrants did not confront the New World with absolutely no financial or emotional support. The mass immigration of the late nineteenth and early twentieth centuries reflected millions of individual decisions, usually made in concert with, or with the assistance of others. And international travel became easier as the industrial revolution progressed. The evolution from sail to steam reduced passage time from Western Europe to 10 or 12 days. Many cargo ships, such as the tobacco freighters that steamed into Bremen, were glad to have emigrants for the otherwise empty return voyage. As the railroads spread in Europe and the United States, immigrants had an easier time making the overland journeys, both to the port of embarkation and from the port of debarkation to their ultimate destination.[1]

The crowded crossing in the densely packed steerage class is an oft-told story. Anthony Tapogna, interviewed in 1975, recalled his crossing with his parents in 1920, when he was 10 years old:

We came over—I remember the passage. It took us from Italy to America here, with a stopover in Portugal. It took us darn near a month to get here— 25 days or so, in the poorest type of accommodations; just like cattle in the hold of the ship, with no privacy, no nothing. Everyone just huddled together. Animals, I think, travel better today than we did in those days coming across.[2]

Such stories reflect steerage conditions, in which upwards of 2,000 passengers often were accommodated in large dormitories filled with two-or-more-tiered bunks and little air or privacy. Emigrants either crowded into galleys to cook their food or stood in long mess lines. Separation of the sexes frequently was casual, both in the crowded dormitories and in the all too few and sometimes filthy toilets.

But change occurred around the turn of the century, as both the United States and European governments insisted upon improvements. Ships were inspected before sailing. The vessels themselves were greatly improved, and the huge new ocean liners of the Cunard and White Star lines provided more comfort and a speedier voyage. By the twentieth century, many shipping companies had added a third class, which usually accommodated six to a cabin and provided galleys, dining rooms, smoking rooms, bars, more plentiful toilets, and showers. Yet even as these improvements were advancing, older and smaller lines were still transporting thousands of passengers in disagreeable steerage conditions. Steerage probably remained common for most immigrants well into the twentieth century.[3]

"There Was No One to Help Me"

Some immigrants actually did conform to the loner stereotype. Certainly that is true of Walter Mrozowski, who emigrated from Poland sometime after the Russo-Japanese War in 1905. (The story of his life up to the decision to emigrate appears at the end of chapter 1.)

I decided I would go to America. I had heard about the United States and what a grand country it was. I had enough money to pay my way over, so I went to Hamburg and got passage. I went on board the *President Lincoln*. I was leaving my homeland and relatives, but I had made up my mind. Nothing could stop me from seeing the United States. Anyway, after the boat headed for this country, I knew I had to go along with it.

As I could speak German, I met a man on the boat who spoke that language. He asked me if I had an address of someone in the United States. I told him "No." He said I would have to have one when I landed or I couldn't get off the boat. I did not know what to do. I did not know anyone in the United States. So he helped me out. He gave me an address of a woman. I found out later it was the address of his sister in New York. I did not go to her. She did not know me.

So when the boat landed in New York I found there were two classes of people: the poor ones and the ones who looked like they had some money and were dressed that way. I was among those who looked like I had money, so I had no trouble getting off the boat.

Do you know when I left the boat I had only $10 in my pocket. I was in a new world with but a few dollars. But I said to myself, "Walter, you have got to get a job, you are far away from home." I kept my courage up. I had to. There was no one to help me. I was a young fellow with no relatives or friends I could call on. It was a tough spot I was in, but I made up my mind I would make the best of it. I could not go back to Poland as I did not have the money to buy my ticket. So I walked around New York for the rest of the day. As night came on, I felt tired and sleepy but I knew I could not spend any money for a hotel room.

I thought things over again. I said, "Walter, you have got to hang on to that $10 or the best part of it—it's all you have." So I kept walking and finally found myself where there were some freight cars. I walked along and saw one with the door open. I looked in and saw it was empty. I said to myself, "This is where I sleep tonight and save my money." So I got in and went over in the corner and lay down. I was soon asleep. I don't know how long I slept, but I woke up and found the train was moving. And it was going at a fast clip. So I decided to stay in the car and wait until the train stopped. I stayed awake for an hour or so and then went back to sleep. No one bothered me. I got a good rest and in the morning I was all ready to leave my hotel.

The train did stop and I left the car. I went into the town. I still had the best part of my $10 in my pocket. I did not know anyone. I saw a man who looked like a foreigner and I went up to him and spoke in German. He understood me. I told him I had just gotten off a freight train and did not know where I was. "You're in Torrington, Connecticut," he said. That did not mean anything to me. I told the man I wanted a job. He could not help me. So I sat around for about two weeks, that is when I was not going to some factory looking for work. I found my money was getting low and knew I had to do something pretty quick. I went to one factory every day, and I guess the man got tired seeing me every day and he decided to put me to work. I asked him what kind of work I would do and he said I was to sweep the floor and make myself useful in anything they wanted me to do.

Before I went to work, my boss sent me downtown with a man to get some overalls, shoes, and other things I would need in the work. I tell you, I felt like a fellow who had come into some money. I had heard about a Santa Claus and now I knew that there was one. But still I had very little money, not enough to get a room, so I slept on the floor of the factory. And I was glad to get such a place. I went along at the sweeping business for a while, and one day the boss said he was going to put me in the machine shop. He said he liked me and wanted to help me. So I went into the machine shop and helped around the machines.

The boss told the men in the shop to help me all they could, and they did. I stayed with the factory for about five years, and when I got through I was a toolmaker. But I did not know much about the English language, and while working in the factory I made up my mind to go to school. I went to night school for three winter sessions. I learned something about reading, writing, and arithmetic, and I want to tell you it did me a lot of good.[4]

Similarly, Mary Strokonos left Vilna, Lithuania, on her own in 1915. She did find a young man from her hometown on board ship, but her dependency upon him led to an unhappy marriage.

When I get to be about 22, 23, I think all the time I come to America. Landlord's daughter come to America, then two, three years come back to see family. Tell big stories about America. She had American clothes and nice things; she bring big blue teapot to mother. I listen to stories like baby listen to stories at bedtime, you know. I think I go to America too, have same things as she has.

My people do not like me to go when I tell them, so I play like fox and no say anything more about plans. Every time I go to market I keep little money for trip. Three, four years go, then one market day I don't go back home. I walk long time, then farmer give me ride on hay wagon. Ride all night, fall asleep on soft hay. In morning farmer shake me awake and tell me I am in city. What city? I can't think of name now.

I go down to where trains are and I ask the man how much it cost to go to America. He laugh and say you can't ride train all the way to America. But he nice man, he put me on train and I finally get to town where I take boat. Where do I get boat? I think in Germany, maybe Berlin. I can't read or write, so I can't tell. I get to boatman after long time in town. When I told him I wanted to get boat for America, he ask for my money. Then he take some, put some in bag and give it back to me, and tell me I need this in America.

When boat sail I am downstairs in boat. Many, many people down there, very crowded. Everybody very sick. I am so sick I cry and cry, I think I die, then I wish I back on farm. On boat is a young farmer from near town I come from. I lonesome and he is nice to talk to.

After boat rock like cradle back and forth we stop at island. Doctor come in and see if anybody sick, then he let everybody out on island. We wait long time, then we get to America. I get scared when I see so many people and buildings. I walk along street and I come to a shop they have windows full of cakes and goodies like only rich in old country can have. I go into store, but I can't speak English so I point to man and then to cookies. He put them in paper bag and then I show him money and take one, two pieces. I am very, very lonely and I start to cry and it gets very dark but I don't know where to go. I walk along and then I feel a hand on my shoulder. It is a cop and I think I am going to be put in jail, but he take me to a house where the woman is a Lithuanian. I am so happy I kiss his hand, but he only laughs. The woman gets me a job in hotel doing work, but I don't know American way and I am very dumb; everybody laughs at me. I am very saddened; every night I cry.

One day when I leave the hotel I met Walter Stroknos who I met on boat. I am so happy to see someone I can talk to that I hate to see him leave. I come to America in summer and I marry him in fall. We live in New York for a while, then we come to here to farm. We work for people who own farm. It is so nice! People are nice. We live in shed where chickens live now. Old lady in house give us a bed and table and two chairs and a stove and mirror; she give us pans and dishes too. We very happy. After little Walter and Josie were come, old man die and old lady go to live with son. She sell farm to us for $300. Walter get money from man on paper—you know, he sign his name. After we move into big house, Albert and Mary and Vera and Peter were come.

Now Walter is not so nice and one day he throw stick of wood at me. It hit me and cut my head. He get doctor and he sew it up, then he tell him he send him to jail if he do it another time. I don't like my life no more. I wish I don't marry Walter. He work hard but he very mean, say bad things.[5]

So too Nathan Nussenbaum, an Austrian Jew, immigrated in 1896, alone and with no one to greet him. But as he said, he could speak German and Yiddish, and once in New York, he was befriended.

So, the desire to come to America got so that I finally decided to make the trip. I said "Good-bye" to my relatives and friends and went my way. I only had a few dollars in my pocket after I paid for my passage, and I decided I would hold on to it as long as I could. I could speak German and Yiddish, and I knew I would meet people in New York who spoke those languages and they would help me get work. I was 19 years old when I came to America. That was about 44 years ago. I was quite young for a fellow born in a foreign country to seek his fortune in the United States, where he did not have any friends. But I was determined to try my luck in this country. I was never afraid of hard work. You see, I am pretty well built, so with a lot of courage I faced my new experience.

I want to tell you I was thrilled when I arrived in New York City. I saw tall buildings and thousands of people. We did not have anything like that in my hometown, and after I landed I just stood still for several minutes and watched people as they came and went. Nobody spoke to me and I did not speak to anyone. It was not because I was afraid but due to the fact I did not know anybody.

I walked around all day, hoping something would break for me but it didn't. When night came on I began to think about where I would sleep. In my home in Austria I was used to sleeping in a pretty good bed. I wondered if I would in New York. I counted my money and found I had but a few dollars. I had to eat, so after a light meal I wandered around and finally came to a dock. I saw other men sleeping under ice wagons and I thought it would be all right for me to do so. I lay down under a wagon and kept my hand in the pocket where I had my money. I knew if anyone tried to get it, I would wake up and there would be a battle. But I was not disturbed. When I woke up the next morning the sun was shining, and after a small breakfast I began walking again. I did not have any luck in getting a job and was beginning to lose some of my courage.

I slept under wagons for about three or four nights and no cops bothered me. I was in fear they would. Finally one night a cop did come to me and after waking me up, he asked what I was doing there. He was a Jewish cop so he and I got along all right in our conversation. I told him I had just come from Austria and was without a friend in America. I showed him the few dollars I had in my pocket. I said I was saving all I could until I got a job.

The cop said he believed me and he would tell other cops on that beat not to bother me but to let me sleep under ice wagons, as I was a friend of his. And he also told me he would try and get me work. I slept under the wagons for a few more nights and my friend, the Jewish cop, came to me and said he wanted to meet me the next day. He was going to take me to a friend who would give me work.

I certainly was tickled. I counted my money and found that I had about $3 from the $9 I had when I landed in New York. I had no trade but that did not matter. I wanted work, because my funds were getting quite low. So the following morning I met the cop at the appointed place, and he took me to a storekeeper who used to sell dry goods and other lines, to the homes. He had a talk with me and told me he would pay me $3 a week and give me my room and board. Was I happy? You bet I was. I did not like the idea of sleeping under ice wagons and I took the job.

He gave me a pushcart and told me what neighborhood I was to work in. I did not know the ways of this country and trusted everyone. I worked hard every day but was more than glad when night came and I had a good bed to sleep in.

A funny thing happened one day. I was pushing my cart as usual when a cop came to me. He looked me over and said he thought I needed a pair of new shoes. I thought to myself but did not have the money to buy them. After we had talked for a while, he said he had a pair of good shoes at his home and he would sell them to me cheap if I would go with him. So we went to his home and he showed me the shoes. I asked him what he wanted for them, and he said they were worth $5 but I could have them for $1.50 if they were what I wanted.

I thought it over and said I would sure like the shoes as the ones I was wearing were about gone, but I did not have the money to pay. I told him I had some money but it belonged to the man I was working for and if he would go to the man with me and tell him about the shoes, the man might give me the money to buy them.

So we went to my boss and the cop told him how I wanted the shoes but did not have money enough of my own to buy them. I did not get the money or the shoes and I found out afterwards that it was a "game." My boss was in with the cop to find out if I was honest. I thought it was a mean trick to play on a young fellow who had just come to this country. It taught me a lesson I never forgot.

I kept the job pushing the cart for about nine months. Then I got a job in a factory. I got it through my friend, the Jewish cop, I met while I was sleeping under ice wagons. He proved to be a good friend to me and was always trying to get me work. . . .

Well, when I went to work in the factory, I got a room for myself. I felt I was finally getting along all right, and every evening I would take a walk. Something happened on those walks that made me mad. I really was quite mad.

My first name is Nathan and in Yiddish it is Nisn. I remember the first night I was out walking. The sidewalks were so crowded with people that I had to walk in the gutter. I was going along minding my own business when I heard someone holler, "Listen." I thought they were calling me, that the fellow knew me. So I turned and said "Hello" in Yiddish. No one answered me and I thought it strange. I heard several other people say "Listen" as I walked along and each time I answered but got no reply. This went on for a few evenings and finally I got mad and went to my rooming place and told my landlady about what had happened. She explained that when folks said "Listen" they were not speaking to me. What they said sounded like Nisn, my name. I saw then they were not fooling me and had no intention of hitting up a conversation with me. I felt much relieved after things had been explained to me.[6]

If the loner was not typical, neither was the family that managed to migrate all together. An unidentified member of this family described their arrival from Scotland:

I often think how fortunate even the poorest, humblest person is to be born an American. I was not. I obtained my Americanism the hard way, through heartache, homesickness, and grim determination to make my adopted country really adopt me as one of her sons. The hardest part after the excitement of packing and planning is over is to face the fact of possible hardship and the breaking of family ties and friendships. It is almost like death must be to leave people who are dear to you, knowing that you will probably never see them again, for poor people do not run back and forth across the Atlantic even if in this day and age it is not so much of a feat. It takes money and time, and the great multitudes of the middle class do not have an oversupply of either. I am an American citizen now and no amount of money could ever induce me to give it up. I talk, dress, eat, live, and even think just as every other American does in my circumstances. All thoughts of any other country or people have long ago left my mind completely.

My parents came to the United States with my two sisters and my brother when I was about 10 years old. One of my sisters was just a babe in arms. Why they ever thought of leaving their home and families in Scotland and coming here I do not know. Most likely it was the great tales we had heard of riches to be obtained almost for the asking in this country, and then too my father had the restless blood of some long-dead pioneer ancestor flowing in his veins. If my mother had let him, I believe we would have spent our lives moving about from one place to another in search of that nonexistent utopia where all dreams come true without any particular effort, but one trip was enough for my mother with four small children and not too much money.

There are parts of the trip that I do not remember, but the general impression of it will never leave my mind. We came over third class and our fellow voyagers were a mixture of every nationality in the world, all bound for a new life and happiness in the United States. For the most part they were all kindly people trying hard to help each other out and to make the best of a trying trip, even though they could not understand a word the other said. Most of the responsibility of that trip fell on my mother. My father was too full of excitement and plans to be much help. Small as I was, I realized this and tried in every way I could to help my mother out.

There were certain things that my mother could not bring herself to leave behind us in Scotland, such as dishes and bric-a-brac of various kinds, and we were all loaded down with packages wrapped in string bags, newspapers, and cloth. My particular charge was my young brother and two large white china cats that my mother prized most of all her possessions. They were wrapped in newspaper and made an awkward, bulky package for a small boy to handle, but I delivered them right here in Bridgeport without so much as a nick taken out of them. So between caring for my china cats and keeping my younger brother from falling overboard, I did not have too much time for romping and playing on our trip over. My older sister and my mother somehow between them managed to care for my baby sister and keep all of our possessions together and get us all through the journey without too many mishaps.

There were only two places in the United States that we had ever heard of. One was New York, where we were to land, and the other was Bridgeport, where a friend of my father's had settled several years ago and who had sent us a postcard labeled Seaside Park, Bridgeport, Connecticut. When we were finally permitted to go into New York City we were a tired, bedraggled family and must have made a rather pathetic picture. My father was very well pleased with New York and was all for staying there a while and looking around, but my mother refused even to spend the night in such a place and insisted that we go on to the other place, Bridgeport. We had no idea how far away it was, nor how to get to it. We tried making inquiries, but although we were sure that we could speak English, no one understood us. Finally an Irish cop took pity on us and after my mother had rummaged around in her various packages and produced the picture of Seaside Park, he finally understood where we wanted to go and directed us to the place where we could get a train.

Once inside of Grand Central Station, we were more lost than ever. We were so loaded down with the baby and our packages that we could not even open doors without setting something down, holding the door open with a foot, and then loading up again. This time a colored porter came to our rescue, but again when we tried to tell him where we wanted to go, he just shook his head and rolled his eyes until the magic card of Seaside Park was shown and then he gave us a white-toothed smile and beckoned my father to follow him to a small cage where after a great deal of delay our tickets were obtained.

We were directed to a track number to wait, and there we stood for over an hour. There were chairs and benches around, but my mother was not going to take any further chances, but kept us all standing there amongst our possessions for over an hour, and it seemed like a day to us children as we were tired and hungry. We finally all got settled on the train for the last lap of our journey and although I fought desperately to keep awake, my eyes just would not cooperate, and I went sound asleep before the train was hardly under motion.

The next thing I remember was my mother shaking me and getting off the train. The station here in Bridgeport looked then very much to my sleepy eyes as large and confusing as Grand Central. After we were all loaded up again, we started to walk—where, none of us knew. We just walked. My father tried making inquiries to locate his friend, but did not meet with any success. At first we walked straight ahead and gradually left the busiest section of the city behind us. We finally started to turn in and out side streets, still with no definite plan of where we were going or what we were apt to find ahead of us. When we were all so tired that we could hardly take another step, my mother sighted a church which she was sure was a Catholic church and she turned out to be correct. We all piled into the church and sank gratefully into a pew while my father went off to look for the priest.[7]

"My Mother Cried a Little"

Most immigrants seem to have had some traveling companions, or at least some assistance at home or when they arrived. Many had been preceded by relatives or friends. Certainly 20-year-old Antonio Almeida of Portugal was glad to join his brother in Providence, Rhode Island, in 1919 after an unpleasant voyage.

When the ship start go up and down, ev'rybud lay in bunk too sick to get out, just stick chin over side and puke. Best on top bunk; somebody on below get sick, stick out head, fellas on top puke on him too. First day out, ev'rybud happy out on deck in the sun. Somebody play the accordion, somebody play the guitar, ev'rybud sing, dance, laugh, pitch the horseshoe; but second day, ungh! then she start. We stop in St. Michael's for put on the meat and next in Faial, in the Azores—that's all.

I not sick at all. Little time before each meal, cook come to door where Portuguese is, and wallop on the pot with wood spoon. I find out, right after this noise, two more cooks come and pull big trough filled with stew by two ropes through where we are supposed to sleep, if she no stink so much. They run like hell, yell, holler like hell too, stick in the cup into the trough to get good filled with bucket they give for eat. If other guys in the room no too sick for talk, they yell, "Shut up, fat fool, get away with the rotten bucket. You are the big pig, can eat no mat' what happen."

Eight days go by like this, then I land in Providence. My brother meet, we go to the not-speak [speakeasy], and to New Bedford.[8]

Liberato Dattolo's brother sent him money in 1914 so that he could join him in Bridgeport, where there were several other people he had known in Italy. Dattolo, who was interviewed in 1939, recalled:

I came to this country from Italy in 1914 because everybody was coming here that we know on the other side. I worked on the farms with my father, and we used to work for almost nothing. My family was always poor. And in Italy, if you were poor it was too bad. . . . My older brother came to this country and he got a job in the American Tube and Stamping Co., so he told me that there was lots of work here and to come to America. I came here when I was 15 years old with the blessing from my father, and he told me not to forget the family; and every time that I could send him some money, to do it right away. My brother sent me that time about $40 for expenses to come here. Everybody used to hear the stories that America was a rich country; and when anybody from the village would leave to come here they used to say, "Don't forget, when you go to America don't forget your friends."

I landed in New York, and when I saw all the buildings I was surprised because I never saw anything like that in my life. I used to see the people pass by me and they were different than the people in the old country. These people that I saw used to walk quiet and they looked like they mind their own business. In Italy when anybody walked on the street they used to whistle and sing. Here they looked like they were mad.

My brother came to meet me at the boat and then I walked with him and my friend to see some of New York, and then we came to Bridgeport with the train. I asked my brother how Bridgeport was like, and he said that it was not like New York and there was a lot of factories here. He said that Bridgeport was the best place because there was a lot of people from the old country that we knew in Bridgeport.[9]

John Lukasavicius, also interviewed in 1939, immigrated from Lithuania in 1923. His father had preceded him in 1907.

When my father wrote and asked for one of us to come to America, my brother was satisfied and didn't want to leave, so arrangements were made for me to go. I was glad of the chance because after having talked to one or two of the people who had been there and returned, I was sure that life would be better for me in America. They had told me about the way people lived there and it seemed that even though the work was hard, pay was better and many of the marvelous things they described were worth seeing. Workmen bought fine clothes and jewelry in that country and lived in houses with floors in them. Anything you wanted you could buy instead of making it yourself.

I was glad to go to America because I was young and thought that I could get rich instead of being a poor farmer all of my life. I didn't have any idea of politics or whether people in Lithuania were free or oppressed. All I knew was that everybody hated the Russians and the old men talked about how great Lithuania used to be in the old days; but since I didn't know any different, the way we lived was all right with me. I knew too that if I went to America, life would be easier for those of the family remaining because there would be one mouth less to feed and one body less to clothe.

A day or two before I was to leave for America, we had a big party at my house. My mother prepared many dishes and the two village musicians played for dancing. All the village came to the party and everybody donated as much money as they could spare for my journey. My passage had been arranged and paid for by my father; the donations were to be used as I needed them. Everybody was glad that I was able to go, and I remember that night I made several promises of presents to my friends after I was working in America. My mother cried a little when I was leaving and asked me to be sure and write her all about my father, who had been gone 16 years, when I was leaving.

Coming to America I intended to work hard, earn a lot of money, and later return to my village a rich man. I didn't know what kind of work it would be but everybody said that if you wanted to work, in America you could always find it.[10]

John Larson, a Swedish immigrant, arrived in New York in 1895. Like many immigrants, Larson intended to return. His sisters already were in the United States, and his experience was relatively serene when contrasted with some of the other interviewees.

My father came from a long line of farmers. We have over 200 acres of farmland which has been in our family since 1795. The present house was built in 1880. I lived in the town of Bara on the island of Gotland on the Baltic Sea. My mother came from the same town. My mother's family were farmers also. The original John Larson bought the land in 1793 and built a home there. That house burned down. The land was bought from the Swedish Crown and today there is not any mortgage on the property. My oldest sister's son runs the farm now. We are very proud that we have been able to keep the land in our own family for so many years. My father was a good manager and lived very well.

My two older sisters came to America and procured jobs as housemaids. When I was about 13 years old I began to get the wanderlust and wanted to see the world. I began to dream of America and what a wonderful country it was. At this time, I started to learn a little English from books. My sisters were doing very well in America but they found it hard to learn English. I did not want to stay home with my father and my stepmother. I missed my older sister so much and wanted to be with her. My older brother helped my father on the farm and I felt he did not need me. In America I thought I could make more money. Father did not object to my leaving Sweden. At that time Father was 54 years old and I was 19 years. Father wanted me to come to America for five years and then return to Sweden. I was satisfied to do this at the time I left Sweden. I had no fears of any kind when I was young and unmarried and full of adventure. I was qualified only for farming. I did not know what I would do when I got to America. Probably work in a factory. I expected to return to Sweden in five years, after I had made a lot of money.

My father and my sister helped me financially. I came to America on an English boat called the *Kensington*. We sailed from Liverpool, England. Of course, I traveled third class. I brought most of my own food with me. We had a very good trip over. I only knew one man on the boat. He came from my part of Sweden. We danced so much on the boat that I wore out a pair of shoes.

My first glimpse of America was wonderful. We sailed up the Delaware River to Philadelphia. It was in May and the country was in full bloom and it looked beautiful to me. Of course it was different than Sweden, but I liked it at once. When we got off the boat we stopped for a while in a sort of wooden shed. I will never forget how I bought cake, milk, and a cigar from an old lady who had a stand there. We only stayed in Philadelphia for a few hours. I liked everything I saw. The railroad station was so large and I will remember the statue of William Penn. We took the train for New York a few hours after arriving. I was so anxious to get to New Haven I really didn't notice much in New York. I stayed in New York at the Congregational Immigrant Home. At the time I arrived in New York in 1895, there were no skyscrapers.

We left New York the next morning for New Haven. My sister met me at the station, and I surely was glad to see her. At that time New Haven had about 80,000 people and was more like a town than a city. I thought the center green was beautiful with all the lovely elm trees, especially the large Franklin Elm at Church and Chapel streets. We do not have the tall elm trees in Sweden and I just couldn't get over their beauty. My sister took me to where she was working on Orange and Humphrey streets. I stayed there a few hours and then we went to a boardinghouse on Franklin Street. This house was run by a very kind Swedish woman. At first I did not notice any changes in my countrymen.

It seemed strange at first to have my meals served at different times than when I was in Sweden. Our food was cooked mostly in the Swedish way but served American style. The homes in New Haven were furnished much better than in Sweden. The people dressed in a better style and I liked the American shoes also. The Americans seemed to have such a nice way of walking and so alert and quick in their movements. After I was here awhile I noticed the Swedish-Americans thought they were so smart and uppish because they could speak better English, but I didn't let it worry me. I was so thrilled with America and being near my sister.[11]

Charles Smirnoff, a Russian Jew, discussed the difficulties many immigrants had simply getting to a port of embarkation. He came alone in 1900, but an uncle helped pay for his passage. Like many immigrants, he was assisted by the process known as chain migration, whereby people from a village gravitated to neighborhoods already settled by fellow villagers.

In 1889 a law was passed definitely limiting the number of students who might enter the high schools and universities. This civil law denied the great masses of Jewish youth an opportunity for education. It was a bitter disappointment for me.

After the percentage laws were passed, thousands of Jewish students traveled to other lands seeking the education which were denied to them in their own land. Foreign universities were filled with Russian Jewish students. This situation caused great hardships for the poor, for they had to live on bread and cheese as they traveled on foot to satisfy their desire for knowledge. Many families had migrated to the United States to give their children an education, for their friends and relatives who left not many years before had already established themselves in the new country and had written glowing accounts of their success, happiness, freedom, and opportunities which they found there. At this point I was determined to go to America, not only for my own advantage but with an eager desire to bring my family there too.

A number of emigrants had to steal their way across the Russian border because they could not get passports. Trains, moving constantly through Germany, were thickly packed with refugees, and were on their way to port cities from which the emigrants sailed. German Jewish aid societies had rendered great aid to the frightened and helpless travelers as the trains stopped at various stations. This wave of emigrants from Russia spread to Canada, Argentine, South America, South Africa, and Palestine as well as the United States. My uncle had provided me with the necessary funds for this journey so that I did not have the inconvenience that others had experienced. I was just 20 years old when I left Russia. The ship sailed from Hamburg.

I have often told of my voyage in the steerage of the ship when all the discomforts of travel for over two weeks had to be endured. Bearded men dressed in long black coats and round hats made up a large part of the 200 passengers. The costumes of the women showed a greater variety, but they mostly wore full skirts and numerous petticoats. Yiddish was the chief language spoken among the Jewish passengers. I shall never forget the thrill that entered my heart when the ship finally steamed into the harbor of New York. It seemed that the Statue of Liberty welcomed us to a country of freedom with her hand raised up. The excitement among the passengers grew more intense as the ship entered the harbor, especially among the children, who had suffered most from lack of proper food. The regular meals offered by the ship were of little use to the Jewish immigrants because it was not kosher. Boiled potatoes, herring, and tea were the chief articles of diet. I told the immigration authorities that I was a carpenter and was going to make my home with an uncle in New York. This, of course, was a lie but I was advised to make this statement by one of the passengers who had made his second trip across the ocean. I really was not qualified to do any sort of work because I had just left college in Moscow.

Upon landing, not knowing where I was going, I followed a group of people for a few blocks. I was bewildered at the large crowds of people on both sides of the street, the elevated railroads above, and the streetcars, some pulled by horses. I stopped in front of a store where the proprietor had stood outside to get the morning fresh air. It was on Canal Street, I later discovered, and upon making inquiry of me as to where I came from, he directed me to a synagogue about three blocks away where I would be able to find some of my *Landsleit*. I soon found myself in the company of a man who had lived in our Russian village who had known my father since early childhood. He brought me to his home, where I met the family and I recognized two of the children [young men] who had attended the cheder with me. After partaking of a hearty meal we remained in the kitchen and I was asked many questions as to the conditions in our Russian village and also about the population there who were familiar to us. The next day many other Jews who had come from the same village and had settled in New York a few years before had called to visit me, and they also were anxious to hear of any tidings from the homeland.

As my friends were low and I did not want to impose on the good nature of my host, I went about in search for employment. I found work in a pants factory which was located in a building loft. I had to sit all day at the power machine sewing trousers. The hours were long (from 7:00 a.m. to 7:00 p.m.) and I worked in a small, hot room with a dozen other men for about $5 a week. But fortunately it was not for long, as the men in the shop have joined the garment-makers union and were now to work less hours and receive more pay.

The street I lived on was Baxter Street, a noisy and exciting street with tall, shabby tenements on either side. The pavements were lined with pushcarts containing every imaginable kind of goods. The peddlers would call out their merchandise loudly in Yiddish and brisk bargaining went on. The East Side was the scene of a continuous mighty struggle which went on daily—the struggle for a living. The newcomers went where their friends and relatives were located—where they could find work. This East Side became a great manufacturing center for clothing.[12]

For some the strain of temporary family separation took its toll, as is demonstrated in the recollections of this unidentified Polish woman:

Yes, you're right, I don't take it as a compliment anymore when people tell me they'd never guess that I was born in the old country. Seeing me with Vincent and the boss, if anyone were to hint that they thought I was Polish looking or acting I'd take it as an insult, I guess. Not, you understand, that I'm ashamed of being Polish anymore because us Poles are going places in the U.S.A., especially in this city, like you just said. There's Judge Jamrosy, Joseph Kulikowski, Steve Briekomski, and Stan Mainacki, to mention just a few who've made good in a pretty big way. When, if you don't mind my saying it, there's my own brother, Joe, with his swing band raking [in] more money then 90 percent of them. And he wasn't born in this country like the others. Where was he born? In the middle of the ocean. . . . Sure, I don't know what that makes him, but anyway he's not 100 percent Polish like I am. But he's the closest to it of all the Bodzuchowskis except me, the others being by my old man and that other woman before and after Joe and I landed in this country.

What happened to our own mother? She passed out on the way over from having Joe and being seasick at the same time. She was awful seasick, I remember, and being only 12 at the time and not speaking one word of English, I was too scared to tell the ship's doctor even if Mother had wanted me to. I remember her telling, and telling, and telling me not to go for the doctor even after her water broke for fear it would cost something—and then Joe's arrival wasn't in the cards. Understand? Well, then, let me skip it. What's that they say—"Of the dead, nothing but good"?

Do I know who Joe's real father was? How should I? But what's a woman going to do when she hasn't any money and divorce isn't possible in our church and her husband has forgotten her on the other side of the Atlantic Ocean?[13]

"This City Appeared as a Tremendous Overstuffed Roar"

For many immigrants the first impression of the United States was one of high buildings, noise, crowded streets, and hurry, hurry, hurry. Morris Shapiro, a Russian Jew, came to America in 1923, but not before spending a year and a half in Romania. Actually he was all alone, but not because he was emigrating. He was alone in Europe because his family already had emigrated. He related his immigration experience and his first impressions of New York, "the greatest city in the world," when he was interviewed in 1938.

Leaving Russia, I crossed the border and [went to] Romania. I lived there for over a year, working in the meantime in a candy factory. Then my sister and brother-in-law left me. Their visa came through, and they were lucky enough to be included in that particular quota.

For the first time in my life, I was actually on my own. No family, no relations, and very few friends. I was still young, but I'll admit that I was a bit downcast. The future appeared a little dark, and besides that, I had a premonition that from then on I would have to look after myself without the immediate help of my family.

A short time after my sister and brother-in-law left, knowing that it would be about a year and a half before my turn came to go to America, I packed and went to Bucharest. I felt that it would be best to go to this larger city where I might have a better opportunity of obtaining a job with a higher salary, or even learning a trade. I believed that knowing a trade would somehow help me in America.

I was very lucky in getting a job during my first week in Bucharest. I was also happy in the thought that I would also learn a trade, even though it was not to my liking or fitted in with my plans. This job consisted of being an assistant in the painting department of an iron bed manufacturing company. The pay was meager, but the opportunity was there.

After working hard for six months at this trade, I became a full-fledged painter with a corresponding raise in pay. I worked in this factory until notified that my visa had come through, and that I was included in the coming quota. I finished working and immediately set out for Constantsa, where I was to board the ship. And so, armed with a trade [and] a fairly comfortable amount of money, I set out joyously for the New World.

Twenty-two days later, I arrived in America. Unlike most of the immigrants, I and the rest of the new arrivals did not land at Ellis Island. This place of entrance was so overcrowded that it was necessary to land us at Providence, Rhode Island. After a day of examinations, I was given a boat ticket for New York. There was no extra charge for this ticket, as we had originally paid for our fares to New York. The very next morning I left for New York, and in late afternoon of the same day, I was greeted by my aunt at the docks of the greatest city in the world.

I only remained in New York for a few days, but I shall never forget the astonishment I felt at my first glimpse of this great city. I was bewildered at the sight of trains running overhead, under my very feet, trolleys clanging, thousands upon thousands of taxis tearing around corners, and millions of people rushing and pushing through the screaming noise day in and day out. To me this city appeared as a tremendous overstuffed roar, where people just burst with a desire to live. Before I really had a chance to become acquainted or accustomed to this groaning metropolis, my aunt shipped me off to Hartford, where my sister lived and where I made my future permanent home.[14]

Andrew Kokas came to New York from Lithuania in 1912 at the age of 16. Later he moved to New Britain, Connecticut.

When I first arrived in New York the thing that troubled me most was whether I would be able to live in that heavy smoky air. It felt thick when I breathed it. When I looked at the people I thought that if they can stand it, I can. The things I looked at most was the big buildings and the busy look that everybody had. I thought to myself that in a country where they made things as wonderful as those buildings, anything was possible—even for a farmer boy like me.

I was astonished at the fine clothes my brother wore when he met me and at the way he could get around the big city. Other Lithuanians I met later were dressed the same way and they seemed at home in the busy life around us. I remember some of them were bashful boys when they left our village and now they acted like men of the world. Eating in a restaurant was something new to me and all the different kinds of food you could get was a great surprise. Privately I thought my brother was very wasteful when he left a slice of white bread on a plate after we finished eating; I put it in my pocket with three other slices from my own plate. My brother laughed at me and told me that people ate white bread every day in America. I didn't know what to think. I liked everything we had to eat except the pie we had for dessert. It was too sweet.[15]

Harry Selmquist arrived from Sweden in 1926 at the age of 19. His loneliness in his third-class cabin was alleviated by visits to a fellow villager in second class. His first impressions were of African-Americans, Angora cats, and food:

I was 19 years old when I came to America. I came alone on a Swedish American boat. My brother had loaned me $225. I came third class. Everyone danced a great deal and I would play my accordian. Sometimes I would go up to the second-class cabins and play for the passengers. In this way I earned about $80. One night we had a very bad storm, so it took us nine days to come to America. Once in a while I would go up to the second class and visit a Swedish friend of mine. This made my trip very pleasant.

When I arrived in New York the traffic was most confusing. A Lutheran minister talked to me on the dock and put some of us in a taxicab so we would get to the railroad station. The ride in the taxi shocked me very much, and when we arrived at the station some colored men with red caps wanted to take our bags. We had heard about the gangsters in America and we thought we were being robbed. Finally we got straightened out and had some coffee and cake. The skyscrapers were so large and the city seemed enormous to all of us. I marveled at the size of the station and the way it was built. When we got on the train for New Haven, we couldn't get over the grand seats and the way the train went so much faster than it did in Sweden. There was a colored man selling candy and fruit. At first I was afraid of the colored man but finally I bought an apple. The colored people seemed so funny to us. We do not have them in Sweden.

When I arrived in New Haven, my brother and sister-in-law met me at the station. I surely was glad to see them. Then we went to my brother's home in Fair Haven. I did not notice any changes in my countrymen. Everyone was so kind to me. A few days after I arrived in New Haven, my brother took me to a dance where I met so many nice boys and girls and they all made me feel like I was at home.

My brother had a large Angora cat. I had never seen one before so I asked my brother if it was a bear, and he laughed and said, "No, it is a cat." It struck me as a funny-looking animal.

My brother had a very nice house. The hardwood floors seemed so beautiful to me. I had been used to wide boards in Sweden. In Sweden the men take their hats off when they meet anyone but I noticed here in America they only tipped them. I soon like the American way. At first I couldn't get used to only three meals a day. At home we had six meals. My sister-in-law was a very good cook. We had Swedish and American food. At first I did not like the taste of tomatoes but I soon enjoyed them. The ice cream also was so cold but now I like it very much, also the strawberry shortcake.[16]

Arthur Carlson entered the United States after emigrating from Sweden in 1902. Like so many others, Manhattan's sheer height impressed him. While he had made the trip alone, he nevertheless had a brother awaiting him in New Haven.

I came to America on the Cunard Line in March 1902, traveling steerage. It was a very rough trip. The passage cost about $50 at that time. I brought my own food and was treated very well by the crew. Of course I could not speak English, and that made it very hard for me when I first landed in New York. I had to stay in Ellis Island about two hours and I was treated very well.

The tall buildings impressed me very much. Nothing shocked me. I was so thrilled over being in a new country. I really saw very little of New York because I was supposed to go on a boat to New Haven, where my brother was to meet me. The people on Ellis Island told me I could get to New Haven quicker by train so I took the first train out, not thinking that my brother would be waiting for me at the boat. I was so excited I did not feel a bit lonesome. The train impressed me very much. It was so large and comfortable and went so fast. Of course my brother was waiting for me at the dock, but I did not even think of that at the time. When I got off the train someone kindly put me on a trolley and told the conductor where to let me off. There were two other Swedes on the train who were going to New Britain, and they made me feel better because I could talk to them.

I liked New Haven right away. It was so different from Sweden. It was winter and the lovely elm trees were not out yet, but the people seemed very friendly to me. The conductor let me off and told me where to go. My friend's house was two blocks from the trolley and I did not have any trouble finding the house. My brother lived with a very nice family of Swedish people by the name of Johnson. Well, it was so funny, because I arrived there two hours before my brother. He was so worried because he could not find me on the boat. He certainly was surprised when he came into the house to see me sitting there.

Of course the houses and streets were so different than in Sweden, but I was so anxious to get started in my work that there were many things I did not notice at first. The only thing that worried me was the lack of English language. My brother and the Johnsons were very kind to me. The changes that I first noticed in the American Swedes was in their clothes. They also seemed to have a more free and easy way of living. The furniture was so different also, but we had real Swedish food. I did not mind the changes because everyone was so kind to me and I was my own boss. At first I could not get used to so many sweet things to eat. Of course we had Swedish and American foods also. I did not like the American cheese as well as the cheese we had in Sweden. The American fast way of doing everything in such a hurry struck me funny at first. I was so anxious to get a job and I hated waiting around. The Johnsons took me around to see the city and the buildings. The large buildings and the central green impressed me very much. At first everything seemed strange, but I had a grand time. I only had to wait three weeks for a job.[17]

Michael Daunis left Lithuania for the United States in 1921 because he saw no future on his father's farm, which, according to custom, would be willed to the oldest brother (see chapter 1). Fall River, Massachusetts, was very different from his native village.

When I came to this country everything was strange. I didn't think much about people and things because I was young and everything I saw was different than what I was used to. When I came to my cousin's house in Fall River, Massachusetts, I was surprised at the way he was living. The house had a white toilet inside of the house, and the lights were coming from tubes in the wall and were very bright. I learned later about gas. I met a few fellows who came from the same part of the country I did, and their clothes and watches made me think they were rich because when they left they were the same as I was.

The strangest thing to me about food was that you could buy it in cans. Many of the things I ate were strange but I liked them. The thing I couldn't get used to was tomatoes. We didn't have them in Lithuania, and their taste and smell was terrible to me at first. One thing I liked was the candy, and I remember when I got my first pay I bought a pound of chocolates and ate them.[18]

Maxwell Lear, a Russian Jew, arrived in the United States in 1900 at the height of a presidential election. When he was interviewed in 1974, his impressions were of his initiation into America politics.

When I arrived in New Haven, it was during the fall of the presidential campaign. The candidates were William McKinley and William Jennings Bryan. And one of the earliest assignments I got—they gave me the street in our city called Oak Street. It's Legion Avenue now, and in fact that part of it is gone. Legion Avenue above there is still active. But someone gave me a card of little neckties, bow ties made up with the American flag. This was election time, and I guess they were Republicans. They gave me the American flag things to sell for 5¢ or 10¢ apiece. I don't remember. That was my first job before I began selling newspapers. . . .

The board of education of our city had one nongraded school for foreign children who couldn't talk any language but their own. It was on a little street called Whiting Street. It ran between Meadow Street and George Street. And my teacher, Miss Ford—I'm sure she is in heaven, because people like her can't be anywhere else—dealt with about 40 kids, boys mostly. There were some girls. Some of the foreigners, other than we—we still had our European clothes—but some of them from other nations, Italians, came in flour sacks and any way at all. I remember seeing the kids eating raw turnips—they looked like raw turnips. . . .

My first contact with a black was a friend of my father's later on, who had been the son of a slave. His name was Mr. Thomas. He lived on Rose Street, near where we lived. My father had a little grocery by then. His daughter Carrie was in my class in grammar school. Carrie Thomas was the first black schoolteacher in New Haven's history. . . .

You see, there were three things that struck me. One was that everyone worked. The factory whistles all over the city blew at seven in the morning and at six at night. . . . Secondly, everybody had to go to school until they were 16 years old. School, education, was compulsory. And third, military service was voluntary. In fact, they called them "volunteer," because I know the word "volunteer," from the French that I knew in Russia. I saw one such volunteer on the street during my first year.[19]

But not all first impressions were entirely favorable. Anthony Ausanka of Lithuania recalled a humorous first impression upon his arrival in 1907. But he immediately noticed poverty and the impact of factory work upon his fellow countrymen.

When we landed in New York, I was astonished by the size of the city. I never saw so much traffic and so much streetcars. I went by one place and I saw several people dressed in rags and looking hungry, and I was surprised that there should be anybody like that in a country where everybody made so much money. Near the railroad station I stood out in front of a barbershop for over half an hour watching a man get a shave. I couldn't understand why he was lying on a chair and sleeping while another man was putting soap all over his face. I thought that he was playing a joke and waited to see what the man would do when he woke up. When the barber picked up his razor and started to shave the man, I realized what was happening and I marveled that you could find a place like that. Everybody that I knew had always shaved themselves, and then only on some big occasion.

When I came to New Britain, my cousin took me around and I met some Lithuanians. One thing I noticed about them all was that they had lost the color in their faces. That came from working in the factories all day and not getting much sun.[20]

Nils Sahlin emigrated from Sweden in 1921. While many saw only the tall buildings, Sahlin noticed dirt and high-density living.

I left Sweden on a Swedish steamer that traveled back and forth from Stockholm to New York. I worked on the steamer for quite a while as a medical assistant before I decided to come to America.

My first impression of America was the size of the tall buildings and the awful hurry everywhere. The dirt around the docks disappointed me very much, as I expected to see a new clean country. I could not get over the dirty tenements and the houses so packed in together. Some of the people did not look so prosperous, and I wondered if America was so wonderful after all that I had heard about it. I was mostly interested in the English language. I liked the freedom of the ways of the Americans and their willingness to help anyone.

I did not see any of my countrymen at first. I like the American food and the automat struck me so funny. To be able to put in money and get food was so amusing to me. I did not like to see people eat corn on the cob. It seemed so rough and crude to me. Even to this day I do not like the custom. I think it should be cut off the cob first and then eaten from a dish. I ate some American and some Swedish foods.[21]

But it is left for Morris Kavitsky, a Jewish immigrant who arrived from Poland in 1914, to give voice to the ambiguity of the immigrant experience for many new Americans. He was glad he came; he did not want to return, and he brought his family over. Still, he understood that the choice of the new world over the old required cultural loss as well as gain, and that loss remained very much with him when he was interviewed 25 years later.

I arrived in the United States in the late summer of 1914. The war in Europe had already begun, but America, apparently, was still peaceful and quiet. I had to go through what appeared to me an interminable examination at Ellis Island. Passports, baggage, and my physical condition were checked and rechecked. I was impatient to get to the great and humming city which was so near to me now. I wanted to begin work immediately in order to send money to my needy family.

At last I set foot on New York soil. Before I had an opportunity to look around and examine no more than the skyline, my aunt, who met me on my arrival, bustled me into a taxi and took me to her home. There I was set upon by friends and relatives of the people back home, and I was asked more questions in two hours than ever before in my life. I finally managed to relate everything that had happened back home, conditions existing then, and about the health of all the people that I knew. I was finally allowed to go to sleep in the new country.

The next morning I inquired of my relatives as to what possibilities there were for my getting a job immediately. At first they tried to persuade me to rest up a bit because there were still enough years left in my life in which to work. But I told them that this was impossible; I needed money at once in order to bring my family over. I argued my point until they had promised to get me a job in one of the innumerable fish markets located on the East Side of New York.

A week passed before I was finally told that a job was found for me. During this period I was not idle. I walked around watching the habits, customs, and reactions of my people to the new environment. I noticed at once that all the habits and customs, except religious, of my people living in New York's East Side were almost the same as the habits and customs of the poorer class of Jews in my hometown. They still worked from morning until night, trying to make a living. Although the majority of them wore modern clothes, nevertheless there were still plenty of Jews wearing the old gabardines which they had worn in the old country. Some still retained their beards; others forgot their religion, became apostates, and shaved clean.

Most of the Jews seemed to have lost their health here while working in the sweatshops. I had never seen so many people with false teeth and eyeglasses. Was this part of the process of becoming Americanized? How about tuberculosis and appendicitis? I was shocked at the physical condition of my people in this country. It seemed to me that hardly any one of them escaped the surgical knife. Either his kidneys were bad, his gallbladder rotten, or his appendix ready to burst. Who ever heard of so much sickness back home? It appeared that most of the Jews ascribed their ill health to the weather conditions in this country. The air was damp here, while back home it was clean and dry. But I found that this was not the only reason for the breakdown in health. People worked harder here; they worked twice as hard as they did back home. This surprised me. Where was the great prosperity which was so widely advertised?

A man couldn't even own his own home here; that is, not unless he had a great deal of money. If a man did buy a home, all he would have would be mortgages on top of mortgages which he could never pay off and which, therefore, meant that he never really owned his home. Who ever heard of this in the old country?

The Jews seemed to have taken their lot in their usual docile manner. They walked around as if they were doped. Pasty-faced and undernourished, they worked from morning until night. They forgot their religion and appeared satisfied with the rut into which they had fallen. They went so far as to even smoke and work on Saturday. This shocked me. To work on the Sabbath day was undreamed of. I detested these so-called reformed Jews and still do.

My observations and opinions were cut short when I got my aforementioned job. I say "I got," but it was really my uncle who obtained this job for me in the fish market. I took this job without any objections because I did not have to work on Saturdays. My boss was a Jewish man with whom I had no difficulty in getting along. My pay, compared with my earnings in the old country, was very small. But this did not matter to me at that particular time. I worked very hard for one purpose, and that was to save enough money to bring my family over to this country and also send them a little money each week until the time arrived when we would be reunited. I was better off economically in the old country than I was here. Maybe this was because I lived on so little in order to save money, and God knows that what little money I did save was sent over to my family in order to alleviate the hardships which they had already begun to undergo during the war.

As I mentioned before, I worked very hard and with one purpose in mind. I had very few friends and did not care to mix with anyone. The only leisure time that I had was on Saturday, which I spent in the synagogue. I could think of nothing else but work and my family. I did not even stop to think whether or not I was satisfied in coming here. Neither did I have a desire to go back home. I came here for the purpose of settling and bringing my family over, and I meant to stick to my purpose. Especially so when it became apparent that Jews were not molested here and that pogroms were really beginning in earnest back home.

I finally began to realize that working in a fish market would never enable me to save enough money with which to bring over my family. I had a relative in Hartford, Connecticut, who persuaded me to go there and go into some kind of business. I took a chance and came to Hartford. I have never regretted my decision to come here, and I have made my home here ever since.[22]

Once the immigrants arrived in the United States, there was little time for them to acquaint themselves with their new surroundings. Whether alone or with friends or relatives, most of them had very little money. The first order of business was to find a job.

3

AT WORK IN AMERICA

After locating shelter, the next step for the new arrivals was to secure employment. Indeed, it was the United States' phenomenal industrial growth that had drawn them here. Spurred by technological innovation and the expansion of the railroad system, industrialization had transformed a rural, agricultural, craft-based economy into the world's foremost urban industrialized power. Between 1860 and 1900 the United States rose from the fourth largest manufacturing power in the world to the first. Total manufacturing capital increased from slightly over $2 billion in 1879 to over $20 billion in 1914. The figures for oil refining in the same period rose from $27 million to $326 million; for textiles from $602 million to over $2 billion; for iron and steel from $318 million to over $2 billion; and for machinery from $242 million to over $2 billion.[1] This investment translated into millions of factory jobs.

The new industrial nation required an infusion of workers to run the machines in these factories. The total number of production workers employed in manufacturing rose from slightly over 2 million in 1869 to over 6 million in 1914, and their wages increased from $621,000 to $3,782,000. The average blast furnace increased its labor force from 71 in 1869 to 176 in 1899, and the numbers rose from 119 to 412 in rolling mills. In 1880, 9,869 workers labored in oil refineries; the number climbed to 12,199 in 1899. Similarly, technological innovation in the production of textiles, firearms, locks, clocks, sewing machines, typewriters, and later automobiles provided countless job opportunities. Many of these jobs were filled by immigrants.[2]

For most immigrants, job-seeking was not a solitary enterprise. Family and kinship networks facilitated the search. The relatives who had written home about America and who had assisted in financing the voyage often helped their kinfolk find employment. Friends from one's village might put in a word with the foreman. Numerous studies reveal the paramount influence of family in easing the way into the workplace. As an example, a study of employee files from the Cheney silk mills in Manchester, Connecticut, reveals that over 58 percent of the workers responded affirmatively when asked if they had friends

or relatives in the mills. John Adams, an Austrian immigrant who American-
ized his name, captured this fairly common experience when he said, "I had
an uncle here. . . . He was pretty in with the Cheneys, so he got me a job in
here."[3]

The immigrants entered the labor force at the same time that the modern
union movement was emerging. Immigrant reaction to labor unions was
mixed. Traditionally, historians have assumed that immigrants, coming from
a preindustrial backgound and viewing themselves as "birds of passage,"
saving for the return voyage, were hostile to unions. But numerous examples
demonstrate that when immigrants ceased believing that they would return
home, or when they felt that employer practices threatened their group sur-
vival, they did unionize and protest against what they perceived to be unfair
working conditions.[4]

Many first-and second-generation immigrants were beginning to enjoy some
economic stability by the 1920s. Thus the Great Depression came as a cruel blow.
Although the economic upheaval affected various groups differently, immigrants
were heavily located in manufacturing and mechanical industries in unskilled
and semiskilled positions; consequently they were exceptionally vulnerable. For
example, Ronald H. Bayor has demonstrated that nearly half of New York City's
Italian-born heads of households labored in occupations that were hard-hit in
the 1930s.[5] One result was ethnic tension, and as the interviews in this and
later chapters indicate, there was some measure of gender tension as well. Most
immigrants had come to America seeking economic betterment, but the Depres-
sion served notice that there was no permanent security, not even in the Promised
Land.

"I Knew Some People"

The quest for work was not a haphazard experience. Few are the immigrants
who recalled disembarking and aimlessly wandering about, hoping for the chance
discovery of a job. Most either came with friends or relatives or went to them
when they arrived. Even those who moved from city to city usually had kinfolk
or friends already living at their various destinations. Of course, among the
Italians, the stories of the padrone who contracted for work for large numbers of
his fellow countrymen are well known. But the padrone became less important
as networks of kinship and friendship became established in the United States.
These networks were the best employment agents for prospective employers and
employees. In Manchester, Connecticut, the Cheney silk mills relied upon them

for workers. Ike Kleinshmidt, a second-generation German-American who fol-
lowed his immigrant father into the mills, recalled:

Here my father was, with a wife and four children. I have three sisters and
each one of us, at one time or another, have worked at Cheney Brothers. His
brother came over from Germany a year or so after my father did, and he settled
in Manchester because my father was here, and he became a weaver, and he had
three sons and his wife, and they, at one time, were employed by Cheney
Brothers. There are a great many families here that had somebody, either an
uncle or an aunt or a sister or a brother, that somehow were tied up with the
Cheney Brothers operation. As you go through town you'll find out, you'll meet
these people.

We have records here that go back into the eighteen-, nineteen-hundreds.
I had this family from Texas up here not too long ago that were tracing their
family tree, and they knew that their families, somewhere along the line, was
connected with Cheney Brothers. I like to help these people out because they
can get a good smile on their face when they can find these records. We
did find [them]—we were very fortunate to find out that she had a great-
grandfather and an uncle and an aunt that worked here at Cheney Brothers
and it kind of helped her to conclude her family tree. They worked here many,
many years ago.[6]

John Kluck arrived in the United States from Austria in 1904.

I came over here to Manchester. I was 17 years old at the time. [A friend from
his village] was a velvet weaver, and I wanted to go to Torrington and learn the
machinist trade, and [his friend] said, "Well, velvet weavers, they make pretty
good money, pretty near as good as a machinist." So he asked . . . and they said
they would hire me. But I had two weeks I went and I didn't get paid anything
. . . to learn weaving velvet, and then after that I had one loom and . . . it was
mostly piece work and I made around $6 or $7 a week until afterwards, when
you made $10 dollars. That was big money at that time.[7]

John Adams emigrated from Austria in 1910 and initially went to New
Hartford, Connecticut.

53

I had an uncle here, Andrew Adams. He was pretty in with the Cheneys, so he got me a job in there. So from New Hartford I came over here [to Manchester] and have been here ever since.[8]

From Italy came Ignazio Ottone, who had been preceded by several friends:

Well, I heard [about Manchester] from the people who was coming here. I didn't know nothing about Manchester. . . . People was coming to Manchester; I had quite a few friends before me from my town. There were quite a few guys here from my town over here. When I got here, those boys helped me to get the job, you know. . . .

Well, I went down [to the mill] . . . a girl used to bring me down, see? She was going to school here; she knew how to talk. And I went to . . . well, they gave me a job. The first time I went around, they sent me down and I didn't know what he said; I came home. Next day I went again. He sent somebody with me to the office; you have to go for examination, you know. At the ribbon mill, I started to work.[9]

Michael Califi emigrated from Italy to Fishkill, New York, in 1905. His recollections are revealing because although they portray a man on the move, he always had contacts at his points of destination.

Me had to work. So one day my brother and my cousin talk to the boss in the place where they work [a brickyard], and they say to me, "Mike, tomorrow get up early and go to work with me." I was very glad because me pretty near finish all the money I took with me from other side, and I say to my brother and my cousin, "Thank you very much, much oblige."

He hated the drudgery of the brickyard, however.

I got sick and tired, and one day I say what the hell with this kind work. I think I go some other place, and I make up my mind and I go to Lawrence,

Massachusetts, because I know some people in Lawrence, Massachusetts. And I know that this people in Lawrence, Massachusetts, work in a factory, and they good friends to me, and they sure get me a job in the shop—yep, the same shop they work. . . .

Well, my friends was working in a texty mill [meaning textile mill]. They work over there a long time, and they talk to the boss and ask'm to give me a job, and the boss say o.k., tell'm to come in tomorrow and I give'm a job on the bobbing machine, and the next day I go with my friends and they show me the boss and he puts me to work on the bobby machine [meaning the bobbin machine].

Califi had a run-in with his Irish boss and returned to Fishkill several months later.

Anyhow, I work little bit here and little bits there. I can no remember all those places. Anyhow, in 1913 or 1914 I make up my mind I want to go to Bridgeport. Over here I had some cousins and I know some friends. My cousin was in the banana business, and some more friends was in some other kind of business, too. I know Jimmy Leon, the big shot; in that time he had not even a penny. . . .

So anyway, when I come in here, in Bridgeport, I go to see a friend of mine that I know him from the other side. That was John Joseph. He work in the Crane Valve Company, and I ask my friend if he can get me a job in the Crane Valve, and he say to me: "Mike, I try, maybe you get in and maybe not; maybe you get a job quick and maybe you got wait a little bit, see." Anyhow, I say to John, try. Anyway, no cost nothing to try. But on the same time I look round for something else, anyhow. But I no like to go some other place because my friend told me they pay pretty good money in the Crane Valve, so I say myself "what's use try get a job some other place? I be glad to wait a month and two months, so long I get in the Crane Valve, see?" . . .

I think I wait two and maybe three weeks. One nighttime my friend Joseph come home, and he say to me "Eh, Mike, come here, I got something good tell you." And I go to see what he want, and he told me he got me a job in the Crane Valve Company. "OK," me say, "tomorrow morning I get up quick and early and I go with you. Thank you anyhow."[10]

Similarly, John Lukasavicius's father, who had immigrated to Pennsylvania from Lithuania, sent for him and helped him secure employment in the mines.

When young Lukasavicius decided that he didn't like the mines, it was friends and relatives in other towns who helped him secure employment.

When I arrived at Castle Garden in New York, the authorities at first refused to let me in the country because my eyes were weak. I stayed there for two weeks and the day I was to be deported, it was arranged to let me enter. A friend of my father's put up a bond of $5,000 for me. Those two weeks were the longest in my life; every morning I awoke with the idea that perhaps today they were going to send me back, and I didn't know that my father knew I had landed because the agent he had bought my passage from had told him. I didn't understand why they wouldn't let me into the country and so I sat, being afraid of everything.

I joined my father in Pennsylvania and he made arrangements for me to work in the coal mines. I soon found out that living in America was not much better than in the country I had left. We lived in a boardinghouse with 12 other miners. It was crowded and dirty. Working in the mine was hard and dangerous. Every day someone was getting hurt. During the three weeks I spent there I never saw the sunlight, because we went down in the mine before the sun came out and we finished work after the sun had set. I never saw any other part of the world around except the mine and the boardinghouse. Only Saturday nights we used to go to a local saloon and sit around and play cards and have a few drinks.

After three weeks I told my father that I didn't like that sort of life and asked him to go with me to some other place. He told me that there was no better place to work than in the mines for greenhorns, but if I wanted to go, I could. I left the mines and went to Grand Rapids, Michigan, where I had a cousin. There were several Lithuanian families in that city, and soon after I arrived a job was secured for me in one of the furniture factories. Compared to the mines that job was heaven. I carried around fresh pieces of lumber and helped the cabinetmakers. The sun came in the windows all day long and the pay was better than what I had in the mines. In the mines, my father and I worked two weeks to earn $10 and in this furniture factory they paid me $1.25 a day.

At this time of course I couldn't speak English, so that until I learned a few words it was hard for me to understand what people were asking me to do in the factory. When I wasn't working, I went out with my cousin to the dances that were given once in a while. We played cards with friends and visited with the Lithuanian families. Reading papers printed in Lithuanian, I gradually learned a little about the things that were happening in the world. Discussions that I listened to among the Lithuanians also helped me to see the differences in the government here and that in the old country.

I began to like living here better, as I gradually learned that you didn't have to have a passport to go from one section of the country to another and you didn't have to be afraid of men in uniforms. I remember how scared I was of the conductor on the train that took me from New York to Pennsylvania. When he took my bundles and put them on the rack over my head, I was afraid that I couldn't take them with me, that he was confiscating them. I didn't know that he was just helping me out. Another time in a saloon I was with a group who started discussing the government and the president. I wanted to run out when they swore about it. I thought for sure that we would be sent to prison. When I mentioned it, everyone laughed and said I was just a greenhorn.

After I was working in the furniture factory for two years, my father wrote and said he had been badly hurt in the mine and he asked me to come and stay with him. I went back to Pennsylvania about 1906 and went back to work in the mines. The accident to my father had crippled him, so I had to work and support both of us. After I was working in the mine about three months, a piece of coal from an explosion hit me in the face and I was unable to work for about four months. During that time, the miners in the house we were boarding in paid for living expenses, and because we both belonged to the union, they sent us a doctor. I was glad of that because we didn't have any money; I had spent all I saved for doctors for my father. I went back to work in the mines after I recovered and stayed there until 1910, when my father died. I came to New Britain then. I had some friends here, and they found a job for me in the factory where I am working today.

Of course during all this time I had been sending money home when I could spare it. Later on my sister married and her husband worked the land and my mother lived with them until she died. My brother opened up a shop in a town 10 miles away from our village and still lives there.

During the years that I have been working in the mines and the factories, I haven't encountered any more than ordinary trouble with my jobs. When I didn't understand English some of the men I worked with made fun of me, but I didn't understand them so it was all right. None of my bosses troubled me and the men I worked with, though they laughed at some of my mistakes, helped me out when they could.

In the mines one time, I saw one of the tricks they play on greenhorns and was glad that my father was there to show me the way around. A Polish miner played this trick on another Pole who wanted a job. The Pole had just come to this country and when he asked the miner for a job as his helper, the miner said he would have to test him out and see if he was strong enough for the work. The miner picked up a thin steel bar and bent it in a hook, then threw the hook over one of the electric wires that was used to run the cars in the mines. These lines carried about 250 volts. The miner then told the job applicant if he could hold on to the hooked bar, he could have the job. The greenhorn, not knowing any better, took hold of the bar. The shock threw him to the ground. He got up again and took hold of the bar and the same thing happened. About this time the mine boss came down the tunnel and seeing what was going on, stopped the goings-on. The man was lucky to be alive; the only thing that saved him was the fact that his clothes were dry and that he stood on one of the few dry spots in the tunnel.[11]

Liberato Dattolo of Bridgeport emigrated from Italy in 1914. Once again, his experience reflects the essential services provided by relatives, as well as the tension that competing ethnic networks could provoke.

When I got here I was glad to see all the people that came from my place, and they started to make a good time for me. They made a party, and they had wine and *biscotti* [dried cake biscuits], and lots of meats and macaroni. I was surprised that we had macaroni, because I thought that they only had this in the old country.

Then my brother said to me that he had a place for me to board with some people that he knew—my brother was staying with some other people and they didn't have no room for me—so I said yes, and I went to stay with these people. These people had four big rooms and they had four boarders, all Italians, and they treat me good. After two days my brother took me to the shop that he was working in and his boss saw me and he gave me the job. They made me "cold passer," and the work was hard, and the shop was hot. I never saw anything like this in Italy. We were always used to work in the farm, so this was so different that I was afraid that maybe that I would lose the job.

All this time I used to meet all the other people and they used to take me to the Italian stores to play a little bit cards. That time all the Italians on Saturday or Sunday, they would stay on the corner on Manino's Loan Office and they use to talk all about Italy. They used to ask me and some people that just came from Italy how Italy was, how the people live there now, and what we think that is going to happen that a lots of people come to this country. I said that if someday Italy get better then I like to go back. That time some of the people that I knew they couldn't get used to this country. They used to go back, because when the Italian people worked someplace, some other nationality would bother them and sometime they would make trouble. My brother said that if anybody tried to make trouble with me not to talk, just to mind my own business. In the American Tube and Stamping

I was getting about $8 a week, and I put in from nine hours a day and sometimes more, and five and a half days a week.

There was a lot of Polacks in that place and they never liked too much the Italian people. They always used to call the Italians "Wops," "Guinea," and lots of other names. So the same time we used to call them Polacks and something that I can't tell you. These people they started to call names first. The Italians were always minding their own business, and the Polacks start the trouble. We had 23 men in one department and only 7 were Italians.

Lots of times we had a fight in the shop. I was almost 16 years old that time, and one time somebody called us names too much, so I told my brother and other Italian people that I would fix him up. In the afternoon when the boss was in another place I told this man that we would fight behind the pile of junk. That time I almost killed him. If I killed him I know that they would not put the blame on me, because the other guy started the fight; I was defending myself. That was the only thing that bothered me. I wanted to work just like the other people and here a couple of Polack, the son-of-a-gun, they don't want to leave us alone. What for did they want to bother *la Christianita* [humanity]?

I stayed in this shop for almost one year and then I was laid off, because they have no work for me and some of the other people. Ten people, Italians and Polacks, were laid off at the same time. Then when I was laid off I felt bad, but my brother said that in America it was easy to find a job right away.

One day I was walking on Barnum Avenue and I asked for a job in the Remington and I got the job. When I first asked the man he looked at me and he said, "Are you Italian?" and I said, "Yes. You have a job for me?" . . . He said, "All right, I'll give you the job, but you have to do the work good or you don't stay long." I said, "I'll do anything, and I'll show you that I am a good working man." So he gave me the job. I worked in the scrap room, and it was a dirty job, and I made almost $10 a week. All the scrap that come out of the machine we had to get it, me and another man, and then we put it in the press and had to make like a big bundle out of all that thing.

I worked on this job for over five years and then I heard that the Holmes and Edwards, the silver shop, was busy making the forks and the knives. So I left the job in the Remington and I went to look for the other job and I got it. Here I was making about $14 a week and that was good pay in that time. I worked on this job for almost a whole year, and then there was no more work because some people said that the factory was going to move out of Bridgeport. Well, I went to look for another job and it was not too easy to get a job; then I saw some friend of mine and he told me to put an application in for the state highway job. So after a little bit I got the job working on the roads. We used to repair fences, fix holes on the roads, and do everything. I got $16 a week for this and I stayed on the job for one year. Then the boss said that there was no work, but I don't believe it because he was a lousy

Irishman, and he didn't like the Italian people that worked with him. Nobody liked this man. Even his nationality that worked with us used to hate him like poison.[12]

"I Knew It from Italy"

Not all immigrants arrived without applicable skills. "Lateral migration"— immigrants practicing the same trades in America as they had in Europe— was certainly more common in the early nineteenth century, before American industry was transformed by mechanization. But even early-twentieth-century handcraft workers were subject to some of the same discipline that characterized factory work in the United States, as Lucy Richardson makes clear. Richardson emigrated from Portadown, Northern Ireland, to Manchester, Connecticut, in 1915. Her mother and her sister had been hand-loom weavers in a village called Bann Foot. The "putting out" system in Ireland was a far cry from the routine of a modern factory, but it too required a certain degree of regimentation:

We had a weave shop, we called it, built onto our home. It was big enough for four of these looms. They are quite a large thing and they have a treadle. My sister was 10 years older, and she was a weaver and my mother was a weaver. But me being little, I was about five, and I remember winding the bobbins to keep my sister going with her loom. My mother was provided with the bobbins, and I didn't have to worry about her. Sometimes, now I think of it, I was just a child, and I really rebelled, and sometimes I wouldn't have the bobbins in time. My sister would holler for the bobbins, I'd bring her a hat. So that really was my life at that time. Of course I was going to school at that time. We started school at three years old in that little village. Well my life was happy; I didn't know anything different. There wasn't anything much to do. . . .

They had to go over this river Bann to get a new thing to weave into the cloth—it's a beam. Then when they would weave that, finish that, they had to go over this river Bann again to the inspection place and get their money for it. . . .

Yes, and they had to bring their cuts, they were called, when they had it ready for the place. They called it cuts. They would have to bring that over to this place over the Bann where the inspection office was, and it would have to be inspected, and if anything was wrong, of course, you'd be fined. Then they got paid.[13]

On the other hand, Louise Gaggianesi had worked in relatively modern cotton and silk mills in Pavia, Italy, before she emigrated to Thompsonville, and later Manchester, Connecticut, in 1917. She noticed very little difference in the work—as she put it, "just like here at Cheney's, spinning." When she arrived in Thompsonville, her relatives were already employed in the Bigelow carpet factory.

My cousin, she knew how to speak English, so she got the job for me. . . . [Her first job was] winding; it was the skeins; they were long skeins. I used to pull rope and put the skein up and I had a big spool on the machine. That was the winding. And then the Bigelow had orders to make soldiers' blankets so they put me in quilling. I used to get $14 a week. It was good at that time in 1918 when I got that job. [When she started out] we was in piece work. We used to get $10 a week, eight hours, five days and a half. [Did she like it at Bigelows?] Very. It was just like Italy. I used to work in Italy in the factories, you know, and one job or another, you're gonna get used to it.

[Then in 1919 her sister married someone from Manchester.] That's when my sister, in January 1919, got married with a Manchester man, so she stayed [in Thompsonville] until the first week in March and then she moved here. Her husband found a job again in Manchester, so we moved to Manchester. . . . [At Cheney's] first I went to work in the winding. An Italian, she showed it to me. An Italian girl, she teach me how to wind. . . .

[A man from her village got her the job.] We went to the main office and he talk for me. He asked me how many grades of school I had. I said the third grade of school. And then he said, "I think I've got a job." And I went to work. The foreman was wonderful. . . . Then in the quilling, they need quilling people, so they put me on quilling. I knew it from Italy, and at Thompsonville I used to do quilling, so it was easy for me to learn.[14]

C. Guerra, an Italian mason, came to the United States believing that his skill would guarantee permanent employment. However, he soon discovered that American technology was rendering his hard-earned experience increasingly irrelevant.

The concrete foundations ruin the mason trade. . . . I was born 1885, in Italy. City population was 17,000 that time, and they work most on the farms. Most the people have to work on the farms because there is no money, no place in the city, and the people are lucky to learn something if they have chance. Sometime the man sends the son to work helping the mason, black-smith, and the barber. To learn the trade takes long time—not like this country.

In Italy, where I come from, if the father have the trade he want the oldest son to have the same trade. When I was 10 years old I start to help my father on the mason trade because he was mason and his father was mason. If the father have the same trade, then they make easy for the son because he don't have to start work hard on the foundations. If the mason have helper, small boy 10 years old, they make start them on cleaning and doing all the hard work. They have to help the master's wife and buy all the things for the master and for the wife. They have to be like servant and work like horse. In America the mason can't tell the helper to do something because if you tell him and he don't do it you can't do nothing. In Italy it is like law they have for the trade—the master says, and you do. When the boy is 15 years old, he have to know how to mix the mortar and do it right way. When the boy is 19–20 years old he knows the trade and then he have respect like all the other masons. When he is learning, he don't have respect like when he know the trade. That's the way it is. In Italy the good mason is like the sculptor; the engineer, he is higher class. The barber and the tailor is low class. The shoemaker is low class because anybody could learn the shoemaker, easy.

To be mason you have to know just right everything and that's hard thing—that's why they have respect. In Italy I even have the women work for me and they carry the stones and they do some light work like cleaning. The boys have to do the mortar.

I come to this country when I be 30 years old, and right away I find jobs in Pittsburgh because they are building there that time. My friends get me the job. Pretty soon I was contractor and I have men to work for me. After I finish some jobs there I get the chance to come to Connecticut and work. I help to build some school and some shop building in this place, Bridgeport. I get married and I have my family here—two daughters and wife. Now I am getting old and I don't have much work and my wife have to help supportin' the family.

I do little bit work now but not so good, because the foundations they make from cement, and not stone like before. They build the houses on the East Side [federal housing] and the houses on East Main Street and they don't have use for masons because they make from concrete. Stone is cheaper like concrete, but they build from concrete just the same. That's why people don't care to learn trade like this no more. If they learn something they don't learn mason, because there's no more chance for the mason. Some people I know, they are working in the shop because they can't get this kind of job, but I'm too old for shop so my wife have to work. Sure, the people they want to learn this if they have place to go when they learn, but where's chance?

When I first come to this country, I have lot ambitions and good chance

to make money. I have a house for myself and everything good. Then contractors start to use concrete and ruin the mason trade. That time if I have a son
I send him to learn my trade; now if I have son I send him to shop instead.

Kids now, in this country, be too fresh and don't learn nothing. When they
want to learn something they go to trade school and they don't learn nothing
from the masters. They tell the master how to do—this way they don't learn
nothing. I have two daughters and they don't learn nothing because they's
nothing to learn. The girls have to go to the shop. Instead if I have the chance
to work in my trade, I send them to learn something that they need'm. This
makes lot difference.

All the trades dying now because the people work in the shops and they
make enough to live. Nobody sends the boys to learn nothing because the
trades no good, they have everything machine. Man put something in one
machine and comes out all finished; pretty soon the machine do all the work
and the people have nothing to work. Tailor the same thing. All the suits they
make in the shops. When I have money I buy tailor-made suits—now I buy
from store. Before, mason makes foundations by hands—now machine makes
with only one man what takes before 15 men. This is the same all the trades.
Shoemaker makes shoe repair one time—now they make cheap shoes and the
people buy cheap shoes instead to repair old shoes. Barber before have good
business—now they have barber school and people have cheap haircuts and
the barbers have to have cheap prices because this. So how you expect people
to learn trades if they don't have chance to get jobs with the trade?[15]

"The Trade Itself Is Now Considered Obsolete"

*Like Mr. Guerra, others discovered that the skills they had acquired in Europe
had fallen victim to the onslaught of American technology. Two interviewees,
whose entrance into the United States was separated by 61 years, explained how
their European training differed from the apprenticeship programs in the
United States. Mr. Havanich, a Slovak who emigrated in 1888, was interviewed
in 1940; Michael Bilger emigrated from France in 1949 and was interviewed
in 1981. Havanich had incorrectly believed that his training as a cabinetmaker
would serve him for the rest of his life in America.*

I came to this country with my father when I was only nine years old. He
came here for a four-year stay, and in that time he made enough money to
go back and buy a small house and a plot of land. While he was here he

worked as a track-walker; in the meantime I was going to school. I was interested in drawing and planning while in school, and when I went back with my father I was sent into apprenticeship with a cabinetmaker. At first my father wanted me to learn forging, but I couldn't stand the rub of metal on my fingers. [I had two fingers shot off in an accident] so it was decided that I take up cabinetmaking.

I served in apprenticeship for a period of three years, during which time I learned the trade from top to bottom. In Europe it is necessary that after one learns a trade he must travel to other places so as to get a wider knowledge of his trade. I traveled to many of the principal cities in Europe, learning all styles of work, and as I went along, because of the experience that I had gained, I was able to elevate my own standard. I succeeded in doing this and at the same time I established a reputation as a first-class cabinetmaker. In Europe the tradesmen must know their work to perfection. The shoemaker has to really know how to make a pair of shoes; the carpenter has to know all the tricks of the trade; and the cabinetmaker has to be able to make every piece that goes with the work that is assigned to him. At the present time, with all the advances in machinery, the cabinetworker in this country can only work on a production basis, and it isn't necessary any longer for him to be experienced along the regular line. All of the other trades have taken the same course, with the exception of the mechanics trades that have to do with the present time.

I came to this country again in 1899, this time to stay for good. I was then about 20 years of age and I got a job with a friend of mine who worked in the same line [cabinetmaking]. I stayed at this in New York for a couple of years, and then I came here. While I worked in New York I attended evening school for the purpose of learning the language and architectural drawing. I was very much interested in drawing because it had something to do with my work. Later when I came to Bridgeport I found that I could use both to a good advantage. I set up a repair business on the East Side, where at that time there were a large number of Hungarians; this made it possible for me to engage in other things besides the repair business. Soon, with the spreading of the news that I was able to deal in foreign exchange and mortgage holdings et cetera, I became better known to the Slovak element in the section, and from that time on I was able to make a good living in this section of the city. There have been many changes since that time. When the cabinetmaking business gave way to modern development, I found it necessary to specialize in foreign exchange, mortgages, real estate; and I also acted as agent for steamship companies. At that time, with the immigrants going back and forth, I was able to do good in this business. Now, because of conditions, there is very little business in the agency branch.

At the time I abandoned my work, I began to do business in the sale and repair of musical instruments. I had learned this on the other side in the course of my travels as a tradesman. There the Gypsies were the leading musicians, and oftentimes, when I had stopped in one of the cities, I had the opportunity to engage in this work. My liking for this work lay in the fact that I had always had a desire for fine work. In Europe, unlike here, the essential thing is fine work; to make it durable, and to save and work with the least amount of material possible. That is the thing that determines the good mechanic. Well, when I began to deal in musical instruments [here in Bridgeport], I established a good business because I became known to most of the Bridgeport musicians, and they in turn gave me most of their work. This business continued prosperously until about 1925 and up to the time the movietone set in the picture houses. With radio coming in, the lesser musicians dropped the playing of instruments; it became so that people turned their ears to mechanical music. Now that the educational bodies are stressing music in schools, and music appreciation is becoming more popular, the people are once more turning to the study of music in one way or another. Lately I have had a few calls asking for musical instruments. This the first time that I've had any business in the line since about 1929, the time of the "crash." . . .

The reason that I have not followed the cabinet trade in recent years is because machinery is able to do what we cabinetmakers attempted to perfect years ago. The true mechanic [cabinetmaker] had to learn the science of wood shrinkage, application of finishing materials, and also the styles of furniture. At the present time all of this is being done through machine processing and the final assembling of the work takes but a few minutes. In other words, those working at the trade are no longer considered to be craftsmen; instead they are assemblers, just as in any other type of work. They are no more cabinetmakers than a man fixing a wooden crate. The work is done by absolute machinery to the extent that the trade itself is now considered obsolete. And that's the reason why no opportunities exist in this field. If any of the younger people follow the carpentry trades it stands to reason that they won't take cabinetmaking. However, there is a good chance in carpentry itself, but we cabinetmakers never considered *that* a fine profession. The chances are that a young man taking carpentry as a trade can make a fair living because wood construction is always called for in the rural section of any city.[16]

Bilger was apprenticed to the Peugeot company in France at the age of 15:

Well, I was born in France in 1925, about 35 miles outside of Paris. When I was a young boy, at the age of eight, I moved to the east of France, near the Switzerland border, to live with my grandfather, grandmother, and my father, after my mother passed away. In that part of the country in France, the only industry was Peugeot Manufacturers, who make the Peugeot car. I did my grammar school, I went to high school, I finished high school, and at the age of 15 I entered the four-year apprenticeship program for toolmaking. The big difference in Europe, especially in those days, was the amount of young boys who would go for the trade. In a small plant like Peugeot, where I was, which is divided into four or five plants, we were 167 applicants for toolmaker. It was an 8,000-hour program, the same as it is in this country in 1981.

When you apply for it, the speculation is if you graduate after four years, you have to sign a contract with the Peugeot plant for seven years. The only thing which will break a contract is if you pass away, or if there is a war. Otherwise you are in the Peugeot plant for seven years, and can quit only after that. You do your apprenticeship program as a toolmaker, in the old days, by first of all handling a file. They will teach you how to use a file, they will teach you how to use a chisel, they will teach you how to use a hammer. These are the three tools of the trade, to start with, back in 1940. Then after, you will do all the parts required by the teacher. By hand, you will do parts to fit into each other, including dovetail, radiuses, angles, all by hand. You always finished them to fit perfectly; what we call in this country slip fit. That's the way you finish the parts, because when they send an inspector, there cannot be any light in between the parts. Even in those days, we had dovetail cutters to use on the milling machine. But you had to learn to do it by hand first, before you graduated to go into the milling machine or other machines in the toolroom.

I come out of a shop where we have apprentices. A young boy now doesn't know how to chisel, doesn't know how to use a file. The first thing, when he comes into the apprenticeship, we'll put him on a milling machine, as an example, or a lathe or a grinder, whatever the case may be, and the teacher will teach him how to use the machines. But to use a file . . . In those days, freehand was 80 percent of the trade, because we did not have the tooling. Many parts could be fit by freehand, by filing, by stoning, et cetera.

The technology . . . in the United States, when I came in 1949, was already ahead of us by about 10 years, in Europe. We had some too. When I first started my job here, I found tools that I didn't know existed, coming here directly from France. I enjoyed very much, and I found out, in my 32 years in this country—I got kind of proud of it, because a couple places I went to work for had nobody to do freehand work, and I did it. To some of the American people—they really don't know how we could do it. To us, anybody in this trade in France, or in Switzerland, or Germany, for instance, in my days, could never graduate if they couldn't do freehand.

That was nothing, in my trade, at all. I feel sorry for a lot of the young boys here, who don't know even how to handle a file. But of course, if you talk to one of these young boys, he'll tell you, "You're old-fashioned." Maybe so. But sometimes it helps. Sometimes it helps. . . .

I can give you an example that happened to me only nine months ago, after I got laid off from Timex in Middlebury. I went to work for a company here in Oakville, and the company was just starting a toolroom, and there was nobody in the toolroom who really was a toolmaker. They had two or three young draftsmen from Kaynor Tech in Waterbury, which is a state college. One day, one of the young boys came up to me, and he said, "The piece I want is this shape, but we cannot do it, can we, on the milling machine or lathe?" I said, "No, you can't. Not the way you want it, not the way you draw it, as a draftsman." So he said to me, "Well, then, is there any other place where I can send the job out?" I said, "I didn't say you had to farm it out. I said you cannot do it on a machine." He had compound angles and compound radiuses all over the place. "But I didn't say that I cannot do it." Then he asked me to do it. I said I would rough it out on the milling machine, and on the lathe, and on the grinder, to get as close as possible, and then after I would freehand it. Of course, I had the advantage that I knew freehand; I also had the advantage of gauges, which in my day, back 40 years ago, I did not have. I had to make two parts fit together. But there I didn't have to have the other parts; I could make the male or the female, one or the other, it doesn't matter, because I had gauges technology brought us, radius gauges, angle gauges, feeler gauges. For measuring. So that's what I used, and I made the parts. Back in my time, I wouldn't have been able to use the milling machine or the grinder to rough it out, I would have had to rough it out with a chisel. But I used a miller to rough it out, and then I went on to the bench, and I went on my vise, and I finished it completely by hand, with a file. . . .

The point is, if a customer needs a part, maybe a part to an old machine, or something new, something dreamed up, maybe the part has to be made that way. Sure enough, I know that with technology in this country we can stamp it out, press it out. But in that case, I only made a prototype, one machine. So you can't buy a press and set up a die, all this to make one part. That's ridiculous. So, the young people who work in a prototype plant are going to find out that a lot of prototype parts have to be finished by hand.[17]

"I Turned Over Every Penny"

The immigrant family functioned as a collective economic unit far more than did the typical middle-class American family. (The various economic contributions of women are discussed in chapter 5.) Children were expected to help sustain the family, a necessity that frequently required the sacrifice of education and the postponement of independence. Whether at simple household tasks or in outside employment, children were considered a familial economic asset. Some of them resented being plucked so abruptly from childhood. Undoubtedly many, like Lucy Richardson, expressed their rebellion in childish pranks. Seventeen-year-old Lucy no sooner arrived in Manchester, Connecticut, than she discovered that she had to go to work:

Yes, I had to [work], and at that time I looked so tiny. The landlady that my father had, she said, "You know, you're gonna have to put your hair up; you'll have to get a long skirt, because they won't give you a job." So finally I went, and I got the job. And weaving, imagine, and silk weaving is entirely different to linen, that I was used to [in Ireland]. Oh, I hated that job! And I really didn't care whether I worked or not. I was only young, 17, and I had girlfriends, and sometimes we'd go to the ladies room and we stayed there for a half hour or so. I always remember. Sometimes I would leave my loom going, and when I'd come back there would be something damaged in the web, and it would have to all be ripped out again, and oh! I got scolded for that. I hated the weaving! Finally I didn't want to work at the weaving anymore.[18]

For Mrs. S. and her brother and sister, children of French-Canadian and Irish immigrants, the bitterness ran deep and the experience nearly culminated in tragedy.

I believe you had most of the details of our family from my sister Mary [Mrs. C.] last week. You know I am next to Mary in age. I can talk freely this morning as my mother went to Worcester for Easter. I stayed with the family here for the weekend. My husband went to Long Hill this morning. He is chauffeur for the W. family up there. He has worked there 10 years.

You see we are only married a few months. We were married just before Advent. Sometimes I don't know what to say about these parents of mine. They sure are a problem. One thing I can honestly say—they are mismated. We, the children, are the ones that had to suffer for their mistakes. Ever since my early childhood days all I heard was arguments; my mother calling him lazy, my father telling her how he was tired of her nagging. Then my mother would become angry. The children got the brunt of all this when her temper was up.

I did not have the opportunity of high school education. Mary did. I just graduated from the eighth grade. I had to earn some money, my mother informed me. I secured a position one week after graduation at the Style Craft pocketbook factory on Myrtle Avenue. This factory was owned by a Jew named Wolfe. He blew in here from New York. Just one of the typical New York sweatshops. He had labor trouble in New York, I understand, so moved himself into Connecticut like all of his type were doing at this time, I mean all the sweatshops.

Well, I earned from $6 to $8 a week here—starvation wages. I always thought I had more pay coming to me than I received. He always had deductions made in the pay of all workers, claiming deductions for merchandise he said we spoiled. He tried this stunt on everyone. Finally the labor people caught up with him. He had worked the females over hours allowed for them. Well, a delegation from the shop met with union leaders. Some of the workers walked out and marched to the mayor at City Hall.

Finally a union was formed. We all went back to work. Now we could make a living wage and had better working conditions. I began to earn $14 a week. As far as I personally was concerned, I had to hand my pay envelope over to my mother and it didn't help me. She handed me what spending money she thought I needed; allowed me carfare and 5¢ for a cup of coffee. I always took a lunch from home. Believe me, my allowance was very small. This was discouraging as I would like to have dressed better than I did. My clothing was cheap. The other girls in the factory were well dressed. Most of their mothers only took board from them. They let them have the rest of the money to clothe themselves and have a little amusement or recreation money. If ever I suggested this at home, my mother went in a rage—didn't speak to me for days, called me ungrateful and all mean names.

Mary, my oldest sister, said "Don't be a fool—just pay board. I was afraid, she always tried to scare me." Mary said, "That was one reason I wanted to marry and get away from her constant nagging." After my father cleared out of the house, we dare not say our soul was our own. I don't blame him for clearing out. I worked four years steady at this factory; then became an instructor at $16 per week. I got my younger sister a job there when she finished the eighth grade. She was a good student, always high marks and good reports. She begged for a high school education. She always spoke of teaching. My brother and I tried to have my mother consider sending her to high school.

He worked every day and was a good boy and gave his pay envelope to my mother. But she said "No." So "no" it was. Well, my brother said, "If the kid can't go to high school and three of us are going to work, I am going to clear out and marry." Three months later he did leave home and married. My sister was very dissatisfied with factory work. She did not care for the type of people we worked with. They were rather bold, rough-spoken, and some even swore. Of course, some very nice refined girls worked there, but very few. My sister is very pretty. I thought if only the poor kid could go to school. She always read during our lunch hour. She read books that educate you, not silly novels. She was a good French student and read many books written in French. She took lessons in French from the French nuns. She paid for these lessons herself. She took care of a baby after school hours. The lady gave her $1 per week. For a wonder, my mother let her keep 50¢ for the French lesson. Wasn't she mean not to let the kid have all the money?

After she worked here a year at the pocketbook factory, we heard we, with a lot of others, were losing our jobs. We knew, due to hard times, many factories were closing. We worried. We knew jobs were scarce. We were disgusted at home. My mother's boyfriend was having dinner at our home every night, and also Sunday dinners. He was an Irishman, like herself, Irish descent. He didn't go over so big with us. We knew our father should be there. If not our father, no one. He paid well for his meals. He seemed jolly, rather witty. He was a tavern owner. My mother never indulged in liquor, so could not use drink as an excuse for her nasty temper.

One day my father was in town. As he passed our street corner, he saw him talking in front of our house. Later he inquired about him. We told him he was Mama's boyfriend. He called him Irish this and that and then some hot names. But that's as far as it went. I think he was too yellow to tell her these things to her face. You see that's the way these French Canadians are—sneaky. Well the final notice for the layoff came. My sister and I, on our way to work that morning, went to the drugstore and bought a bottle of poison.

At noon we drank it—jumped from a third-story window in the factory. You see, we figured it was no use living. We could see no reason to live. We dreaded the nagging at home when unemployed. I broke my leg in the leap. My sister was severely burned and cut. People sent for the ambulance. They rushed us to St. Vincent's Hospital, where the stomach pump was used and we recovered. We were terribly burned. My sister was in the hospital many weeks. On account of the broken leg, I was there months. My, how the papers wrote us up in the headlines. I don't think we will ever live it down.

Now for our hospital bills. Who is to pay? But first let me tell you; my mother tried on the day after this to get our pay at the factory. You see how cold-blooded she was—money first. We then were not even off the danger list. Well, I guess our boss, Mr. Wolfe, had a talk with her. Anyway she paid my young sister's bill when she got better and took her home. So she had it better for a while. I stayed until I was better and left the hospital with a promise to pay when I again worked. I made good later.

My father came and took me where he was caretaker in Newtown. His employer gave him permission. This, I think, was the first break I ever got in my entire life. It was a fresh new start in life. When I got able to walk, I cooked, took care of things for my father. This lady he worked for was a writer. She told me to go over to the big house and sit on the veranda. She gave me permission to use her library. She was so kind. One day I inquired from her if she thought my father was lazy. She said "No," he was suited to caretaking, gardening, and working at her stables. He was a little slow but trustworthy. This made me feel better. This lady always left in winter. So outside of keeping fires in the big house, my father did not have much work. Of course, another man took care of the cattle.

So I tried to get work. During the holiday season, this lady of the house notified us she would spend Christmas at her home. She said to hire a woman or two for the work. Well, we hired a cook. I was the other helper. She entertained lavishly for the holiday season from Christmas to New Year's. I told her I would like to do housework. So she said a lady, a musician, a friend of hers she entertained, told her only a few days before she wanted a girl. She said she wanted a girl to look out for her two boys, ages 10 and 12, and also wait on table. This woman lived in Monroe, Connecticut. She telephoned to find out about it. I got the job at $25 per month. Of course, this included keeps; $25 was like clear profit.

I was to learn to drive the car so I could drive the children to and from school when she was away on concert tour. The boys were nice children, not hard to care for. Do you know this woman even taught me to play the piano. She said she was so glad I would stay with her, as many girls did not like it back in the country. It was here I met my husband. His employer's wife was a great friend of my employer. He called every day and always came in and chatted. At first I thought there might be objection; but she said no, it would only make me more contented and not want to return to the city. After a while, when his work was over, he became a steady caller.

After dinner nights, the boys and the two of us played cards—bingo, especially if the children's mother was away. Sometimes we all went roller-skating down in Bridgeport. Finally we became engaged and after two year's courtship we married. I still worked but we had a little rent in Long Hill—four rooms. I didn't stay at my employer's anymore at night. Of course, the boys were older by two years. The cook in the house stayed there.

My husband is Swedish but married me in St. Theresa's Catholic Church rectory in Long Hill. My mother came up to see me married. I did not call on her very often. This is the first time I ever stayed there since I tried to end my life. I only stay now to look out for Mary's daughter, as Mary cannot stay out of work. My mother will be home tonight. The people I work for are in New York for the Easter holidays. I don't let my husband see a great deal of my mother. His parents are in Stockholm, Sweden. He came to America with an older brother. He said he has an aunt and uncle out here. They wrote him thrilling letters. He hopes to bring the old folks here. He didn't think much about this until Russia and Finland had trouble. He has a married sister in Minnesota.

I think Swedish people are ambitious. My husband saved considerable. We paid cash for all our furniture. Of course, we only have four rooms. We have a secondhand upright piano. We paid $50 for it, cash. Our radio and all the rest of our furniture was cash at D. M. Read's store. Even our General Electric refrigerator is cash. I hope I can work another year. We want to save and build a home. Of course, then I would like to have children.

My husband receives $28 per week. Our rent is $16. Of course, it is on a back road. It wouldn't do for anyone who had to go to the city to work. We own a '38 Ford bought on a used car lot. My husband knew the party who turned it in for a new car. So he knew it was a good buy and in good condition. My husband brings my father every Wednesday night for dinner. Of course, in the summer he won't be able to come. Every Sunday we are through our work at noon. So we have dinner at home and come to Bridgeport to a movie. Then we go to some little restaurant after the show for a little to eat. We agree on all matters. So far we have had no disputes. We are very agreeable. Everything is on a fifty-fifty basis. Our clothing bills are small as my husband wears a uniform as chauffeur. I wear maid's uniforms; both are furnished us. So only when we go home, we have no occasion to wear regular clothing. Our food bill is small as we only eat dinner at home.

I am very happy now. My young sister is working in a chain store in town, and is better satisfied. She likes the type of girls there better than the factory workers. She does not seem interested in boyfriends. She is still a reader. Every spare moment she is buried in books.[19]

Many others accepted their early work experiences as a necessary element in family survival, and their subsequently satisfactory lives seemed none the worse for it. Frank Stamler's father, a Hungarian immigrant, operated his farm while working in the Cheney silk mills. Young Frank labored on both the family farm and other farms. Later he followed his father into the mills.

We always grew pigs. We always had chickens; we always killed them all and my father always made Hungarian baloney. . . . I can remember sitting, not in a high chair, but he'd put things in a chair like this, and he'd be making baloney, and I was the one that had the job of taking a pin, and air would get into the casings, you know, and I was the one that had to prick the darn thing and let the air out of the casings. Of course, he always made his own wine, and I never did drink it. I never drink any today. I grew up with it and I never drink it. . . .

We had 20 acres of land . . . and we farmed it all, all by hand. We would get Mr. Loomis or Mr. Ofiara to plow it. We had one horse. We'd cultivate it, but the rest of the hoeing was all by hand. . . . The only thing we sold from the farm . . . I'll never forget that—was beans or anything like that. But we sold beans to J. W. Hale grocery store, and that was the first self-serve grocery store, I believe, in the nation. We would pack it in 50-pound bags and everything. . . .

I worked on a farm when I was 11 years old. I worked at home before that, but I mean I went out to work when I was 12 years old on a farm. That's the only way you could get by with 12 kids. . . . I turned over every penny that I ever earned until I was 18 years old—every penny. Same thing [with my brothers and sisters]. . . . My mother never worked outside the home, no, no, but she had enough work at home, and at that time the Hungarians would never, like today, have a sandwich for noontime, no way. I mean, on a weekend she would cook three times a day. And that would be cooking with no electricity. I mean no electric stove . . . wood and coal; we used to burn coal.[20]

Michael Steinberg, a Russian Jew, immigrated as an infant with his parents in 1890. As he grew up, he helped his father in his Springfield, Massachusetts, blacksmith shop, sold papers, set up pins in a bowling alley, and worked in a florist's shop. As an adult he and his Italian-American partner prospered in a large produce firm.

You know, those people those days were devoted to the family. They worked hard. I used to have to bring him down breakfast in the morning before I went to school. Quarter to seven, half past six. My mother would get up and make breakfast. We didn't have furnaces in those days—we used to have a big kitchen stove. They always had big kitchen stoves—all the people did. Regardless of race or color they had big, big kitchen stoves. And we used to have parlor stoves in all the rooms. Kerosene stoves. And little coal fires. We used to live in a big house. I chopped wood at night, bring up the wood. Scuttles of coal. And I'd make the fire so that my little brothers and sisters could get warm. Springfield is a cold city in the wintertime. And we'd make all the fires. My mother made breakfast for all the children. And I'd go down to my father's blacksmith shop and bring him his breakfast. Had a good hearty breakfast. And then you know he used to shoe horses. And they'd have a lot of customers come in—merchants, to shoe their horses, and they'd have breakfast in there.

There was a saloon on every corner in Springfield in the old days. I was only a kid. They'd let kids buy beer. They had pitchers and pails. So they'd send me over—for 10¢ you'd get a big pail of beer. And the policemen would come in there too to watch my father working there. He had a few men working for him too. And they'd drink beer. Like you're drinking out of this glass, they'd pass the pail around and they'd all drink. They didn't think about sanitary conditions. And they'd go over to the meat market and they'd get a long tenderloin steak, et cetera. They'd rip it off. My father was good on meat. And they'd put it in the fire. They had two big burners. One on each side. And they used to burn soft coal. It used to be hard work. And they'd throw the meat in the fire. Coal would go over it. And they'd turn it over with pinchers. It wasn't sanitary. Then they'd take a big newspaper—no, they had beer barrels. You've seen beer barrels. So they would take the pinchers and throw the meat in hot water. And then they'd take it out and throw it in the cold water. And then they'd put it on those big pieces of paper—longer than this table—and they'd clean it off with a knife—the smut from the coals. And then every man would go over and pull off a piece. And then they'd have rye bread too—go over to the Jewish bakers, they'd have long rye bread. And they wouldn't cut it. They didn't have cutters unless you did it with a knife. And each one would pull off a piece of bread. The policemen would take off their hats, unbutton their coats, and sit down and they'd have a breakfast. I remember that it tasted wonderful. But they'd eat this meat and drink beer. I'd go over sometimes four or five times in the morning before I went to school to get a pail of beer. And they'd all drink beer and eat the meat, eat the bread and they used to have a good time. They used to love it. And they drank whiskey too, also gin.

There was a little town in Massachusetts—Agawam, Massachusetts. They used to make Agawam gin there. It was a gin mill. They used to manufacture it there from corn. You know how much it used to be a pint? I tell it to people. My father would buy about 20 pints and keep them in the blacksmith's shop. Fifteen cents a pint. And whiskey used to be a quarter a pint, the cheap whiskey I guess. Probably as good as it is now, I don't know. But they didn't have any taxes like they have today. And the men would take the bottle— they used to have it in pints because it was easier to drink. And each one would take a swallow and give it to the next person. My children told me that I ought to put a movie on and relate some of those things. Thank God I'm blessed with a good memory and I remember all those little details. But they were good people.

Well, I went through grammar school. They used to have nine grades in Massachusetts years ago. And I went through the ninth grade. Then I went to Norwalk High School for about six months. And it isn't I didn't want to go to school. We needed money. I went to work. I used to work—I told you I had newspaper routes. I was a hard worker as a kid. And I used to set up bowling alley pins. And then I got a job as a florist, from a florist shop. The firm is still in Springfield, Massachusetts William Schlatter and Sons. They were very good to me. And I worked for them after school. And then my uncle came down from Greenwich, Connecticut—Mr. Cohen. My mother's brother. And he liked me. And I was 16 years old. He brought me to Greenwich, Connecticut. He shanghied me, I'll put it that way. He wanted his mother, my grandmother, to have a companion in the house. My grandfather was gone. So I lived with my grandmother for a good many years. And I worked in Greenwich, Connecticut.

Then after a while I went into business myself. The name of our firm was Berman and Steinberg in Norwalk, Connecticut. Then in 1929 we merged with the biggest produce firm in Connecticut, Musante and Pastine. And the firm became Musante, Berman and Steinberg. It was a big firm. We sold the building about five years ago to the city of Bridgeport. There's a big bank on the building now, in the heart of Bridgeport. And I became the general manager, treasurer in the M. B. S. Company. And thank God, I'm the only one that's left of the eight people of the board. We used to employ about 75 people. We were the biggest wholesalers in New England. We used to be carload receivers. Everything. Oranges, grapefruit, cherries, peaches, et cetera. You mention it. Spinach, lettuce, everything. We used to sell to wholesalers. All over the state. We'd go as far as Providence, Rhode Island. And I would say I became fairly successful.

I worked awfully hard. And I've always been charitable, honey . . . regardless of race, color, and creed. And I've been very fortunate. I'm a life member of the YMCA in Norwalk, Connecticut. I'm on the Norwalk Hospital board. Twenty-five years with the Norwalk Hospital, 24 ½. I wanted to resign a few years ago. They wouldn't let me. So they made me a life trustee. They gave me an award. I have it there. And they gave me a pin from Tiffany's with my name inscribed on it with all the years I served.[21]

Sando Bologna's parents emigrated from Italy in 1910, and he was born in 1915. He was proud of the fact that as a boy he carded buttons at home, worked for a shoemaker, and delivered newspapers. But he also was determined to acquire an education.

I would see my father come home at night and I knew he must have been working hard; he was what was called a pickle-tub operator, which means he would dump brass in boiling fluids, acid, et cetera. He would come home with his hands burned at times. The hot acid burned his hands and arms, and sometimes his face. I know that he worked hard and didn't earn much, which was all right because that was the way things were. I said I never wanted to work in a factory. I felt that I wanted to do something better! . . .

The mothers would go to a factory about a mile away (the factory is still there), the American Easterner Company where they would get "the snaps," the fasteners for garments. The ladies were given large bags with snaps and cards, which they brought home. The children would fasten them together on cards, usually 12 to a card. They would count the cards by the dozens. It was kind of fun and drudgery for the children to sit around the dining room table and do this "homework." The girls were usually faster than the boys and more conscientious. I'll never forget this; the black snaps were harder to fasten because they had more shellac on them than the white ones. They were of many sizes. Many times we would get calloused thumbs as we'd put the snaps together. We would get a nickel or a dime for doing a dozen cards. I never was good at it; my sisters were better workers. At the end of a week a family would earn as much as $10 or $15, which was a pretty good sum of money. The mothers didn't seem to mind doing their share of work. The money meant a great deal to them. I think this gave us what you might call "the work ethic." Work was an important part of life, it was a way of life, and it was something that you accepted, something that you were expected to do for the rest of your life. All the kids sat around the table. They didn't go out to play unless they did your quota, or cards, and sometimes they didn't eat until they finished a prescribed dozen of cards. It was an interesting moral building, training.

Sometimes I wonder why they called it child labor or sweatshop operations, or why they said that it wasn't proper and legal. It wasn't so much the fact that we earned that money, which was welcomed, but the fact that we were taught the value of the dollar and that we had to work in order to earn. I think, in a sense, it is sad that some of these kinds of conditions do not exist now. But I'm on the minority side. When I was 10 years old, I got a job working in a shoemaker's shop. There again this kind of employment is illegal today. The employer was an old Sicilian shoemaker who taught me to work at the machines. I was only in the fourth grade, and I was getting 10¢ a week, but the gentleman had a nice wife, and I would run errands for her between the shop and her home. She was a friendly lady [I think a former teacher, because he would call her *la maestra*—the teacher], and she would always give me a tip, maybe a quarter or some other reward, for running the errand. Here again it was a moral thing.

Later I worked for another shoemaker who came from northern Italy, and his first name was the same as mine. He was an educated man who served with the Italian army during the war. He was good-looking, and he thought he was a romantic person like Valentino. I thought he was a braggart, and I really wasn't too impressed with him. But many years later after I left him, he told me he tested the boys who worked for him, and he said, "You're the only boy who did not steal from me." I was surprised to hear this because I never did steal. He said that all the other boys who worked for him stole money. He said, "I left money in certain places just to see whether you would steal it. But the money was never touched."

When I graduated from grammar school in 1929, I was asked by my father what I wanted to do. I had already signed up for high school, and he said, "You go to work." In other words, he didn't encourage me to go to high school. But I did want to go to high school. It's interesting, the counseling that was given at that time. My principal was John Brophy, whom the students called "Long John." He was tall and thin. He had his own disciplinary method. If a boy did something wrong, he would give him a free sample, which would be a whack with a strap on the open palm. I was strapped a couple of times, but I never held it against him. I don't know what I did that was wrong. But he was a fine person, and I loved him. When we were to graduate he said to me, "I see that you have signed up to go to Crosby High School. Why do you want to go to Crosby?" I said, "I want to go there to study Latin." I don't know why I said that, except that I used to write letters to my grandmother in Italian, and I tried Italian in books. He asked: "Do you plan on going to college?" I said, "No, I don't." So he said, "You are not going to Crosby; you are going to Wilby," and that was the counseling that I got. Wilby was a commercial high school, and it was attended mostly by girls. I never regretted going there because I learned to type and take shorthand. I studied two years of Italian, and I had the most marvelous teacher of English who just worked on me, particularly when she found out from me that I wanted to be a reporter. She helped me a great deal. She concentrated on me with Shakespeare. She was really the greatest teacher that I had. I learned commercial law and salesmanship. They were very practical subjects, so much so that when I went into newspaper work, I think I had a good basis for understanding business and law. My knowledge of shorthand and typing were great assets.

The reason I was able to attend high school was because about two days after graduating from grammar school, I was standing near the shoemaker shop—the man who was paying me a dollar a week when I quit him. Along came the foreman of the mailing room of the *Republican American*, who knew me because I had been peddling newspapers for two years. I used to make about $3 or $4 a week delivering newspapers. He asked me what I was doing. I said, "Nothing, just graduated from grammar school." He said, "Then you come down to work in the mailing room on Monday." I took the job. It paid 50¢ an afternoon. We worked from 1:30 to 4:30. We would roll up the newspapers; we would deliver them by automobile, jumping off and on the car's running board. Every day I think I would run about three or four miles, delivering heavy bundles of papers. Within a few months the Depression came, in October 1929. I earned enough money to buy a pizza every so often and to go to the movies. I worked Saturday night and Sunday morning. I was earning $7 or $8 a week. I also delivered Sunday papers. This went on through the four years I was in high school.

Boys who were working in the circulation department decided to become pressroom apprentices. Others transferred to the composing room, and they became apprentices. I thought I would be different. I wanted to be a reporter. I knew that it would be a long shot, so I inquired when I had just graduated from high school and learned that I did not have the qualifications to become a reporter. Frankly, I thought there was some prejudice against me because I was an Italian boy. I still was determined. I spoke to the publisher and the editor-in-chief. They indicated that I just didn't have the qualifications. One day, a newspaper delivery car driver talked about me to the city editor of the *Republican*, whch is the morning paper. I told him I wanted to be a reporter. He invited me to the city room to observe reporters at work. He said, "You can do some work, you can write some stories. You're not going to get paid for it," which was all right with me because it was like going to school. So I did this routine night after night. I would to the newspaper room from 7:00 p.m. until midnight. I would take stories on the telephone. I would go out on assignments. I even had a press card. I received no compensation for it. Today, this is illegal. I did it for a year and a half, learning the basics of newspaper work.

In 1933 when I graduated from high school, it was the depth of the Depression, and the government was adopting work progress programs, such as the WPA, FERA, and the CWA. One phase of it was the institution of community colleges. They put these programs into cities, and in New Haven a community college was opened at the YMCA. The teachers were mostly graduates of Yale or grad students at Yale. I thought I would like to go there. After I read about it in a New Haven paper, I signed up and commuted, leaving Waterbury at 7:30 on the bus, getting to New Haven at a quarter to nine, walking to the YMCA, going to classes until 1 p.m., and returning to Waterbury. At night I would go to the city room to work. By December of 1934, I guess I was well known by a number of people in the city room and I was hired as an office boy at the grand salary of $14 a week, working seven nights a week from 7:00 until 12:30, then walking home. My mother would always be up waiting for me. I would get up at 6:30 and take the bus to New Haven three times a week. It cost 95¢ round-trip. I would eat in a cafeteria, sometimes not have much, like crackers and coffee. I selected subjects that I knew would help me, commercial subjects, mathematics, English, and of course Italian. I studied a course in journalism. Without bragging, I knew more than the teacher, a grad student from Yale. I studied contemporary history. I think that I learned a great deal which I was able to apply at the newspaper office because in 1936, I was already a cub reporter, earning $18 a week, which was a good salary.[22]

Anthony Topogna emigrated from Italy as a 10-year-old with his parents in 1920. He sold papers, worked in both tobacco fields and a pickle factory, and in a dry-goods store while in high school. But his story differs. His father saved his wages for him, and with parental assistance (and a bit of luck), he graduated from college and law school. Thus he viewed his childhood work experience with pride, considering it a valuable component of a successful, upwardly mobile life.

The first thing to determine was, where do we live? We shacked up with some relatives that he had or close friends that he had here, and then we found a place to live on Front Street. I showed some pictures of the flood there; that's where we lived—on Front Street in Hartford. And we lived there because housing was very, very scarce. It was living in a tenement, four-room tenement, and there were then five of us at the time. And then from Front Street we moved to Kilbourne Court, number 6 Kilbourne Court. And there were four rooms there too—no bathtub, just a toilet. There used to be a public bath house on Connecticut Boulevard in those days, and that's where we went once or twice a week to take a shower and to clean up. We were in Kilbourne Court for five- or six-odd years, and from there we moved to Kilbourne Street. Now we had reached it, because there we found a bathtub. We had a bathtub there. So there were five rooms there. The family had grown by that time, and we could use the five rooms. We remained there—my father was a pushcart peddler and also had a store on Front Street. . . .

Grocery store—well, mostly fruit and vegetables. Some groceries. And a pushcart that he pushed all day long. And he had to go to the regional market and the farmers market in the morning. Get up at 4:00 in the morning and buy his produce—his vegetables and fruit and so forth—and bring them back with him and then travel through the east side of Hartford to sell them. And he might have to make one or two trips in the course of the day, pushing that up the hill, the Morgan Street hill, up around the east side, come back, load up again, and do it all over again. And that would take him to maybe 11:00 at night, from 4:00 in the morning to 11:00 at night. And that was hard work, and that was the key word that has become rather profane these days. Work, work—that is the thing that people don't understand today. They want. We have so many bleeding hearts, so many do-gooders today who—perish the thought—don't like to find favor with the word *work*. But that was the key word in those days. Everybody pitched in. We sold papers in the morning. Got up at 5:30 in the morning to catch the trolleys coming in from across the river from Manchester and Glastonbury to sell 50 papers to make 50¢. My brother did the same. And then, during the summer it wasn't a vacation for us. We worked in tobacco fields, we worked at the Silver Lane Pickle Company, and then I got a job, while going to high school, at a dry-goods store on Front Street. And sold and worked every afternoon and night and even on Sundays because my employer was Jewish and he observed the Saturday holiday and I had to go along with it. And there we were.

One time I got a job at the Okay Bakery on Albany Avenue from after high school 'til about 10:30 or 11:00 at night, got home, and then did my homework. But in spite of that I still found time to belong to the inter-high orchestra. I played the violin. I was in the various clubs and then—mind you, I came to this country on July 4, 1920. That's a little subject that I want to talk to you about—education. We came to the Brown School, we started at the Brown School, without the benefit of any training . . . and these good teachers at the Brown School took this raw material, without the benefit of language I say, and turned us out to a finished product so that we understood English, we wrote and read English. In four and a half years we were qualified to go to Hartford High School, which in those days was one of the finest high schools in the country. And three years later I—this little immigrant boy without the benefit of language—became the editor of the *Outlet*, the newspaper of the high school. Now, I don't claim that as a personal triumph. That was common. That was common among a lot of these children. . . .

No, not too many went to high school. I grant you that. That's true. Because a lot of the parents in those days, they were poor, poor. You know today we talk about the poor. If the poor today . . . if the poor of those days, rather, of my generation, had anything similar to what the poor have today they'd be considered rich. So when the kid became 14 he was qualified to get his working papers and many parents said, "You better get your working papers." So there were few, only a few, who were able to succeed and survive to the point of going to high school. I was one of the fortunate ones. But we worked. We worked. Every one of us worked. Every one of the children worked. Had to contribute something.

Let me give you an example: In 1929, when I got through high school, I had the fabulous sum of $1,500 saved up from working—in tobacco fields, in the bakery shop, at the Silver Lane Pickle Company, the dry-goods store, and so forth. I had $1,500 saved up. So I said to my father, "Do you think there's a chance that I might go to college?" He said, "Well, you know where you stand. You're the oldest of nine children. I've got others to consider. But you've got $1,500 saved up." In those days tuition was $300; $450 would take me through with my board and lodging. He said, "You've got two years, and then we'll see what happens."

Well, I put in two years in college. I went to Georgetown. I took, as I said, a business course. And in those days some schools didn't require college boards. Georgetown was one of them, and Ohio State was another, and I was admitted in both. So I chose Georgetown—it was nearer and I was able to make connections with a woman who ran a rooming house. And incidentally, I'm going to come back to that. I lived at 3307 N. Street, N.W., in Washington, which later became the home of John F. Kennedy just before he went into the White House. Now, I lived there for three years or four years, going to Georgetown, and then I moved away from there to get nearer to the law school, which was downtown Washington. I put two years there and the $1,500 expired. Then what to do? Well, I was in law school by that time and I became assistant librarian, which paid my tuition. My father was able to send me $50 a month; that took care of my board, which was $45 a month, and I had the whole sum of $5 a month for spending money. That was my spending money. Then in the last year . . . during the summer I went on some sort of an affair and I sat next to a politician and we got friendly, we talked. And he said, "Would you feel hurt if I sent you $50 a month? Only if you pay me back." And he said that, not because he was anxious to make sure that I paid him back, but so that he wouldn't hurt my pride. And I said by all means, that has to be a condition. So he gave me $50 a month. That plus the job that I had as assistant librarian got me through the last year. And I paid him back. Gratefully I paid him back. Later on.

Now, that's the way I got through college. That's the way I struggled through college. And then I got out of college. I took my bar exams, and as difficult as they were in those days I passed the first time around, which was quite amazing. And I was one of the few, one of the few if not the only one at that time to get through law school and pass the bar exams living on the East Side. We were still living on Kilbourne Street.

Historically, six months after I got through law school my father died. He was only 46 years of age at the time, and here I was the oldest of seven children—two had died by then. And my mother said, "I'll continue the store. I'll carry on with the store." She wasn't making anything in that store. She was too generous. If somebody came in for a dozen bananas she'd give them 15. And that went on until . . . the first flood came along in 1936 and water had gotten up to the second floor, where we lived, and my mother said, "After the water recedes and subsides, we'll go back and clean up." She insisted on remaining because she had a circle of friends, she felt at home. . . .

It wasn't a question that I earned this money and I became the keeper of it. No. I turned it over to my father. He would keep it for me. And if he opened up a bank account, he would open it in his name dedicated maybe someday for my use. But he was the one. There wasn't any such thing as my paying board to my father for the privilege of living there. Oh no. The family unit was close and there were rules and there was discipline that we had to observe.

Today, you know, I can't understand it, the family unit is breaking up. That reverence for family life has been lost, I think. That's why you find a lot of kids finding their way away from home, setting up their own apartments even though their parents are more than able to keep them home. We didn't have that luxury. At least we didn't think that it was a penalty for living home. That was what was expected of us and we enjoyed it, even under the worst of circumstance.[23]

H. S. emigrated from Poland in 1905, when he was 10 years old. He and his siblings worked in his father's Bridgeport bakery, but his father permitted him to attend trade school and become a successful machinist. The immigrant success story was not without a wrenching poignancy, however. While the Old World family was maintained, it did not always emerge from the immigrant experience unscathed. As the father attained old age, no children were willing to assume responsibility for his bakery.

After we had been in this country for about seven years, my father had saved up enough money to open up a bakery of his own. Both of my older brothers had to pay board to my father, and with the money he earned he was able to save enough to go into business for himself. He was a good baker, and the people liked the things he made and we done a good business. All of us had to help him, and even my mother would come down to the shop and help him to make the bread and other things. My two sisters and I used to wait on the customers as we knew how to speak English and to make change. Most of our customers were Polish people, but they used to send their children to the bakery and they couldn't speak Polish very good so we could speak English to them. We made good money in the bakery, and my father decided that we should look around and see if we couldn't buy a house so we wouldn't have to pay rent to someone else. We bought a house up on Cherry Street and my father took out a mortgage on it. It was a two-family house and we got rent from the family upstairs. They paid us $18 a month and that paid the taxes, so we were getting our rent almost free.

I didn't like the bakery business, so my father let me go to trade school and I took up machinist work. That is how I got the job I got now. I got my diploma for machinist work and then I got a job at the Ashcroft Company as a machinist's helper. I worked there for about three years, and while I was there I started to learn something about the toolmaking trade. The toolmakers get better money than the machinists, so I figured that if I learned that trade I would be able to get a better wage. When the war broke out the papers were full of ads wanting all kinds of tool- and die-makers, so I got a job with the UMC Company as a toolmaker. I made as high as $100 a week. I didn't have to go to war, as when I was given the test I was found to be exempt because one of my eyes was very poor. I was certainly glad of that because what I have seen of those fellows that have come back is that I was very lucky.

After the war I lost my job at the UMC and I didn't work for about six months, but that didn't bother me as I had saved up enough money. I paid my father $10 a week board and the rest I put in the bank. Those were the days—everybody was wearing $10 shirts and everybody had money. Both of my brothers had a good job and my father was making good money with the bakery. My two sisters were still helping my father and both of them were engaged to Polish fellows. . . .

I am now a toolmaker at the Singer Sewing Machine Company. I have had this job for four years. We get paid an hourly rate of 72¢ an hour. We work 40 hours a week and my pay amounts to about $30 a week as sometimes we get in a few hours overtime. Most of the workers in my department have been with this company for years. I am one of the workers having the least number of years. Some of them have been with this company for over 50 years. Most of the workers in this department are either English or German. I get along pretty good with all of them, only there is one German fellow who is always bragging of how good the Germans are at tool- and die-making. We are always having arguments about what nationalities make the best machinists. I know that the Germans are very good machinists but it burns me up to have this fellow always bragging about it. . . .

The only thing that bothers my father is that there will be no one to take over the bakery when he retires or dies. He wanted one of us to be a baker, but none of us liked the business. He used to tell us that in the old country it was an honor to be a baker. Because you are making something for people to eat and that they have got to have a man who knows his business and that they can trust and not a man who didn't know his business so would not get as good a bread.[24]

Immigrants during the late nineteenth and early twentieth centuries frequently were described as reluctant to support labor unions, but many did. A Scottish woman, identified only as Miss Y., had worked in mills in her homeland and became an enthusiastic union member in Bridgeport, where her first job exposed her to what today would be considered sexual harrassment. Her experi-

ence demonstrated that ethnic groups could cooperate during strikes and further-more, that local business sometimes supported unions.

The first job I got in Bridgeport was at Carpenter's on Railroad Avenue. I used to work on the presses—it's really men's work. The presses were hard to work, and dangerous. We used to stamp out and shape tin measuring cups and things like that. I'm short, and it was difficult because I had to lean over them. I used to get $16 though I was supposed to get at least $20. I was a good worker. I found out the boss was fixing my time. He was sore because I would na' go out with him. I finally left because of him. If I knew then what I know now, he'd never have gotten away with it.

In 1936, I went to work in Casco's. I have to say this: they have the finest presses. I liked it there. I used to get about $25 a week—never below $20. I worked in three different departments there. I made above average the first day I went to work, and the old workers were sore because they thought I was going to scab the job. When I first went there, I was on the night shift—from 3:00 to 10:00 p.m. They have what they call a 54-minute hour; you can rest 6 minutes out of every hour if you want to. Then they started the layoffs, but they kept me on days because I was a fast worker. The boss of the pressroom told me just the other day, "You're a fool—you could be working now. You'd make a good forelady." I said to him, "What do you want me to do, throw my button away?" [She pointed to the CIO union button on her sweater.] I told him they wouldn't do it. I'm too fast an operator.

The UERMWA came into Casco's in March 1937. When the company saw how fast the workers were signing union cards, they started to organize a company union. They wanted us to sign yellow-dog slips. Of course, I would na' sign it. Cohen—that's the president of the company—used to come around and give us pep talks. He'd tell us that if we'd stick by him, we'd get a 10 percent bonus and everything else. Then he wouldn't sign even a company union agreement; he would na' put his name to paper. He wanted us to take his word by mouth. Instead of gaining with the workers, he lost out.

The chairlady of the company union joined the CIO. We soon had the majority of the workers. We tried to negotiate with the company for a contract, but we didn't get anywhere. Finally the union agreed that if further negotiations were not successful, all the workers would sit down. On the day agreed upon, the assembly department and the automatic lighter department sat down first. The company got wind of it, and immediately spread the rumor that the union organizer had ordered the workers to walk out. The workers got confused and started walking out. But the two departments still sat. When the organizer got there, he found the majority of the workers on the outside.

When we tried to get back in, we found the company had locked us out. All Bridgeport came out to see the sit-down strikers. Food was brought to them, and bedding was prepared. Some of the workers managed to get in by scaling the windows at night.

The company called in Mayor [Jasper] McLevy to convince the workers to g[et] out—that is, the sit-downers. Very late that night, the union agreed to call out the workers provided that no strikebreakers would be allowed in. The workers marched out in orderly formation at 12:00 midnight. Picket lines had been on the job. Our picket lines formed every morning at 6:00. Everybody was out but the office force. We had strike meetings every day at Rokoczi Hall on Bostwick Avenue. That was our headquarters. A lot of the workers were Hungarian. We were helped a lot by the Bridgeport stores—the bakeries gave us bread, meat was donated. We set up a kitchen at the hall, where we served meals to the strikers. The first sit-downer, a woman, was in charge of the kitchen.

We were negotiating every day, sometimes until 1:00 and 2:00 in the morning. I wasn't on the negotiating committee; I was busy organizing, getting workers to sign up. I thought that was most important. I was out on the street every day from 5:00 a.m. to 8:00 at night, talking and visiting, signing up, and getting money for the strike fund. McLevy wanted us to compromise for "peace sake," but the union held out for a month. We demanded a 10¢ an hour general wage increase; we got an 8¢ increase generally, but some got 10¢. I got—in my department, that is—10¢ increase. We won vacations with pay, seniority rights, recognition of the union as sole collective bargaining agent, time and a half for overtime, sanitation improvements. We gained a lot. We went back to work. I was the committeewoman in my department. It took about three weeks to get the prices adjusted.

Then came the Depression—or recession, or whatever the devil they want to call it. I was laid off January 1938. There was no discrimination against me; it was lack of work. Up till now—when I was na' working, I've been organizing. For a couple of months I was the paid business agent of the local, but now the funds are low, so I'm still doing it, gratis. The president of the local was discriminated against, but we got him back in through the National Labor Board; we got lots of people back to work, 50—easy. It was a lot of work and took days.

I'll show you how the union works. [Miss Y. went to the telephone and called the employment manager at the Casco plant.] "Hello, how are you? What's doing? Is that right? That's good, hope it lasts—he's a good little worker. How about the buffers? You'll have something new this week? Gee, that's good. How about the women? In a couple of weeks? No sign of anything brightenin' up? Oh, by the way, what about these three new machines I've heard about? Who told me? Oh, the name? I don't really know—you know there are lots of people in there I don't know the names of. Will you be sure and have that list for me? No, I can't stop in tonight. I've got to go to a meeting at 5:00. No, I'll just be able to pop in and pop out. Have that list ready. Well, don't do nothing in the weekend I would na' do. So long. Oh, you rascal. Good-bye."

[She came back to the tale.] He's going to make a list of all those hired during the week and their seniority dates, for me. He hasn't hired one woman this week. The union office is open every day from 12:00 to 1:00. I used to do that even when I was workin'. You know last year, when they were hiring they used to take them from the U.S. Employment Service—from anyplace, people who never worked in this plant. I told him—the employment manager—"This year you're not gonna do that. I suffered last year—now you're gonna suffer wi' me. You're not gonna hire one person that did no' work here. I don't care whether he's a union member or not, just so long as he worked here before." Why, they had people from pocketbook shops who didn't know anything about the job, working as foreladies. He wanted to know where I get all my information. He told me I'd make a good government investigator. I told him, "Get this, I know what I'm talkin' about. I come down here with facts." Once he asked me why we didn't get unemployed workers relief. I said to him, "What do you think? We workers aren't sleepin'." I've taken them down to get city relief lots of times. There were 1,200 working at Casco's before the strike. It's down to 400 now. Ordinarily they employ about 700; when the layoffs came, it went down to about two overnight.

Once when we were in negotiating, Cohen said to me, "I've no faith in you. All you want in this factory is for your own selfish ends." I said to him, "I do, eh? Well, I'll make a bargain wi' ya. I've got bills up to my neck. You pay all my bills, and I'll stay out of your old factory." "Let the union pay your bills," Cohen said. "What do you want to work for—the union's paying you." I leaned over the table at him, just like this, and I said to him, "Oh, no. I do it for love—for love of the workers, Mr. Cohen." I get awfully sarcastic wi' him. I told him I know everything that goes on. He asked me how I knew so much, and I told him, "I've got a lot of little canaries, and I get a peep-peep here, and a peep-peep there." The president of the local says he wouldn't miss those meetings for the world. And I've got the nerve to expect to get back there to work.[25]

Often immigrants were uninterested in unions if they believed that their work was temporary and that they would be returning home. But the following two interviewees, B. C. and Matilda B., were both second-generation Italian-Americans who lived and worked in Stamford, Connecticut. B. C. began work at 14 and had worked steadily except for periods of childbearing. She was 27 when she described her union activities.

I left school when I was 14. I was in the eighth grade then, but I had to leave to go to work. The first job I had was in the Royal Society silk mill, in the packing department. I was so young then that I had to go home early. I used to get $11 a week, and I worked 34 hours. I guess I worked there about three or four months, but I wasn't satisfied there. I wanted to learn how to sew. The owner of the Stamford Waist Company is a friend of my father, and he gave me a job in his place. I started at $8 a week, and I worked there 50 hours a week. Sometimes we worked overtime and got extra money. I stayed there about two and a half years. When it got slack I went to work in Murphy's—the five-and-ten—and I stayed there about three or four months. I used to get $11 a week. We had to work from 9:00 to 6:00 every day, and on Saturdays from 9:00 in the morning 'til 9:00 at night. Then I went to the Stamford Waist for a while until it got slow again. I got about $10 then. Then I went to New York to try my luck there. After two weeks, I got a job with the International Tailoring, as a floor girl. I used to carry the work out, because they were piece workers there. I used to get $18 a week. I felt swell, like a lady. I worked there for three years. During that time, I didn't get any increases. The job was too soft. Then they got slack, and I got a job in the Willow Cafeteria. I got $14 a week there, with four meals. We came in at 6:30 and worked until 4:00.

While I was working at the Willow, I fell down the subway steps and hurt myself. I had to stay home three months. Then I tried to go back to work, but the job was too heavy, and one day I fell down in the kitchen with a tray. The manager told me he would transfer me. It was just a gag, though. Every time I went back to go on the easier job he had promised me, he kept stalling me off and telling me that he would have the job for me next week. I finally got wise to myself and came back here—to Stamford. And then I got a job again at the Stamford Waist Company.

I started at $12 a week, but when I was there two weeks the NRA came in. When I had come back, there were still workers there getting $7 and $8. After the NRA I got $14 a week, and my hours were cut to from 8:00 in the morning to 5:00 p.m., and no work on Saturday. Two weeks after that the union came in. The boss didn't like the idea of the union at the beginning. We had a strike—that is, not really a strike. We just waited around until the boss came to an agreement. You see, we were beginning to work on the cotton blouses, and the boss wanted to cut our prices about 17 percent. The girls didn't like the idea of the cut, and the union managed to get the boss to only cut the prices from 12 to 15 percent instead of 17. The union got our pay raised from $14 to $16 and then to $18 and $20 on some work.

That's why I don't understand why the girls crab about paying their union dues. After all, they owe it to the union that they got their pay raised, and the dues are only about 35¢ a week. Of course, when I joined the union I only had to pay $2 initiation fees; now they have to pay $10 to join.

The work is seasonal, and I'm still working there; that is, I'll go back when business picks up. I've never been unemployed there for any length of time. Usually you work from January to April steady, then it's slack through the summer and starts up again in the fall, in October. Usually there is a slack period where you work part-time to December. I work as a sewing machine operator. And when I go off during the slack period, I got my unemployment insurance through the summer. I get about $7.50 a week. It's swell. Before that we didn't know what to do.

Of course, I knew all about unions. When I worked at the International Tailoring, they had a union there, and the men used to get swell pay. They wouldn't let me join, of course. They were getting $45 and $50 in their trade, and I was only getting $18. Now in the shop, every time I open my mouth about the union, the chairlady at the shop says, "All right, you keep your mouth shut. We know all about it, you know all about the union."[26]

Similarly, Matilda B. had been working since she was 14. As she made clear, she was an organizer and a leader. Her interview also reflects the heightened ethnic tensions during the Great Depression. She was 27 when she was interviewed in 1939.

I never used the transfer I got from the New York school. Shortly after I came to Stamford, I got my first job in the Individual Laundry, where I worked on the shirt press. I got the job myself, and I had some hard time before that. You were supposed to be 16 to get a job, or else have working papers. I didn't have working papers but I told them I was 16. I used to go to work at 7:30 in the morning and work until 6:00. On Saturday we worked a half day [51½ hours per week]. I got $14 a week, and I'll never forget that first paycheck. I worked there two years. No, I never got any raises in those two years. All the girls in the place were dissatisfied. We all know we worked too hard, and too long for the money we were getting. But they were all afraid to talk. Well, I got the girls together so we could ask for a raise and we approached the boss. The boss asked the girls who started the strike, and some of them told him I did. So I was on the outside then, and all the girls went back to work. They put me up at the wall, because they knew I was the spunkiest talker. I got fired.

I was out of work for about two or three weeks. Then I got a job at the Anna Costume dress shop, as a finisher. We used to have to sew buttons and snaps on a dress and turn up the hem by hand. I got $1.95 a week in that place. It was owned by an Italian then. We used to go in at 8:00 in the morning and work until 5:00 or 6:00, depending on whether there was a lot of work or not. I worked there two weeks. When I saw that the boss was handing me down $1.95 for a week's work, I nearly raised the roof in that place. I had an awful fight with the boss, and I quit.

The following day I got a job in Piper and Salerno—a coat shop. I was a sleeve folder—that's when you finish off the sleeve and lining at the cuff. I got $10 a week there; that wasn't so bad. We worked from 8:00 to 5:00 and a half day on Saturdays [44 hours]. I was satisfied there, but after six months the place went bankrupt. That place was owned by an Italian and a Jew.

From there I went to the National Pants—that's the Genovese Pants Company now. It was owned by Italians and still is. I got $3 a week for work from 7:30 in the morning till 6:00 at night and Saturday a half day [58 hours]. I worked on the buttonhole machine for about six or seven months. After that I asked the boss for a raise. He got sore, and he said that work was slow and he wasn't getting paid much for the work, and all that sort of thing. So I stood there till I found a job in the five-and-ten—want to know the name of it? G. C. Murphy. I used to work from 9:00 to 6:00 every day, and on Saturdays from 9:00 in the morning till 10:00 at night [52 hours]. I got $14 a week, and I worked there two years. Then I got into an argument with the manager. It was during the Christmas rush, and I was on the outs with one of the stock girls. I had an empty space on one of my counters, and during Christmas you're not supposed to let any of the spaces get empty like that. Well, the manager balled me out, and I got sore. He called me a "Wop," and I called him an "Irishman." And I told him to stick the job where it belonged. I guess that was telling him in plain English. I quit there on a Saturday, and the next Monday I got a job at the Stamford Waist Company. Sure, I got the job myself. Nobody ever helped me find a job.

I've worked at the Stamford Waist for about nine years now. I started as a learner—on a sewing machine. I got $11 and I worked from 8:00 to 5:00, with a half day on Saturdays [44 hours]. I kept getting $11 until 1934. One day the organizer from the ILGWU came into the shop and stopped the power and told us to report to a special meeting at Carpenter's Hall right after work. He said the town was 100 percent organized, and if we didn't join the union we couldn't work, because this was the only shop that hadn't got a union.

Everybody turned up at that first meeting. The girls asked me to get up and ask some questions about conditions in the shop. Oh, questions like— why we weren't allowed to talk at our machines, and why we weren't allowed to go to the ladies toilet without being followed like a dog. The girls in the shop were afraid to talk, but I wasn't and I asked the questions.

The bosses always have a stooge around, you know that. The next day someone reported me, and the forelady wouldn't give me any work at the shop. I couldn't figure it out at first. I kept asking for work, and she kept ignoring me. Then I went to the phone, and I called up the union and asked for Mr. Barcan, our organizer. I told him the whole story. He told me not to leave the shop—to sit at my machine until he came. I sat down and waited, and when Mr. Barcan showed up at the shop there was a riot. The boss didn't want me in the shop; he was sore because I had told about the conditions. The organizer told the boss he'd have to pull the shop out on a strike. Well, they finally got it settled, and I stayed in the shop, and the forelady had to give me work, too. Since then everything has been all right. I've worked there steady, except in the slack seasons, of course.

During one of the slack seasons, I got a job at the Flossie Dress shop. That was owned by a Jew, but they had an Italian foreman. It was a union shop, but we used to work at piece work. I used to make about $1.70 a week. Can you imagine! They used to keep us waiting around three or four hours every day, and then they had their old girls and they used to give them the good work. One day I just got sick of waiting around, and making such little money, and I approached the foreman. I told him I came to the shop to get my bread and butter, not to watch him fool around with the girls. Of course we had an argument, and I quit.

Before that, during another slack season at the Stamford Waist, I worked in the Flossie Dress shop. That was the time I nearly got killed. Do you want to know about that? Well, they had fired a couple of the girls. Now you know the union doesn't approve of firing unless there's a darned good reason. The boss refused to reinstate the girls, so the union was forced to call the shop out on strike. The union called on their best and most active members to help—to encourage the girls to stay on the picket lines. So I ran right down there and went to work. One day when we were on the picket line, I saw the boss looking out at us. When I seen the Jew looking out the window, did I get sore! I had my scissors in my pocket and I took them out and pointed them at him, and told him to "Come out, you dirty Jew." There was a policeman across the street, and when he seen me point the scissors he thought I had a gun in my hand, and he pointed his gun at me. The policeman on our picket line saw him, and he took me by the arm and swung me behind him so I wouldn't get killed. I really owe that policeman my life. Of course I was scared—sure. I stayed on the picket line just the same. Always show the union spirit. You know what the union slogan is, don't you? "One for all, and all for one."

The next day, the boss hired taxis to get the scabs to the shop, and he bought them ice cream and lunch so they wouldn't have to come out and face us. So we framed the girls—the scabs—one day. We made them think that we had gone home, so they could escape like rats in the hole. You should have seen them jumping into those cabs at night, like rabbits; the foreman used to come down with them and push them in and then slam the doors. This day, we hid behind the cars. There were some young fellows on the picket like with us, and together with the girls we grabbed the foreman when he came down. We pulled his pants down and made him stay that way, in his undies. We laughed like hell. He got pushed back and forth along the picket line, in his underwear. You should have heard him. He begged us to let him go, and said he would join the union the next day. We told him to never mind tomorrow, but to come to the union hall right then and there in his underwear. We let him go after a while, and the next day he came down to the union with the forelady. She was Italian too. They both joined the union, and everything was settled. We were like one big happy family together. In fact we all had a big party together in the shop, and all the fights were forgotten.

After the union came into the Stamford Waist, I got an increase all right. [From] $11 to $16.80 a week, and no work on Saturdays. Besides that we only had to work until 4:00. Our hours were reduced from 44 to 35 hours a week. And we had better conditions, and our jobs were guaranteed against firing. We had the union behind us, and we were respected better than we were before we had it. Now if we want to ask for a raise we don't have to be afraid of no enemies, or having the boss know which one of us started anything. I can certainly say I've enjoyed my life better. And besides that, I've gone to so many places with the union and had such good times.

We had a two-year contract; when our contract was renewed we got another raise. We got an increase of $1.40. Now for the same hours I make $18.20. And just lately, the union gave us insurance. In case of death the union pays $150, and anybody you want can be the beneficiary. We only pay 35¢ a week dues. And the initiation fee if you joined when the union was first organized was only $1.95. Now it costs $15.95.

Do you want to know the activities of our union? Five years ago the union helped us to get a chorus started. There are about 30 union members in the chorus. We have a swell teacher that comes down from New York. The union pays for it. We've been everywhere—to Randall's Island, to Carnegie Hall, at the Adelphi Theatre, and two years ago we went to Atlantic City with the whole ILGWU chorus to entertain the convention. Once we broadcasted over WOR. We did have a dramatic club and a baseball team a couple of years ago, but that's all gone now. We put on two plays, one at the Italian Center, and one in New York at Labor Stage. We've had so many good times, and gone so many places. You know, before times were bad we used to go down to New York about three or four times a year. But it is an awful expense, and now we don't go as often.[27]

After work, immigrants devoted much of their leisure time to family and community activities. Just as the workplace saw cooperation as well as conflict, so too did relations with kin and neighbors.

91

4

FAMILY AND COMMUNITY

More than four decades ago, Oscar Handlin's Pulitzer Prize–winning account of immigration, The Uprooted, *offered a nostalgic view of the immigrant family. The Harvard historian contended in a now classic portrait that in Europe the family had been an integral part of the village community, and through an intricate web of relationships no one could live except as a family member. The family reflected community values and the community reinforced family standards. However, once families left the village as a consequence of emigration, the set of relationships became unglued. Families were on their own in the new land. And in a country undergoing industrialization, like the United States in the nineteenth century, individual family members found themselves further isolated as they moved into factory work.*[1]

Such an interpretation tends to oversimplify. Since not all European immigrants had lived in villages—many came from an urban background in countries already enmeshed in industrial capitalism—and since the nuclear family was common even in preindustrial times, it is questionable whether emigration and industrialization led to a "breakdown" of the extended family. Kinship— and friendship—continued to play an important role in the new country. As suggested by John Bodnar, as well as many other contemporary historians of immigration, family and friends provided access to jobs, homes, and information generally useful to a newcomer: "In the movement to a capitalist world and in the initial decades of settlement, familial and communal networks abounded." The family economy was often sustained by mothers and sisters who looked after boarders or took in "homework" while the males worked outside the household.[2]

The oral histories in this chapter reveal cohesion and conflict within the home. As with most aspects of immigrant society, group cultural differences and individual temperaments helped to explain different relationships. Generational differences, however, appeared to cut across ethnic groups, with the tensions between parents and children exploding in a variety of ways. Often, immigrant parents compared their children's behavior to what it was like in the old country and found such behavior wanting—although not always to the extent of the construction worker who believed that raising children in America was like raising "animals." Respect for authority and discipline receive a good deal of attention from our narrators, with the latter ranging from shrewdly innovative to brutal. Some of those interviewed also contemplate the ways they relate to their own children in light of the ways their parents interacted with them. As the son of a Sicilian immigrant explained, his father disapproved of his grandchildren being spoiled "by trying to bring them up so that they will be able to stand on their own two feet later in life." The son continued: "We want them to be broadened, independent, and self-sufficient. . . . I only wish I had been 'spoiled' half as much." Often public schools received the blame for separating generations, for teaching a new language, for filling heads with new ideas. In many instances, immigrant attitudes revealed ambivalence about the value of education. On the one hand, it was needed to advance in the new society; on the other, it divided parent and child.

The schools were only one of many institutions in the immigrant community. Neighborhoods served as coordinating points for a multitude of activities, from the preparation and sale of food to the promotion of prayer. Familiar sounds and smells marked one's territory. Institutions as diverse as saloons and churches vied for neighbors' attention. Many places, such as Michael Steinberg's father's blacksmith shop (described in chapter 3), functioned as gathering places for the community. While different ethnic groups often lived in close proximity to one another, many voluntary associations—both newly created to meet immigrant needs and transplanted from the old country—allowed individuals to maintain their group identity and to associate with people like themselves. Such newcomers, then, could live together by living apart.

Politics worked to unify different ethnic groups and simultaneously divided them. National leaders such Franklin D. Roosevelt, remembered at the conclusion of this chapter by those who spoke to the WPA, tried to enlarge their parties to encompass a coalition of multicultural voters. Local politicians attempted the same, but parochial rivalries often pitted Irish against Italian against Jew or other ethnic group. Community, then, had to withstand strong forces of division. Ethnic group cohesion frequently militated against universal cooperation, but the bonds of community often adhered. Commonalities such as the one expressed by Sando Bologna when describing his neighborhood—"The world was poor as far as we were concerned"—may have served as a unifying force. The need to survive motivated many and suggests a reinforcement of the sense of community among the newcomers, even as strong antagonisms ripped at the foundations of the community. Like the old country, the new world was not an easy place in which to live.

FAMILY

The family was the backbone of the immigrant community. It provided financial security, a sense of continuity with Old World traditions, and the emotional support that enabled immigrants and their children to adjust to the rapidly changing demands of American society and culture. Yet those demands eventually weakened the family structure. The strain usually appeared first among immigrant children, who were caught between the traditional world of their parents and the modern culture outside their homes, which they encountered every day at school or on the neighborhood streets. The allure of American culture did much to fragment the immigrant family and in the end led to the decline of the immigrant community itself.

Some parents, such as the Italians described below, developed close and affectionate ties with their children.

He [his father] was basically a farmer and I think his character was handed down to his children. You know the people who live on the farm are real good people, and that is why I like farmers, because they are solid individuals. The Chase Manufacturing Company, which is now the Chase Brass and Copper Company, offered land to employees where they could grow vegetables. It was what today one might call moonlighting, or leisure-time activity. There were many acres of land which was not too far from where we lived. It was a good half hour walk, to get there from our home. During the summer, he, like most of the other employees, would be given a certain share, for example, two acres or more, where they planted whatever they wanted to. So every summer my dad would plant potatoes, and corn, and vegetables and other commodities. I would walk with him because we never had a car, and I would spend hours with him planting, tending and harvesting, but I never really was that excited about it. It didn't appeal to me much, maybe because it was confining work. At harvest time we would sometimes rent a truck or have a friend help him bring the crops home. It was a great source of food for us. It was better than getting food stamps and canned goods like so many people get today. This was the kind of companionship that I enjoyed with my father at that early age, say up until about ten or so when I broke off and was close to my mother, because she enjoyed going to Italian shows and visiting friends. . . .

She was a good mixer, and she was a pleasant person. I think she favored me in a lot of ways because I was her only son and I was the oldest child, so I always felt a strong tie to her. Even though she never went to school, there was something about her that used to amaze me. How could she figure out the expenses of the week; how could she add and subtract? She never learned that in school. How could she determine values on food, on clothing, and how could she find out if certain things were necessary? All these things I couldn't understand because of the fact she never had any training in these matters. . . . The other thing that impressed me about my mother was, perhaps one night a week, she would spend it mixing dough. Another night she would be washing the clothes by hand on the scrub board, repairing the clothes, or making dresses for my three sisters.[3]

It would be misleading to present an overly idyllic picture of the immigrant family. As this interview of an Italian immigrant showed, parents and children grappled with the influences of American culture at the same time that parents struggled to preserve respect for their traditional viewpoint and authority. For this unidentified construction worker, raising children in America was like raising "animals."

Now I know how these children are in this country; you can't tell them nothing because they mix with all kinds of people that are different from Italian people, so they learn not to respect the father and mother. In Italy the father and the mother—they have all the ideas made for the children, and the children have to do like they say, and that's the way how they learn right. In this country it's like you raise up the animals, to raise children. . . .

See, everything changes. The people now are more like the American people. Before, all the people come from the other side they used to be strict with the children just like myself; now what's the use. This is a different climate and the children they are growing different. Before, the children used to do all the things that the father says; now they do what they see and what they think is alright. Now you don't know the difference with the Italian boys and the boys from the other nationalities. For my part I don't care now; what's the use. But I think that the boys should not forget the country that we come from because it's not right to do this, because there is lots of things that is good from their Italian habits—that all the nationalities could learn.[4]

Another Italian immigrant affirmed these sentiments.

That time the Italian men they were more strict with the family and with the wife. The wife had to be in the house all the time, and she could only go with the husband when she had to go someplace. Now, the women they go to the show with the children and they go to anyplace when the church makes the good times and they have more liberty. The children they could go anyplace that they want; before, they had the orders that they have to stay near the house and they could not go far. Now the children they go to the clubs for the boys and the girls have their clubs too, and they meet all kinds of people. So these things we never had a long time before. When our children they grow up they will be Americans and you never know that they are Italians. . . .

Long time before, all the Italian people they had the children follow the ideas from the old-country style, but now you could see that all these things they don't mean nothing because all the Italian people born in this country they are not like the Italian people that come from Italy. When I was in Italy my father and mother they were the ones that tell me what their father and mother was doing and how I should follow the ideas that they had. The father in the family he was like the teacher, and everything he said we had to do. This was the way that everybody was brought up. When you try to do this thing in America you can't do it. Because the trouble here, you tell the children one thing and they do it for one day, then they go outside and they see the children that they have the different ideas because they are other nationality. Then they come home and they say that the other children they don't do the same things I want them to do.[5]

"My Mother's Mark and My Father's Mark"

The issue of family discipline marked the memories of many oral history narrators. Paul Goodwin, a Russian Jewish businessman who was 56 when interviewed in 1975, discussed how children were kept in line in his family.

Now, my father was a good storyteller. He was a very nice man; he was a personable man. He was for most of my life a sick man. He was a very bad

97

asthmatic. . . . He was quite a learned guy. He was not the person in the house that ran the discipline of the house; my mother did that. My father would just sit by and watch it all. However, I think you had the feeling, though, that he was the next judge that you might have to appear before if you didn't toe the mark, without ever really saying that. But I think you had the feeling that you were going to have to answer to him. Now I must say that my father never raised a hand to any of us. I don't remember any physical punishment any time from my father to any of us, nor even threat of it. My mother wouldn't hesitate to give you a little bit of a crack across the rear end. I always remember my mother for this because I think that it's probably one of those things that every kid has a memory of his mother about.

I was about 11 years old. I came home about 7:30, 8:00, I guess, and my mother said, "I thought you were going to the library." I said, "Yes, I was in the library. But we got kicked out of the library for making noise." That is the one time I remember my mother physically taking a strap to me. The idea that anybody could ever be asked to leave a public institution was an anathema to her; that she couldn't tolerate. And I remember getting a good strapping for that. And it did it, because that's the way we were brought up. We still, I think—that mark is with us—we are like that. We still [think] that the law is the law; we're really that way. I think all my brothers are like that.

When asked about the upbringing of his own children, Goodwin reflected on a different generation and continued to stress the impact his parents had upon him.

I think that's been a very sore spot to me. I don't think that I have been as tough as I should have been. I think, at any rate, that bringing up children in an affluent society is a much more difficult thing to do than in a very modest set of circumstances. I try. There are many times in which I try literally to remember my mother's sternness about things. And sometimes I assert myself along those lines, and my kids give me a lot more lip about it than I would have ever dared give my mother. But I'm afraid that's the nature of things today.

But I think my mother's mark and my father's mark on us is very, very strong. Tremendous. I think on all four of us. I've said this many times. They were never people who would be didactic in telling us things. But what we learned about behavior or people I would say was all learned around the kitchen table. A great deal. And I still believe that. That's where a good deal of your approach and teaching comes from. In a very informal kind of way—

listening to reactions, to people, or reactions to circumstances, reactions to one another. What was tolerable, what was not tolerable. And I think that's where all of our standards, most of our standards, came from. I still believe that that's the place that it all comes from.

That's why I believe that you can spend a fortune in education, but if the fundamentals weren't right in certain stages, I think it's pretty difficult to overcome. I won't say you can't, but I still think those are critical times for people to set standards. And they set them—I'll tell you they set them. Our interests in community and so forth all stem from mother and father.[6]

Mr. Dugas, a second-generation Slovak-American, 50 years old, down on his luck, and unemployed except for some occasional real estate dealings when interviewed in 1939, told about discipline in his family.

Because I was one of the first Slovak kids to be born [in the neighborhood], I naturally know how most of us grew up. The parents in those times [treated] the kids like little slaves. They used to make us dress neat as far as [that] went, but they used to boss the hell out of us. All of the parents in [those days] considered it a disgrace if the children were not kept clean. I remember [my] mother and father giving my neck and face a careful examination before I would go outside. They used to tell me that the people would talk about the [family if] the children were not kept clean. Because of this habit I found that up [to this] day, although I don't wear fancy clothes, I find myself looking in the [mirror] before I go out anyplace. Even now in this section you can find that no [matter] how poor a family is, the kids are always spick-and-span.

We were [taught] that time to respect our elders and not to talk back to them. If we ever [argued] then my father would get a strap and tan my hide. The kids of today are a [bit] different; the parents are not as strict as they used to be. I believe [that a certain] amount of this is alright, because it makes the kids follow the good [aspect] of parents. I wouldn't be where I am now if I had taken my parents' advice [about going] into the priesthood or some other profession. Some of my best friends are [professional] people and they are making out pretty good while I am here doing [nothing.] I don't mean only for money but also for the sake of keeping occupied.

The parents in those days used to horsewhip us if we as much as [stole] an apple. I remember the time that I went up on the other side of Tube Stamping Company, when I was only 12 years old. I hopped the fence in one of those places and I loaded my shirt full of apples. When I came home I was proud [of] my pickings and I showed all of the apples to my father. He asked me where I [got] them, and when I told him that I had gone into somebody's lawn for them he told me to put on my jacket and take him to the place. When we got there he made me throw all of the apples under the tree and then we proceeded home. When we reached the house he saw my mother and told her to go to the store for something and in the meantime he marched me into the kitchen. He made me get the strap and told me to bend over. After I had done this he started to swing and in a little while he whaled the hell out of me. Well, let me tell you I never went to [steal] apples there again. And if sometimes I did get some apples I would never let [my] father know about it.

Well, this is no exception; all of the parents then did the same thing. Discipline was the important thing in those days. The old-timers believed in that system and there was no getting away from it. [Plenty] of times I went hungry because I hookied away from school or because I did [something] wrong. The only thing that I have against this kind of treatment is that sometimes they carried it too far and it had the opposite results. This is, as I see it now. A certain amount of discipline is alright, but not too much.[7]

If apple theft was treated with the strap, smoking met another fate, as related by Mr. P., a 58-year-old German-American Bridgeport resident who had been brought up on an Iowa farm.

My father bought a farm there in Dayton Township and by a great deal of hard work and good management succeeded in having one of the most prosperous farms in that part of the country. Everyone who knew my father liked him because of his honesty and square dealing, and I believe he had more friends than any other man in the state of Iowa. He was strict on discipline, however, especially with himself, and never used tobacco in any form and was a complete abstainer from any kind of strong drinks.

I'll never forget one time he caught my brother and me smoking cornsilk back of the barn. We could tell the way he looked that we were in for it; and both of us stepped forward to take the usual punishment for a wrongdoing, which was to grasp the lobe of the ear between his thumb and forefinger and besides bearing in with the thumbnail, he would give a twist on the ear that would almost lift us off of our feet. This time, however, he just told us to go to the village store about four miles away and bring him two corncob pipes and a package of "Mrs. Miller's" tobacco. I'll never forget that name as long as I live. We had to walk both ways and it was almost dark when we arrived home. We were darned good and tired and hungry as bears.

Father never said a word; just took both pipes, filled them with some of the tobacco, and beckoned to us to follow him. Just as he was going out of the door I caught him winking at my mother and wondered what it was all about. He led us to a little old shed just about big enough to hold us and handed us the pipes. "Now, you boys go ahead and have a good smoke, and when you have finished with the pipeful, I will fill it up again for you; and remember I want you to smoke hard so I can see it coming out through the cracks." Well, we smoked hard—knew better than to try not to—and I suppose because we were so darned tired and our stomachs so empty, it didn't take much to put us under but we never did get to the second pipeful. You can bet we went to bed without any supper and I do not believe anybody could ever be as sick as we were that night. I had grown to manhood and had a family of my own before I ever smoked again, and my brother has never used tobacco in any form to this day.[8]

"My Children Have Been Brought Up My Way"

Joseph Lazzaro, who emigrated from Italy in 1920, was 72 at the time of this interview. The father of 10 children, 8 of whom were girls, he voiced some common fears immigrants had about raising Americanized children.

My children have been brought up my way and the Italian way. This I mean is that the children should always ask the father when they want to do something that they are not sure of. In Italy I was taught that what my father said was right. I have done this with my children and they have to do it; if they don't, they can't live in my house. What I say is the law in my house. They say that the older a man [is], the wiser he is. I think that this is true; if it wasn't, then my father wouldn't teach me these things. Once the father has the children get the best of him, then it is too bad, because they will try to tell him what to do. In Italy the father has the right to whip his children if they do not do right, no matter how old they are.

In this country it is no good. The children tell the father what they want. If it is no good the father doesn't care; he let them get the upper hand. You read in the papers that a son has beat his father; that's a shame.[9]

Sometimes the battles between parent and child were fierce enough to turn the child against her heritage, as seen by this confrontation between a strong-willed Polish-American daughter and an abusive father. One should note the conclusion of this segment, which ends with the daughter's condemnation of her parent as a "damned foreigner."

How long were we on Ellis Island? Not very long. The doctors there took little Joe away from me after they'd looked me over. [Her mother had died in childbirth during the ocean voyage; she was coming to America in pursuit of her husband, who had abandoned her for another woman.] They sent for my father and he took us back with him to Waterside. I was given a good beating and told to call the other woman "mother" and her two kids, Stanislaw and Piotr, my brothers. It always looked to me as if he considered me his first failure since the other woman had given him two boys and my own mother Joe. Poles always want boys rather than girls. But I came on the scene old enough to work, whereas Joe and Piotr were still at the breast and Stanislaw just able to walk. So, fortunately, I wasn't needed about the house.

The old man took me up to the factory, where he got me a job sorting parts of small locks as they came down the conveyor—you know, tumblers, facings and such. There were half a dozen Polish girls on this job but all older than I was by several years. They asked me how old I was and when I told them 12 going on 13, they said I had better not admit I was that young if I didn't want to lose my job and have to go to school. They said my father must have lied about my age, which is just what he did do and without telling me anything about it. He knew I couldn't speak English and that the foreman couldn't speak Polish, and he knew that I was too afraid of his stick to risk talking out of turn. What he didn't know was that I'd be willing to work anywhere so as to be able to stay away from that other woman and her two squalling brats and from my father also, as much as possible.

She went on to describe the house in which she lived.

Mother of God, it must have been the worst in the Polish colony of Waterside: ramshackle, tumbledown, with no running water or electric light and no bath or indoor toilet—only a backhouse behind a pump which ran dry in the summer. . . . We didn't [bathe] except in the Rippowam, which ran almost under the house, and into which it finally tumbled after the spring floods of 1923. But that was after [we] had left it, or had been put out of it, rather, by the city authorities on account of its not being safe.

But in those days, I might as well tell you, it didn't seem so bad because then I hadn't learned that it's dangerous to be cold in the winter, to sleep on a mattress on a drafty floor or eat food that's spoiled or been cooked in a pot babies' didies have been boiling in. Dirt and filth was second nature to all of us, so much so that looking back I consider it only a miracle of God that any of us survived.

But survive we did, all of us, in spite of Father's blows and that other woman's efforts to feed us. In those days, I couldn't imagine where all the money went that father and I made at the factory. He used to stand right outside the door next to the pay window and pounce upon my $4.40 pay envelope the moment I got it on Saturdays. He was always too fond of money to spend it on liquor, although he liked it well enough when somebody else paid for him getting drunk. It was only after the authorities put him out of the house by the river and the truant officer caught up with him on my account that I'd learned enough English to find out. He was salting almost every cent away in the savings bank.

The interviewer asked her to explain how the truant officer discovered she was absent from school.

Not on my account, I assure you, although he beat me almost to death for it just the same. It was the new pastor of our own Holy Name of Jesus Church who first told him that I ought to be in school when he found out that I couldn't even read Polish—a girl of 14. As a matter of fact, I couldn't even write my name, not ever having had to. Where we came from in what was Russia before the war, education was the last thing a girl was likely to get. Even in Poland today I hear that the condition of women isn't much better off even though it is a republic.

The interviewer asked her what happened when the priest told her father that she should be in school.

Plenty. The father couldn't do anything with him even after he'd been down to our place twice and had the president of the John Sobieski Society

103

talk to him too. The little runt couldn't get it though his thick skull that girls rate the same treatment as boys in the U.S.A. To him a girl was good for just two things—work and producing boys who'd grow up and help the family out financially. She might even get a husband who'd be willing to live in and do the same if he was dumb enough like they are in Poland. But education—hell! A girl was born with all she needed.

Well, the father and the president of the John Sobieski Society, to which Father belonged, couldn't do a thing with him on account of the fact they all came from parts of Poland owned by different countries in the beginning, with different standards, if you know what I mean. So the father just turned the matter over to the truant officer. He came over with an interpreter and when the old man found out it would cost him a great deal more to keep me out of school than to let me go, he gave in. Anything that ever came up to threaten his bank account always has its way with [him]. But even to this day I think he still has it in for me as being the first one to oppose his plans. Joe and I kid him about it sometimes even to this day, whenever we go down to the house, which isn't often because he's still a damned foreigner who doesn't know what it's all about.[10]

Growing up in a Sicilian household ruled by a domineering father, a second-generation Italian-American, interviewed in 1940, not only rejected his heritage but refused to impart it to his children.

Our neighborhood was not an especially good one, and I with my sisters and brother attended the Smalley school. My playmates were Italian, Irish, Polish, and American, and aside from making sport about my name, we got along very well. Looking back I can hardly see how I endured my childhood, living in that old shack on Oak Street [in New Britain]. Our yard was rather big and was always littered with barrels and piles of wood. We had grape arbors all over the place, and in the summer my father and his friends would sit out there drinking and playing cards while my mother worked in the garden.

My father was a small, stout man and rather blustering in appearance. He continually fought with my mother, and we, as children, were always afraid of him. Italian was the only language spoken in the home and my father, being what he was, disliked American customs and ways. He was a strong defender of Mussolini from the start, and as Il Duce grew in power my father praised him more and more. My mother, on the other hand, was hardworking and very religious. She put up with plenty in order to keep peace in the house.

I got off to a bad start in life, being christened Giuseppe. In school I was the object of crude remarks and when I got into the ninth grade I decided I wasn't going through life with a name like Giuseppe. I talked with my history teacher and told her I should like to have my name changed to Joseph. She fixed it with the principal, but when my father learned what I had done I got the worst beating of my life. However, from that time on, in school and to my friends, I have been known as Joseph. I feel that since we are living in America we should have American names and not be subject to derision by others.

At age 10 he brought a violin with money that he had saved shining shoes and selling newspapers.

We lived in a five-room tenement and we were always crowded. . . . All meals were eaten in the kitchen, as our dining room was used for a bedroom. My father and his friends often sat around the big table drinking wine and talking in loud voices about politics, work, and Italy. There was always a lot of noise in our house, with the children running around and my father's friends dropping in at all hours. I sometimes had to take my violin up in the attic in order to practice.

Manners and etiquette were entirely foreign to me until I reached high school age. Prior to entering school, whatever English I used was learned from my little playmates and neighbors who gathered around a small grocery store where we lived. We played in the street and in our schoolyard but never in our backyard. My father would never have any kids around the house. He said they spoiled the grass.

When I entered high school I went out for the football team and was accepted. My father, however, refused to sign a slip stating that I might play and so the coach called one night to talk to him into it. I was embarrassed as I sat listening to my father damning the school for what it was doing to the kids. The coach could not make the old man see straight and finally left before he got thrown out. Coach Cassidy was somewhat of a politician and he talked to one or two prominent Italian politicians who came to talk with my father. They told him it would be an honor for an Italian boy to be on the team and should make him very proud. This, of course, changed my father's outlook and he gave his consent.

After graduating from high school he entered college, working at a variety of jobs to pay his way. But his father lost his job during the Depression and began demanding that he return home to help support the family. He quit college after two years and contributed most of his earnings to his father for the support of the family. Eventually he began to chafe under this arrangement, and after he met his future wife he unilaterally cut his contribution.

My father did not like this, nor did he like the girl with whom I was going. She was Irish and was from a very nice family, and this was often the cause of many hot arguments. My father talked much of Italy to me, and of Mussolini, and of how I was an Italian and should find some nice Italian girl to go with and get married to. When I opposed him he would get red in the face and call me all kinds of names. He blamed the school and my American friends for spoiling me and used to say if this were Italy, things would be different.

Eventually he married and got a job in an insurance company in Hartford. As the father of two children, he was committed to raising them as Americans, which meant a wholesale rejection of Italian culture. Ironically, his son still seemed to express an interest in his heritage. It is not uncommon for the third generation to try to repossess the heritage that the second generation tried to forget.

My children are Americans and are being brought up as such. I have given them nothing of Italian ways and culture. We treat them as individuals and talk to them intelligently, as we would to grown-ups. Even now when my son asks me about the foreign situation we try to explain to him just what happened. He is very young, of course, and doesn't understand a lot of things, but already he is interested in knowing the answers to many questions. We are trying to bring them up so that they will be able to stand on their own two feet later in life. We want them to be broadened, independent, and self-sufficient. My father, of course, wholly disapproves of this method of bringing up children. He tells me I am spoiling them. I only wish I had been "spoiled" half as much.[11]

The public school also caused friction between parents and children. It helped to quicken the pace of assimilation and provided a path to social mobility and a way out of the immigrant neighborhood. Ironically, as this interview of an Italian-American showed, some immigrant parents encouraged children to use the schools to better themselves and in so doing may have weakened the ties that bound their children to them.

I was born in New Haven. I went to the grammar school, and when it came time for me to go to high school my parents talked the matter over very carefully. They each wanted to have me get an education, at least the best I could. They realized what an education meant to me. They were quite anxious that I get a college education, and they figured how much money it would take to let me have one.

It was not easy for them, but they sent me to New Haven High and when it came time for me to go to college or to work, it was decided that I should get a commercial course. This I did but I will never forget what my parents sacrificed, particularly my mother, while I was taking the course. I feel that I can never repay her for what she did for me, and as long as I live it will be my aim to give her everything I can. She desires that effort on my part.

She took in boarders and she also took in washing so that I could go ahead with my education. My father also wanted me to get all the education possible. They struggled and made as much money as they could in order to give their family everything that was possible.[12]

"You Did What You Were Supposed to Do. You Prepared Your Lessons."

In Eastern Europe and czarist Russia, many Jews were prohibited from attending school and were forced to educate themselves. This gave them a strong tradition of learning. A second-generation Russian-Jewish–American spoke of the high esteem in which his family held education and the educated.

There was no such thing as hooky-playing. There were certain rules that we knew we abided by. It was as simple as all that. Right was right, wrong was wrong. And don't try to be sneaky. . . . It was rather—and I think it was true in most families of my generation—there was a pretty high level of ethics. . . . At school you did what you were told to do; you didn't get into trouble. If you did, the teacher chastised you. No one went to the school to say, "Why did you do it to him?" My father had a rule of thumb: if the teacher did it, she was right, you were wrong, that was it. No questions asked, no running around fomenting strikes.

I don't think they even knew what it meant to question the authorities, so to speak. And school was an authority, the teacher was an authority. Maybe it was an Old Country attitude towards authority. . . . You did what you were supposed to do. You prepared your lessons. . . . And when the report cards came out, they had to be reasonably good or you were awfully ashamed because it was spread around. . . .

Learning—and you'll find this a fact particularly among Jewish people—learning is the greatest thing there is. Studying is even above prayer. That's a fact. I remember that my father's doctor . . . was at the house one day, and I was a grown man, I was in my early twenties. And one day I said, "Hey, Doc." This man was already in his fifties. My father turned to me and said, "Hey, what are you 'Doc'-ing him? What, did you and he feed pigs together? What are you presuming, calling him Doc? You call him Doctor."

This was the kind of attitude that our generation had towards people with learning, whether they are [a] rabbi, or doctor, or lawyer, teacher, principal of school.[13]

Ernie Demao's radical Italian working-class father was an example of an immigrant who took a dim view of the liberating potential of education. For him learning was a tool of the exploiters. The son, however, was determined to fight his father for the right to learn.

I wanted an education. I was a reader—an omnivorous reader. Everything I could get ahold of, no matter what it was, I had to read it—good, bad, or indifferent. My father had no education. He, with his Wobbly background, felt that the troubles of the world came from the educated people and the working class had enough trouble without raising exploiters of the people. So he was opposed, and [there was pressure] to go to work.

I said, "But I work every summer." I had a job after school, selling shoes. I would bring home $8 a week during the school period, plus everything I made when I worked at the plantation [the Clark Plantation in Pequonnock].

I would be reading upstairs. The stairs would creak when my father was coming up. He would listen for the click, putting the light off. So I learned the trick. I'd be right under the light. When he would come up, I would just turn the light enough to put it out, slip into bed, and he wouldn't . . . This went on for quite a while, 'til one day he put his hand on the bulb and it was hot. That was the end of that.

We got into a fight. He went at me. There was an old milk bottle. They used to be heavy, glass milk bottles. I just grabbed that in time and swung, and I caught him on the forehead and staggered him. He'd come at me with a knife. Pretty ugly. I left. A 15-year-old boy, knowing nothing really about life, because I went from school to the plantations. If school was out on Friday, Monday I'd be on the plantation. I worked 'til Labor Day, then back to school. It was a little terrifying. I didn't know where my next meal was coming from. But I did have this job, getting $8 a week, selling shoes (ground gripper shoes) on the second floor, down across from Brown Thompson. Brown Thompson and G. Fox. They were right next to each other. I had to pay my own way.

Now $8, even in those days—it was room, food, clothing, and very often I didn't eat. But I was determined to get an education.[14]

COMMUNITY

"The Atmosphere, the Sights, the Smells"

Upon arrival in America, most immigrants settled in ethnic neighborhoods. These communities were a source of both continuity and change as they helped immigrants to maintain some of the traditions of European culture and provided a sense of security that eased their adjustment to American society.

Despite the poverty and harsh realities of immigrant neighborhoods, they often bustled with energy and excitement. The following description of Hartford's Little Italy in the late 1940s illustrates the many sights, sounds, and smells of a transplanted Old World culture as seen through the eyes of an appreciative Italian-American child. Food and celebration fed neighborhood solidarity.

After the church, I remember them [his grandparents] taking me to the grocery store, to go shopping, because on Sunday they were open, at least half a day. I remember the smells of the Provolone cheese, and all the other imported cheeses from Italy, sausages, salamis, were all hanging in the window. The bakery rushed out—the smell of hot Italian bread, which flowed all over Front Street. It was all over Little Italy, the atmosphere, the sights, the smells, and I just loved it. Of course in the Italian supermarkets, I shouldn't say supermarkets—ah, markets—you'd have all kinds of smells of the herbs, Italian herbs and things. It just was a feeling I had for Little Italy. I was born with it, and it shall be with me for all time.

I remember the old pageantries we used to have on Front Street, Santa Lucia feast, *la festa di sant'Antonio, la festa di Monte Carmelo*, which was across the bridge, the old stone—I shouldn't say old—this stone bridge, I think it's called the Bulkley Bridge. I remember we used to walk from our Williams Street home with my mother and my sisters and brothers and go up to Mount Carmel's beautiful feast. They used to have a mass at Saint Anthony's—I'll never forget it; it'll always be with me. So you know it was a great influence.[15]

Ethnic neighborhoods were often dangerously overcrowded. The practice of taking in boarders to raise extra money intensified the congestion. Newcomers, usually single men, became boarders to save money and to be among friends who helped them to adjust to life in America. As the experience of the following Italian-American woman showed, taking care of boarders normally fell on the shoulders of women.

My husband was working steady that time and everything was alright. I had to take care of the house, and we had four boarders and I had to cook for them. When I first came here I didn't want to do this because everybody wants to have their own house. Well, I change my mind because everybody was doing this thing. That time some of the people that came from the other side didn't have no place to stay, and we took some of the people in the house that we knew. That time even some of the *paesani*, before they come from Italy, they make the arrangement to stay in the house of some relative, and when they stayed here for a little bit they used to send for the wife and the family. This is the way that everybody used to do it at that time. Some of these people that had a good job that time they go to Italy every year because the passage was cheap, not like now. The Italian people were not the only ones that used to have the boarders—all the other nationalities used to do the same thing. But after a long time these people that used to have the boarders, they had their families here and they start to have their own place.[16]

"You Lived over Them, or You Lived next to Them"

The Little Italies, Little Polands, and Little Hungaries of America usually existed in close proximity to one another, but different immigrant groups rarely mixed socially save at work or in the marketplace, as shown by this second-generation Russian-Jewish–American's depiction of New Haven's Jewish community in the 1930s and 1940s.

[It was] not necessarily a totally Jewish community, because in the area of Washington Avenue you had the Italians, you had some Polish people, you had not many Irish people that I knew of in that area. But Polish and Italians in that area, yes. They didn't intermingle. Well, the kids certainly did, but there was no great social life of intermingling. But families talked and marketed together. The streets were full of—the grocery stores, the confectionery stores, and the butcher stores. You lived over them, or you lived next to them. They were all part and parcel of your existence.[17]

Sando Bologna, an American-born son of Sicilian immigrants, described the Sicilian community in pre–World War II Waterbury, Connecticut, where his countrymen lived closely with one another but largely separate from other ethnic groups despite what he called its "cosmopolitan flavor." One thing all people in the area held in common: "The world was poor as far as we were concerned."

Like so many other people who worked in the factories, we lived across the street and half a block up [from a brass factory] with another family, dear friends of my father. That block is still there, the tenement, and my *comare*, who is now about 80 years of age, who is like an aunt to me, is still living there. She is one of the few persons who knew me from the time I was a baby. A strong friendship prevailed, whereby my father used to call her husband and my mother called her in the form of godfather and godmother, which is a sign of strong friendship. Mrs. Sapio became godmother to one of my sisters and I became godfather to two of her sons. This is a strong link of friendship that goes on. I can go on and point out why I am so upset about the new connotations that are given to the word "godfather."

I understand after a few months when my dad was hired that we moved out of the fourth-story tenement and into a factory-sponsored housing project which they used to call sheendeeny, from the word "shanty," or barracks. They were just ordinary wooden buildings, four or five families in one row, what today might be called duplex, I suppose. We had very shoddy furniture, and we had no indoor toilet. As a matter of fact, they were to the rear of the shanty and they were called *backhousen*, which comes from the word "backhouse," or in back of the house. I never knew until many years later, as a matter of fact, that when we say we're going to the bathroom, we'd say we are going to the backhousen. It is an example of how words are formed. It wasn't until many years later that I found out in Italian you don't say back-housen, you say *gabinetto*.

In this shanty area lived immigrant families; the majority of them were Italian and many of them Sicilian. I never spoke English at home. This was a handicap when I went to school, and of course I didn't speak proper Italian. I had a Sicilian dialect.

Many of our neighbors were Sicilians. There were non-Sicilians, but my immediate friends were Sicilians. When I went visiting with my father and mother, we went to only Sicilian homes. The men would play cards and then they would choose the *bosso*, or leader, and then they would distribute wine. Meanwhile, the women would knit and listen to records of Italian music and drama and talk about family problems. It was a close-knit situation. On Sundays we would walk up a long hill road to a farm area. There was a Mr. Luppo (we'd call him Jimmy Luppo), and he had eight or nine children (they are now in business in Waterbury) and many neighbors. Children would play in a large farmyard. The men would play cards and share the wine. The women prepared the meals and gossiped.

I went to a second school, then a third and fourth grammar school, because we moved from one tenement to another as conditions improved and as my father earned more money, but always in the North End section, which is now a predominantly black section. There were, of course, many Italian families, but there was a cosmopolitan flavor of Irish, French-Canadians, and Polish families. Also there were what we called "colored people." It was a good hodgepodge, and the important thing was that they were all poor. We didn't know rich people except from the "boulevard section" or the area where we live in now, which was inhabited by people who were in manufacturing or business. The world was poor as far as we were concerned. Consequently, I didn't think the problem of who was better existed—at least I never felt that way—and the humble atmosphere of the home is the thing that I think stuck in our minds. It still does.[18]

"Yes Sir, Those Were the Days"

Mr. Dugas, a 50-year-old Slovak-American who spoke earlier in this chapter about family discipline, drew a pleasant sketch of how simple pleasures like an outing in a neighborhood park in Bridgeport could play an important part in immigrant community life. He explained also how modern conveniences such as the automobile and mass entertainments such as the motion pictures changed the face of immigrant leisure.

On Sunday all of the Slovaks and people of other nationalities used to go out to the parks. Washington Park at the time was kind of wild and most of the Slovaks didn't want to go far away from home, so that all of the people in the section would be found there on the holidays. The parents would usually buy the kids all kinds of candy, peanuts, and popcorn. Some of the people after they got there would gather in bunches, the women with the women and the men with the men. They would talk about anything that you could think of. I remember at the time that most of the men talked about their jobs, the children, and what they did when not working. They spoke of getting together and playing cards or going out with two or three families. In those days it was a common thing to see two or three families go visiting other people. The women would always talk about how they were getting along; most of them took their sewing bags with them to the park and they would get together and show the kind of work that they had been doing. Sometimes us older kids would sit with the women and they would chase us away and tell us to go with the men.

Most of the kids in the park used to play together and raise hell to beat the band. And sometimes when some of us would get into a scrap the whole park would echo with our hollering. The girls were trained different then, and they were bashful of the boys. The only time that they would play with boys was either when the parents would tell them to or if the kids were kind of young; in that case there was no feeling of being bashful. Sometimes the kids would play with the kids of other nationalities who were also at the park. We got along with them pretty good, but sometimes they would hop on us and then there would be a hell of a scrap. If the older people separated us, then the Italians who formed the other group would apologize for the kids that got into the scrap. They were good in this way not to start trouble.

When I got older I found that a lot of these people that went to the park either had cars or that their friends had cars, and in this way they would go to places out of town or at Beardsley Park, or some other place. I remember that my father got a car when I was about 17, and he took the family and some of his friends out in the country for a picnic on Sundays. In this way they managed to break away to some extent from going in masses to Washington Park, but it ain't the same meeting place that it was years ago.

Yes sir, those were the days. Today they are victims of the machine age and they don't get around to seeing each other like they used to. Well, even the children are different—years ago they used to be satisfied with what they could get in entertainment by going to the park. Today they want too much excitement and aren't satisfied with going to the movies twice a week. After the movies came in I remember that I was satisfied if I went once every two weeks. In those days our parents used to think that the movies were not for the children and that they would spoil us. The movies in those days were considered almost sinful, and my people said that the priest in the Slovak church did not approve of some of these pictures. Because of this we could only go when we could sneak away or when we had enough money.

The Slovaks in those days were strictly home people, and they spent most of their time with friends and never associated with people of other nationalities. Because of this they hardly went to a movie or any kind of a show. Sometime when the Slovaks had religious plays at the church hall on Church Street or when they held one at Sadler's Hall, these places would be filled to capacity with all of the Slovaks. It was considered a sin if any of the Slovaks missed one of these religious plays. I remember many times that there were family quarrels because someone in the family could not go to the performance. Anything that the priest said in those days was like a law. In fact they paid more attention to the priest than they would to anybody else.

A confirmed bachelor, Dugas sadly found himself increasingly estranged from the immigrant community that brought him such fond memories.

I spend my spare time playing the saxophone and piano, which I learned by ear. I like music very much and I can appreciate what little I hear of it. I haven't many friends left on the East Side. Most of them have moved to better sections of the city; some in Stratford and out of town. Some of them come to see me on and off, but most of the time I am by myself. I live in a three-room flat on the first floor. My father had his saloon in what is my living room now. I had this changed shortly after my father died in the '20s. The reason that I had this room changed was that I was sure that Prohibition was here to stay and that the section was losing its reputation of being a good business place. I don't invite any of my neighbors into my house because I have nothing in common with them. Besides, the people there are kind of nosy and are not the kind that you could call good entertainers, because they are old and have different ideas that wouldn't match with my own.

I generally get up at 6:00 in the morning and although I haven't got any place to go, I take a walk around the East Side. Later I come home for breakfast, which usually consists of ham and eggs. After this I sit around a little while and read the *Bridgeport Telegram*. I first look in the want-ad section if there might be a possible job, then I look at the news, and last but not least I take a look at the sports sheet. I'm a baseball fan and I follow up the games from day to day. Around 9:00 in the morning I go downtown to see a couple of the real-estate dealers and I have a chat with them on some of the developments in the real-estate line. We usually discuss sales and how much a house on a certain street might be valued at. After this I take out a book in which I have a list of prospective buyers and I pick out a name. I have gone over this list time and time again and although I know that the sale is doubtful, I nevertheless see them again; it might be that they have changed their minds about some house that they have wanted to get and chances are that I might clinch the sale. That's how the real-estate game is—you can never tell when you might strike it lucky. Sometimes a sale comes out of the clear sky, and then other times it might come in weeks or months. Sometimes I feel like quitting it altogether, and then suddenly I'll get a sale—the whole thing works on a law of averages.

At night, or late in the afternoon when I get home, I get the *Post* or the *Times-Star* and I go over the want-ad section again, and then I go to the real-estate section again. After this I go to the sports sheet and after that I get some of my cooking done. Sometimes I make stew or some other kind of meat; sometimes it's cabbage and potatoes; sometimes it's ordinary kielbasa with cabbage or macaroni. I'm not too fussy about eating, so it doesn't make any difference with me whether I eat cabbage or pie. After supper I go out on the porch and finish reading the paper. When I get tired of this I go into the house and play on the saxophone or the piano. If I don't get any visitors by 9:00 I decide to call it a day and I go to bed. That's all of my routine, and it's almost the same every day; it has been this way since 1925. It's not that I am getting old that I do this, but only because there's nothing more entertaining.[19]

This Polish immigrant, interviewed in 1940, found life in America lonely. Many immigrants who came from rural villages in the Old World found adjustment difficult in urban America. Mrs. R.'s attitude was further embittered by the hard times of the Depression.

When I was on the other side everything was different like here; all the people were understanding how to be good. We lived on the farms and everybody had to work, but at the same time we have good times because the people were closer. The church was one place the people always go, and we learn everything from the church the right way. The people were more like friends than over here, and most of the time they invite all of the families when they have weddings.

Here in this country if one family have it better than the other family, they don't even want to bother. They are stingy because they think they are better and you're low. The people here that have the money, they are like sports. They don't care if you're good friends; if you have it bad they don't want to know you. When I had things in my house better, all my friends was coming to see me; now that we have relief they don't want to bother. When I see them on the street, they say that they are too busy and they have to go someplace. These same people they go to church and they say that they are good to God; just because they have the money they think that it's enough. This is what I don't like, because I was always good to the people. Nowadays you can't trust nobody because one family thinks they are better than the other family. Even one time when the people first come to this country they were better; now they learn the American habits that you don't have to respect if people don't got money.[20]

Mrs. W., an Irish widow who had lived in Bridgeport for 40 years at the time of her interview in 1940, expressed the confusion felt by older immigrants who remained behind after their once seemingly close-knit communities had been transformed by newer arrivals.

I myself could write a book on the different ones that have come and gone on this street. I do not know many of them now, but years back we all seemed like one big family, but of late years it is not that way. You know I do not even know the family who live on the other side of me. At one time I knew them all but that has all changed now. I am so busy with my own activities that I do not have time to confab with the neighbors.

Did you notice when you came into this street that it is all built up. There is no room to build another house, and when I came here there were lots across the street, and along the other side of me going toward Pequonnock Street.

It has been interesting, to say the least, to see the different houses go up and the different families that have come and gone. Some of them I have become acquainted with and others have come and gone and not even known who they were or where they came from. That is sort of like New York where they say one does not know their next-door neighbor.

I do remember this street and the different nationalities on it when it was the neighbor street that I remember it by. There were the Irish, the Swedes, and the English that predominated it. Now Lord knows who are here. There are a few of the Irish left and some Swedes, and there are some Jews and Polish and Italians on the street now. I do not know them, but from their names and their looks I can tell pretty near what they are.

Some of the Jews and Italians have bought the houses across the street and have really done some nice repair work on some of them—also doing a little remodeling. There are two Italian families across the street and they have even gone to the bother of putting up a stone wall across the front of their homes. Some of their places have banks and during the rainy weather the banks run down and they would be regular rivers over there, so these walls have stopped all that.

The flat downstairs here is the payoff. The different families that have lived

117

there is a caution. I cannot keep track of them. Just at present there is a family of seven living there. Husband and wife and five kids. I thought when they first moved in that I was in for it, that the noise would be all that I would need, but such is not the case. The little woman has those children under her thumb. There is not a noise downstairs after 9:00 in the evening. They have sort of tough going as he has a job that does not pay any too well, and to keep those kids fed and clothed is not an easy job.

Yes, I have really seen this old neighborhood grow from a few houses into a fully developed community. This was almost country at one time and now look at it. This section is all built up, even a way out Park Avenue. I suppose the automobile has brought about this big change. People think nothing of living way out in the country now and still come into the city for business. Times have really changed.[21]

Martin Brown, an Irish-English immigrant, explained the importance of ethnic clubs and societies in his social life. These neighborhood organizations provided friendship and financial assistance, and helped ease the process of assimilation into American culture.

I was not here long when I made friends with many other first-generation Irish fellows. At that time there were many Irish societies and every week I would go to at least one Irish dance. I don't remember—it is so long—the names of the societies but I did belong to at least four of them, all of which have passed out of existence today. Then the Irish used to get together like your foreign groups do today and usually a swell time was had by all. I also played cards and spent many a winter's night at a table playing forty-five and pinochle. Sometimes I would win a few cents but more often I would lose. Anyway I liked to play—it passed the time away. On Saturday night the fellows in the house would buy a keg of beer and play cards and drink until 4:00 and 5:00 in the morning. Once in a while we would go to a dance instead, but that was not very often on Saturday night. As for shows, I did not take much interest in them when I first came over. Those large Main Street showhouses were not there at that time anyway, but I do remember going to the Globe in about 1914 and 1915 to see vaudeville shows.[22]

A second-generation Polish-American illustrated how ethnic and community organizations in Ansonia helped to shape his childhood.

Let's say when I was a kid, or say around '40, '48, '49, I belonged to the Falcons, and it was a Polish group that had insurance. They had a lot of youth movement, gymnastics, and basketball teams. They had band organizations, where we used to play in a [fife] and drum corps. It was a big youth organization where they kept kids pretty busy in sports, music, et cetera. There was a place for somebody to hang around, take them off the streets. Also you had your YMCA, which is a pretty good organization where you had the same thing. Anything you wanted to participate in—gymnastics, basketball, swimming—they had. I belonged to that because of where I lived, there was just a bathroom out in the hallway and no heat. If you had to take a bath you had to go in the hall bathtub. It was pretty cold. It was kind of hard to take a bath in cold water, so you'd join the YMCA any time you needed a bath, take a shower at the same time, swim, shower, spend the day exercising, things like that. There was a lot of youth activities and clubs at that time because there wasn't too many youth working, that were able to get jobs.[23]

Gennaro Capobianco, the co-editor of an Italian-American newspaper in Hartford when he was interviewed in 1974, described the importance of mutual aid societies and explained why they declined, but certainly did not disappear, after the government took over many of their functions during the Great Depression.

Now, you have all kinds of Italians, so they want to naturally keep the good old Italian customs and traditions in their hearts by belonging to these organizations. Some of them were founded, besides that reason, for mutual benefits, sick and death benefits! Let's face it, in those early days, from the time they came, in the late 1800s up until the 1930s, there was no Social Security. And insurance companies weren't big like they are today. So who's going to help them out as immigrants with hospital bills? With their dues, they would build up the treasury, and when they needed help, all the members would get together and maybe even collect a little extra money besides for the sick benefits. If a member died, or a family member (funerals were not cheap, and they aren't cheap today), someone had to help pay the bill. And if you were a recent immigrant, where were you going to get that kind of money? So you joined a society, and you got your sick benefits, and your death benefits. If your wife dies you got money; if it was a husband, you got money; if it was a child you got money. Like the Sons of Italy . . . Orphan children—who would take care of the orphan children if the mother died? The father—it's hard for a father to take care of a family, especially in those days when Italian families were big. So the Sons of Italy, of which I am a member, like I told you, have an orphan fund, besides sick and death benefits.

So these are the reasons, the things that would help the immigrant. Although today the sick and death benefits are not necessary because we have so much insurance and Social Security. Granted, though, the death benefits could always help out on a funeral, but the sick benefits have just gone out the window. Many of the organizations have dropped them. We still send flowers to the hospital, and to the funeral home, a wreath if a member dies, and a sympathy card, or Mass card, but sick benefits, as I said, they're going out! There are very few that are paying it.[24]

Born in 1924, Father Theophil Mierzwinski was a second-generation Polish-American and the son of a miner and factory worker. At the time of this interview he was a parish priest in Waterbury, Connecticut. He contended that community churches enabled immigrants to hold on to some Old World traditions and also to adjust to life in America. This excerpt reveals the beliefs and perceptions of a priest about the immigrant Polish experience and are not based upon his own experiences.

I would say the Church in many ways helped the Polish immigrant identify with the country. Because the Church also gave him an identity with others who were Catholic. So he knew he was not isolated by his religion. He knew his religion made him part of a minority. And in the practice of his religion, the Pole was very tenacious of the traditions that he had brought back from Europe. You see, in Europe the Church was able to actually be the form developing culture. To me the astounding thing about the Polish immigrant—I say this even with the awareness that many came from the cities, many had an educated background (the academic world had no trouble). Many of the middle had no trouble. But the vast majority who were peasants had never been given the opportunity for any kind of extensive formal education, and they had to work the fields. Now the only source for them was the Church. And so the Church had educated them, and through its liturgy had taught them their beliefs, and enabled them to express these beliefs in song and in processions and pageantry. And the instruction that they had received was such that when they came here to the United States these immigrants naturally grouped together and formed their own parishes. This was one of the first things they desired: their own parish.

To maintain the ties of religion—and of course the idea that the religion and the education of the young and the preservation of their culture, their heritage, are intertwined. You see, the only thing that kept them as a people in Europe was a bond—you can simply say an ethnic bond. But the ethnic bond now also had the preserving character of another wrapper, namely the religion. And that religion affected their whole life, because they were formed in it in a liturgical way, where the seasons and the liturgy and the work were all intertwined. So the education they received from the Church over there. Now when they came over here they were able to associate with the Church. And to draw them away from this was always a challenge. To challenge their being as religious persons, to challenge their beings as Poles.

When it came to Americanizing them . . . the different associations, the different fraternal groups, the establishment of a Polish home, which was invariably something they did in the communities, all of this was a means of carrying on their social and political activity. And sometimes that would be associated with the Church, sometimes it wouldn't.[25]

The Priest and the Community

Monsignor John P. Wodarski was the son of a Polish-American factory worker and grocery store owner. When he was a child, the Catholic Church played a central role in his life, helping him to retain his cultural heritage and also to adapt to American society. Later, as a Catholic priest, he provided newer Polish immigrants with similar services.

My parents were very concerned, interested in the spiritual welfare of their kids. See, we lived in an area where we were a very small, small, tiny minority of Catholics. This was the Elmwood section of West Hartford, and that was a pretty strong Protestant community. And he [my father] was very conscious of the needs of religious education for the kids. And then also very, very conscious of the importance of their cultural heritage. Even though they were peasants, nevertheless they did have an understanding and great appreciation of the Polish culture into which they were born. So shortly after we began school, my two older sisters and myself, and later my younger brother, there were four of us in the Elmwood School. I think it was when I was three, my father and mother decided that we should be going to parochial school. The closest parochial school was either New Britain or else Hartford. Since there was no [commutation] to New Britain that was very convenient, we went to Hartford. That was a distance of five miles, and I recall that here my father was making $6 a week and he was spending $2 plus for carfare for us kids to see that we got to parochial school.

All parishes pretty much served the same function, the immigrant pouring into the country. And the Irish had theirs, and the Poles had theirs, and the Lithuanians, and Italians, and all that sort of business. But as far as our own experience is concerned, the Poles are probably a lot more loyal, or perhaps a lot more dependent on the services the parish offered. So it was not only the religious needs, and they were very conscious of that, but it was also all these social needs. There were all kinds of parties—you know the Poles are a very, very social people, and so you have parties concerned with the various church functions.

The interviewer then asked whether the Poles, to maintain their culture, had to rely on the Church in the Old Country since in a formal way there was no Polish nation.

You know we can skip through lots of chapters in history, and you find that when the partitions of Poland came, toward the end of the eighteenth century, the Russians and Prussians and Austrians carved up Poland, you find that the political leaders of Poland just took off. Because they had the means. And they took off for France, they took off for Italy, they took off for various other parts of the world, and the only leadership that was, that remained in Poland, was the clergy. So the parish priest, whether he was out in the villages or even in the city, the parish priest was there. Everybody else took off; he was there. Consequently a tremendously close tie developed between peasants and priests, as well as civic inhabitants and their priests. So the priest served not only his basic function of a spiritual leader, but he also took care of the rest of the business.

He was a community leader, in all aspects of life. Education, social needs, the physical needs, all that, that sort of business. So that carried over, so that you'll notice if you study immigrant history here in the United States, you'll find they poured into certain areas where there was a priest, where there was a parish, and they grouped around this. So you have those famous settlements, in Milwaukee out in Wisconsin, in Chicago, and of course you have Detroit, Buffalo, and so forth, and here [New Britain] the very, very famous Monsignor [Lucian] Bojnowski, who arrived here in 1895 . . . just before the great big Polish immigration began. And he was a kind of providential man. He was a man of aggressiveness, a great imagination, and so forth. He arrived when all these famous building hardware factories were geared up to go and they didn't have any help. And so they worked out a deal whereby Monsignor Bojnowski provided them with help, and they got their jobs. It wasn't any problem. So they could get themselves well established. And that could be repeated many, many times.

Wodarski then explained why he went into the priesthood.

That came about because of interest. I guess the parochial school—the sisters in the parochial school used to be talking about kids becoming priests and sisters and all that sort of business, and so when it came time for high school, we had a curate, as assistant priest there, Father Kowalski, who is now dead. My father went to him. Oh, I guess we had a mission, a mission at the church, the [Vincentian] Fathers, the Polish order. And of course the missions stressed the importance of education for kids, and particularly religious education. And stressed the matter about the great need for clergy and all that sort of business. And then one thing led to another. I was an altar boy and this thing became very attractive to me, and so I kind of mentioned that. So my father marched me up to the priest, and said, "Look, what do we do about this?" That was a common practice. Life's decisions, family decisions, were often the result of consultation with the parish priest, on the theory that the parish priest was interested, number one, in our welfare, and he would advise properly, et cetera. So one thing led to another and Father Kowalski suggested that I go to the local minor seminary, which is a high school and a junior college. It was right in town, St. Thomas Seminary.

After World War II, Father Wodarski was named director of youth for the Hartford diocese, which covered the entire state of Connecticut. He related how church services came full circle to the time of his parents.

My job was to prepare youth programs for all the Catholic kids in the state of Connecticut. I was having 250,000 kids involved in our programs. It was a matter of preparing programs and then peddling them down into the parishes. We had the parishes, we had close to 400 parishes there, and through a whole series of middle management sort of things, where the local directors were able to set, model our desirable program for the youth, which then the parish priest would implement.

On the elementary level there were religious education programs—Christian doctrine. Then on the high school level it was a mixture of not only straight Christian doctrine but the social and cultural and athletic programs, the CYO programs—the Catholic Youth Organization programs, that type of thing. These were basically parish programs which in certain situations extended out beyond the parish. Like for athletics in this given area of New Britain you would have a league for the high school group, and right after the war we even had a group for returning soldiers. Then right after the war we had all kinds of programs for young adults. The soldiers were coming back and they wanted to get married, so we had kind of a marriage mart sort of thing, of socials, of thousands of people coming out—dances and marriage preparation. Good old thing, you know, come out and meet the boy or girl or so forth.

See, it was just a repeat of what my parents experienced when they first came over here. The social center, it was the parish. So they ran dances and boy meets girl and the next thing you know they get married and set up a family—and so this was just a repetition of the same thing in a different age. It served its purpose very well.[26]

"I Tell Them God Is in All Places"

In some immigrant communities religious life was not always peaceful, as mainstream churches often battled with ethnic churches for the allegiance of their parishioners. This Polish immigrant, who lived in Bridgeport, explained to a WPA interviewer why she preferred the Polish National Church to the regular Catholic Church in her neighborhood.

The priest in the Polish Naradovi [National] Church is not like the priest for the other churches because he wants to help the people but he don't get no money himself. The other church is more like business because you have to be like rich to belong to that church. In my church you give money when you have it—in other church, you have to give or you don't belong. You have to pay $12 a year to make support that church, and you have to pay for the tickets to get confession. I don't want to send my children there because it would cost me too much, and I never have the money, anyway. Then they don't teach you the right way. They only tell you things about religion and that's all. When they come out of there they are bad just the same. Religion is all the same, only some people they have to make like a business from it.

I used to belong there one time when I was young. After I got married I start to belong to my church that I belong now. There was a boarder in my house that was going to that church, so he was always telling us how good it was, so we tried there, and now we belong there a long time. Oh, I like that church! They don't want money when you don't got it. If you have, you give; if you don't have, they don't ask you. Sometime when I could get $1 I give it to them, but I can't go there all the time because I have little money all the time. In the other church if you don't have it the priest talks about these things in the Mass. Another thing about my church, you can understand what the priest he have to say, in other church the Mass they all in Latin, and nobody could understand. Lots of people they say to me that my church is not real church of God, but I tell them that God is in all the places—if it's Jew or Italian, it's all the same like one God. They show you two times a week how to read and write in my church—they do that after they have the Mass. In the other church you have to pay too much; in my church they have everything cheap because they want to help the people the right way. Now lots of people are understanding these things and we have lots of people that come from all over.[27]

A young second-generation Polish-American, interviewed in 1940, also preferred Bridgeport's Polish National Church to the mainstream Catholic Church.

Goddarn it, talking about religion—I've been having plenty of trouble lately with my girlfriend, talking about religion. I'm having a hell of time trying to pound some sense in her head—but I guess that someday she'll understand, or else. She's been trying to get me to go to church ever since I met her. Well, I go once in a while, but I tell her I want to go to the Polish National Church on Barnum Avenue. She thinks that Saint Michael's is OK, but I tell her that I don't care for that church because the priest runs a racket. If you ain't got the dime you can't get past the front door. And besides, the smarter people go to the Polish National Church. There, when you go, you could see the difference—nobody hollering about putting more money in the basket or supporting the priest so that he could buy more houses. Jesus Christ!—try and tell my girl about that, see what she tells you. She'll tell you that what the priest does is alright, no matter what he does. What do you think about that! There the priest is fooling the ignorant dopes, and like a bunch of goddarn fools they take in all he says.

My girl is one of them, but I'll drive some sense in her head if it takes a lifetime. She wants me to go there when she knows that I don't give a rap for that racketeer. That's all he's running there—a racket. In the other church it's different. There at least they have plays that are sensible, and they learn something there because the priest explains things to the people, but in St. Michael's they don't give a damn. The dumber you are, the better the priest like it. . . .

The difference with the way they run the Mass is like this: the Polish Nationals say the Mass in Polish and the service the same way. That's the right way because everybody could know what the priest is saying. Even when they teach the kids how to read and write in Polish they have a good system. They have regular books so that you could learn Polish the real way. But in the other church the Mass is all in Latin and the people don't know what it's all about. Even when they teach the Polish language, they don't do it right. Instead they go ahead and give them a book that's a regular prayer book and they teach you all that hooey. In other words, you're not learning Polish, you're only learning how to say your prayers in Polish. The young people want to know what the priest is saying just as well as the older people, can you blame them? I'm not crazy about religion, but at least what's right is right!

My cousin Gene belongs to the other church, but he don't go there anyway. When his mother died they had a Mass in church and they had the nerve to pass the basket around and make a collection. And they even passed the basket to the ones that were in mourning. How do you like that for nerve! After the funeral Gene wanted me to go with him and talk to the priest, and I would have gone with him only my dad told me it was no use talking to a bunch of crooks. If a member of that church dies, then the church won't bury them unless he gets the regular price and collects the back dues they owe. You don't believe me? Ask any of them, they'll tell you.[28]

Not all immigrants welcomed the Church in their lives. This Polish immigrant from Bridgeport shunned all churches. He recognized how American culture loosened the bonds of traditional religion for the second generation, and he viewed the Church as a tool of aristocracy and antiradicalism.

I said before that I am different. Maybe different because I don't believe like some of these religious fanatics that all the things that people do have to be connected with the Church. I know lots of Polish people that have no use for the Church. I know lots of people that even talk against the Church. If we look at the background of Poland up to the time that I came here, we could understand why people don't believe these things so much. The more intelligent people that come from there know that the Church was really the institution of the government, and all these superstitions that the people carried from there was carried because the people were in ignorance. The more intelligent people knew this and they even rebelled against the government, but it was no use because the people were few. . . .

The Roman Catholic Church is a big business that wants to keep the Polish people interested in the national spirit; this way they have the people believing in something that does not live. They are religious fakers. The Polish national groups are not so bad, but they are not holy at the same time. They are a little more liberal but they are fakers too.

The Polish nationals believe in preaching the Mass in the Polish language and having ideas that mix with the American culture—but pretty soon all will be forgotten because there is no use to continue the Polish language in this country. The Yankee people have a population of 80 million in this country and all these foreign people will be dissolved in this big pot—maybe not now because the people are blind, but in a few generations. . . .

The old people are the ones that keep up the old customs in this country. They are the ones that make the churches live. Some of the older people stick to the Catholic Church, and then there is the other group that believe that the Mass should be in the Polish language, and they are the ones that belong to the Polish National Church. Like I said before, one church is almost as bad as the other. But there are some people that feel that they don't want to stay with the service—because they feel that if they hear the Mass in Latin they will only hear lots of hocus-pocus. This is the only difference.

Since I come to this country I only went to church once, because I wanted to see what the Church was like in this country. I don't care for the Church since the time that my people were so religious and they wanted to make me go. I had to go when I was a boy, but when I got older I don't care to go because by this time I was learning that the Church was only a way to keep the people in ignorance. This was on my mind all the time, and I believe that anybody that had brains could see the same thing. How do you think the Polish people were kept in ignorance all the time? Do you know that the Polish people were the most revolutionary people in the whole of Europe? Do you know that these people were fed so much baloney from the czar's aristocracy that the people lost all ambition to free themselves? This is why I hated the Church all the time when I was old enough to understand everything—because the Church was the helper to these aristocrats. Does that show why I am against such fooling of the people? I have read all the works of Tolstoy, Gorky, and other even American writers. When I read *The Cossacks, War and Peace*, then I realize that there had to be something done for the people. What these books say is the same thing true with Poland.[29]

"The Priests Want to Put Chains Around the Necks of the People"

Another Polish immigrant saw religion as an interference in his freedom. In the Old Country the Church had often been a source of oppression, and many immigrants wished to escape its hold in the United States.

No, I don't go to church. I'm an independent freethinker. No, I don't belong to any Polish organizations. Before I marry, I belong to some Polish societies, but not now. Religion make a lot of trouble—it's a big bluff. I never push my children to go the Sunday School, go to church. No, I never do like that. My daughter who's living with me—she had some trouble with her husband so she had to come home to live with us—when she's at school, she goes to Christian Science church. Now, she strong for this. It's terrible, this religion. I tell her it's hard for us to live together now, because I don't care much about religion and she's so wrapped up in this Christian Science. It's hard to get along. Religion—it's good for nothing. The priests want to put chains around the necks of the people. I think the world is for everybody, not just the priests. They start with the young children—then they got them for their whole life. No, my wife and I, we're both freethinkers.[30]

The WPA interviewed Nathan Nussenbaum, an Austrian Jew who immigrated to the United States in 1896, and who later became the owner of a window cleaning company in Bridgeport. At first, however, he was a homeless pushcart peddler who often slept under ice wagons (his story appears in chapter 2). A man of deep religious sentiments, he painted a painful and poignant picture of what occurred when he tried to attend a well-to-do synagogue nine months after his arrival.

I told you I was Jewish and like to attend services in the synagogue. There are many days which practically all Jewish people observe. One thing they don't do on those days is work. Well, one of those days came along and I was not working. I did not know how to spend the day. I did not want to walk all around the city all day, so I made up my mind to visit a synagogue. So, with my book in my hands, I went to a synagogue and started to go inside when the man at the door stopped me. He was Jewish and we talked Jewish.

He said it would cost me some money to go inside, and I told him I did not have enough. The least that was given was $1 and some people gave $2, $3, and $5. It all depended on how much they could afford.

I did my best to impress upon the man at the door that I wanted to attend service and had no money. He would not let me in and told me to get outside. Quite a large crowd had collected to see what was happening and when the man told me to get out, I broke down and cried. (I cry at the least provocation.) On this occasion I really felt bad that I could not go inside because I had no money and as I turned to go away, a nicely dressed man came to me.

After he talked with me for a while, he went to the man on the door and told him what he thought of him. He said, "You ought to be ashamed of yourself for the way you have acted. Here is a poor young man who wants to go inside and worship and you won't let him inside because he has no money. Get out of here." And he shoved the man on the door. The man moved away and the crowd went inside. I stood at the steps waiting to see how things would come out.

The man who had taken the fellow off the door came out to me and invited me to go in. He told the new man at the door that whenever I came to let me in whether or not I had money. "This man wishes to worship and whenever he comes, you let him inside." The doorman said he would and he took a good look at me so he would know me the next time.

The man who had gotten me entrance took me by the arm; he had his wife and children with him. He took me right down to the front seats and gave me a shawl to put around my shoulders. That was the custom in the old country, but a man in Austria did not wear a shawl only when he was married. I told him that I was unwed and he said that would be all right. So I sat through the service and walked out of the synagogue with this man and his family.

Once we got outside he asked me if I had eaten, and I told him I had not. "Are you hungry?" he inquired. I said that I was, so he took me across the street and told me to order whatever I wanted. I ate a big breakfast and felt fine. I made up my mind there were a great many people in the world who had hearts like my friend. I thanked him and said I would never forget what he had done for me. He said that was all right and he was glad he could befriend me. He shook hands with me and said I would hear from him.[31]

Just Because a Man Wears a Collar
Turned Backwards ...

William Bradley, a second-generation Irish-American interviewed in 1940, voiced a suspicion of and hostility to religion that would not have pleased the Irish Church hierarchy.

I was raised a Catholic, and while I believe in my religion I don't sanction the commercialism which the priests seem to force on their people. If a man has money he can break any law or rule of the Church and still be among the favored. But without dough you are just a heel. That is true anywhere I guess, but it should not obtain in a church. Also I don't believe in those rules forbidding a Catholic to marry a divorced person, and the rule that a divorcee cannot be buried in consecrated ground is ridiculous to me. There are other things too, but what's the use of going into them? The religion is not to blame; it's the people at the head of the Church. There is just as much graft in the churches as there is in politics and don't let anybody tell you different. Just because a man wears a collar turned backwards is no real reason he should dictate any man's life.[32]

Andrew Porylo, the son of a Ukrainian peasant, immigrated from Galacia in 1911. He showed that the hostility many immigrants felt toward religion had its roots in the Old Country, where the Church was a powerful institution, often backed by the state, which frequently exploited the faithful. Still, they had ways of punishing clergymen who exceeded their authority.

Everybody in the village was religious, and if you didn't go to church one Sunday, everyone wanted to know what happened to you. Everything that the priest said we had to do. The priest was paid by the government, but he took things from the people too. Often people didn't like it. A midwife, for example, always had to bring a chicken and some cloth to the priest when she reported that a child was born. If the people were poor and didn't have any chicken or cloth, he often beat the midwife.

Once a midwife helped a very poor woman with her baby. There was no chicken and cloth for the priest, so he beat the midwife when she came to him. Her brother saw her crying, so he went and beat him up. Everybody knew about it, but they didn't say anything, and the priest kept quiet too.

I read in school that a priest was supposed to get only one kronin for burying people. Our neighbor's father died, and the son went to the priest for the burial service. The priest asked too much money. I said to the man, "You go to the priest and leave a kronin on his table." He did that, and we started to get the body ready to be buried. We brought the body to church. The priest came to the church, but he didn't go to the cemetery, so we buried the man without him. The priest started to charge less.

When my grandmother died, my uncle went to the priest, and he wanted very much money for burying her. My uncle came to my father, and then my father went to the priest. The priest still wanted a lot of money, so my father gave him a beating instead.

Every year the priest sent a wagon to every house in the village to collect things for himself. When a wagon came to my house, my father said, "Well, we have to pay him, and I don't see why." I said, "You don't have to pay him. He gets paid by the government." My father refused to pay and threw the collector out. The people were shocked and said, "What are you doing!" The priest spoke in the church about my father. I went to his [the priest's] house and said to him, "Father, you got too many privileges." And he said, "I know you are a radical. It will be too bad for you." "No," I said, "it will be too bad for you." I told him what I learned in school about what a priest should get. Next year, he didn't send any more wagons to the village. He had his own land, and he got paid by the government. He was well off.[33]

The Evil Eye and Other Folklore

Immigrant churches commonly competed with Old World superstitions such as omens, old wives' tales, and the evil eye, or il malocchio, as it was known among the Italians. Emma Reale, a 45-year-old second-generation Italian-American living in Bridgeport, revealed the intricacies and power of the evil eye.

Oh yes, it is true that the Italians do believe in the evil eye, and that it is carried over from the Old Country. It is quite hard to explain to someone who can't see the result of the evil eye, and I can hardly expect to convince you of its power without having seen it for yourself. I can remember so clearly an old man living near us who used to come to our house when we were ill and pray over us. After he had said the prayer a few times, believe it or not, we were cured. In fact he was called to my bedside so very much, I could read every prayer on his lips as he said it.

Perhaps it would be better if I stopped and explained just what the evil eye means to us. For example, a person who has a headache, backache, et cetera, is said to have the evil eye. Sicknesses that doctors have given up as incurable or unexplainable are also the work of the evil eye.

The interviewer asked how she knew when someone had the evil eye.

Let me explain. We all know that oil and water do not mix. Take a basin of water and put a drop of oil in it. If the oil spreads out and mixes with the water, the person is said to have the evil eye. I firmly believe this because I have seen it done. The procedure is always in threes. The prayer is said in three sections. If the person is not cured the first time, the oil and water act must be performed three times more, and the prayer said each time.

Many people, my husband included, thought I was crazy, but they are convinced now. The idea is that all these actions are done in the name of God and with the help of God.[34]

John Capozzi, an Italian immigrant from Bridgeport, took a skeptic's view of the evil eye.

You know after all the troubles I go through [he had just been separated from his wife and family], I don't believe in anything. Sometimes I don't believe I live. Lots of people over there say if you got big headache you got the evil eye. That's a lot of bull. Then they take . . . a dish and put some water in it. Then the woman that does the trick, puts the dish on your head and holds it. Then she makes the sign of the cross on the dish three times, she makes out she says something—I don't think she know it herself what the hell she says—anyhow, and she takes and sticks her finger in olive oil and she throws a drop of the water in the dish. Then she makes another drop go down, and she do this a few times. Then she looks in the dish; if the oil is gone, she tells you, "See, you got the evil eye." If the oil stay on the top of the water, you ain't got the evil eye. That's a lot of bull because if she gets some water that is not very cold, the oil will go away; if the water is cold, the oil stay on top. Everybody know that the oil all time stay on the top of the water.

One time my mother say to me, "When you get out of the house in the morning, if you meet a lame woman or a cripple woman, you will have bad luck that day; if you meet a lame man, you will have good luck that day." That's more baloney. One day I met a lame woman, and I say, "Bad luck." I walk maybe about 50 feet and I find a dollar bill. Another time I met a lame man and I go around the block, I fell over a rotten banana and got hurt.

The interviewer asked him if he could explain this.

Well, it's like this way. On the other side, in those little towns, like mine and yours, you see very few people. I don't think you meet 25 people all day long. So it is hard to meet a lame man or a lame woman. But you take over here, you meet a million people every day. Well, in the million people it's got to be somebody lame, maybe a woman, maybe a man, and maybe kids.

Those people are crazy, anyway. Another time my mother said, "When you get a whistle in your ear and the whistle is in the left ear, somebody is talking about you and they talk good about you; if the whistle is in the right ear, somebody talks about you too, but they talk bad." I ask you, can that be right? Anybody that believes in anything like that, he sure is crazy, don't you think so?

Here's another one I know. This one will make you laugh. You know that big black bird that comes out at night. What the hell you call him now . . . the owl. Alright, if this black bird comes on the roof of the house and he starts to sing, that means somebody in that house sure is going to pass out and die. How the hell is it that a bird like that was on top of my house every night for a long time, and nobody died? And then they say the same things about dogs around the house. That's just because they come, that's all. . . . And they believe in so many things, all crazy things just like that. No, I never believe in those things; no sir, not me.[35]

133

Politics

Politics was a key part of most immigrant communities. From the Irish immigrants of the nineteenth century to the Latinos of today, it has frequently been an avenue to empowerment and opportunity. The Italian immigrant in this interview indicated that politics was also used to express loyalty to America and even superiority over other ethnic groups—in this case the Irish.

I am satisfied with the United States with everything like it is. You see all the Italian people they want to be like a part of this country, and the Italian people they want to be like a part of this country, and the Italian people more like any other nationality they defend this country. The Italian people they are in politics and they are interested in politics, in the people that they are good. The other people they are not interested in politics like the Italians. Only the Irish people they are in politics more than the Italian people. But someday the Italian people they will be in it more, because the Italian people they are interested in making the things better than the Irish people. The Irish people they are in it because they want to make things good for themselves. But this is the thing about the Italian people. They want to see that everything is just. And when this thing comes from the heart, then it makes a lot of difference, because this is what counts.

The Italians now, . . . they have not been treated good by the Irish and the Americans, and now they want to have their own people in politics so that they could help one and the other. Even now you hear that if there is an Italian that is put up for a candidate, the people of other nationalities don't want to make him win because they're afraid that the Italian will get strong and someday they will show to these people that don't like them just how they will conduct everything when they have power. Before when the Italians were not strong, and when they did not have the citizen papers, these politicians wanted to step on the Italians. Now that they are citizens, most of them, these people they want to promise to the Italians a lot of things so that they will get the Italian votes. But the Italians they are smart to this. Before—that was maybe 10, 15 years ago—the Italians used to believe the politicians, but now they have their own people and they are voting for them. Now we have people from our nationality that are in the professions and they have the understanding that the Italians have not been treated good, and they are the ones that are coming in politics. Pretty soon the Italians will be on the top, and they won't have to trust any of the other nationalities to do anything for them. They never did anything for the Italians anyway.[36]

Some ethnic groups were slow to recognize the possibilities of politics. Joseph Gursky, a Polish-American and unemployed laborer, realized the significance of politics but was unsure whether Poles had the ability to compete successfully with other immigrants.

I think that the Polacks are dead in this town when it comes to politics. It's a shame that they never could get together because that's where the drag comes in. What the hell use is it for some Polack to come around on election day and ask any one of these politicians a favor. The only thing they could say is, "I'll give you my vote if you do this for me: give me a job." But he's only one and he has no backing. Look at all the other nationalities—they are all organized. At least they try to do something among their own people. That's the bad thing about the Polack here, they don't stick together.

That's the one thing I give the Wops credit for—when they get go into something they make a go of it. Look at those Wops—they're always on the job. All year round they're always active in the clubs and they know what it's all about when the time comes for election. And if they're in the two parties— Republicans or Democrats—if an Italian is running, then they give him the vote. When I was in Stamford, I worked in the Yale and Towne [Lock Company], and at night I had things to do in the Democratic Club at night, and I noticed that the Italians always stuck together. You'll never get the Polacks to stick that way. The only thing that they're together on is religion, and lately they're starting to get away from that. . . .

That's the trouble here—they have no leaders. They haven't even got any political clubs, so how the hell do you expect them to get any notice from the other politicians that control the city. Look at the other nationalities—they all get favors done and they're respected, but the Polacks haven't learned yet.[37]

During the Great Depression many immigrant neighborhoods rallied to the support of Franklin D. Roosevelt, whose New Deal made a concerted effort to attract the loyalty of ethnic voters in the cities. The attraction was as much, if not more, based upon economics as on ethno-cultural issues. Henry Masch, a Polish Jew who immigrated in 1885 and managed a clothing store in Bridgeport, explained why FDR earned his loyalty.

You cannot make it too strong about how I feel about President Roosevelt. He is just the man for the office and I honestly hope he will accept the nomination this year [1940]. He is just the man to keep the United States out of the war. He has been tried and has proven he has the right kind of stuff in him.

Do you realize that when he advocated and put into force relief measures, such as the WPA, he saved this country from a revolution? Well, he did in my opinion. There is no question in my mind but what this country was on the verge of a revolution a few years ago. It was averted by the timely intervention of President Roosevelt.

Just look what the man has done for the people of the United States! He thought of an idea whereby those people who had lost their employment could get temporary work and relief through the WPA. I absolutely approve of the WPA. The amount of money most of those on it receive does not make them feel they are independent, but it does bring home the knowledge that they receive some money which will keep their homes going, until they get back into private industry. Yes sir, you must give President Roosevelt great credit for his efforts in behalf of the poor people. Without his efforts this country would have been in a revolution long before now. . . .

So I say, let's keep President Roosevelt in the presidency, if he wants the job again. Let him spend money every year for the relief of the poor. I am willing to do my share in the way of taxes, although I feel we have quite a few taxes at present. I admire the way in which President Roosevelt tackles all the big problems, particularly the one about relief. He does not go at any of them in a headstrong manner, but feels his way until he arrives at what he thinks is best for the country. You've got to hand it to him. He is a very deep thinker, always having the interest of the people of this country at heart.

If he is nominated again, all the criticism his opponents can muster cannot stop him from being elected. He has a great personality while on the air. He just gathers his listeners around him, as he says in a fireside chat. He makes the gathering homelike, very much so. He is the only man I know of who can start his speech with the words, "My friends" and put it over. I love to hear him talk over the radio. That's the only chance I have to hear him. And he always has something worthwhile to say. That's a fine thing. He is not like a lot of other speakers I have heard—they seem to be talking only for exercise.[38]

The sorrow felt by many immigrants when Roosevelt died is movingly told by a second-generation Italian American.

FDR was a hero to the people in the neighborhood. I can remember the day he died very vividly. I was quite young. Maybe I was seven years old, and

I was playing in the yard two doors away and there were some Irish people who were very friendly with the family and the woman stuck her head out the window—she had the radio on the windowsill. She said, "Go home and tell your father that the President died." I ran in the house and there was a Jewish salesman there, sitting down having—it was a warm day so they were having probably a cold drink—and I said, "Papa" (you didn't call him anything else but Papa), "the President died," and he threatened to beat me because I shouldn't say such things. He thought it was a story. But I said, "No, Papa, Mabel said to turn the radio on, the President died." So he did. He turned on the radio, probably WJZ, which was one of his favorite stations, and the news came over that the President had died that afternoon. It was April 12, but it was a very warm day. I can remember that it was very warm, and this Mr. Marion who was sitting with him and he both started crying like they had lost their best friend. They didn't know what was going to happen to the country because he had died. He had been President for so long, I don't think they remembered anyone else.

But I do remember my father coming home from work after the President's funeral—maybe a day or two after—saying that he thought Mr. Truman would be alright. He heard him speak that day, and he thought he was going to be alright. He said some pretty good things.[39]

A successful Jewish-American businessman, interviewed in 1975, traced how his attitude toward FDR was altered by the passage of time and colored by the historical debate on his presidency. Revelations about the Roosevelt administration's policies during the Holocaust and what in the 1990s would be called the "character issue" affected this changed assessment.

I thought he was a great guy. About that time, that was '32, '33, and '34, I was 26, 27 years old. I had just come out of the Depression. He was the figure and the man who set things right. It was the day that he came in. You didn't learn until many years later that all that he accomplished the day he walked in and closed the banks and started WPA and CCC and all the rest of it, you didn't learn until much later, many years later, that same thing could have been accomplished by Hoover if he would have allowed Hoover to do it. But he wasn't about to let Hoover do it. So the Democratic party stymied Hoover from doing it, by just not allowing anything to go through. If there's going to be any credit, they were going to get it. And they did.

During the war—it wasn't until long after the war that a lot of things came out, that decisions which he made which were made in concert with let's say other people, like three or four people, were not exactly what I call the decisions that a great humanitarian would have made. Now when the Nazis offered to swap 200,000 children, or 100,000 children for trucks, et cetera, I think his refusal to swap them the trucks or the money or whatever it was they wanted was an inhumane act. Because we had the war, we knew we were going to end up on top of the heap. We could have, without really hurting too much, given them the trucks or whatever else it was he wanted to save 200,000 little children. He made the judgment not to do it. . . . Many other things just like that. He could have stopped a year of suffering in the year '32, '33, could have been the year when—actually, the year the country did not have to go through that experience. Three years was enough. . . . But you know, he was basically a politician working with some pretty tough politicians, and I don't know.

I think that everybody in the lower economic brackets, people that suffered through the Depression and through the war, thought he was the greatest thing since the electric light. He was in many ways looked at as a savior. Because he was a very forceful man who did what had to be done, got a mandate, a free mandate to do everything he wanted to do. Subsequently I think he got sort of power mad, and he turned out to be—it turned out that he was not God, that he was a man, a strictly human being with feet of clay who had less than the highest set of mortal values. I think in general that like most people, on balance, I would give him a plus.

The fact that he played fast and loose with his wife's affections or whatever problem they had, and his kids, that's the personal end of his life. It colors the man a little bit, takes some of the aura away from him. But generally speaking, I think he was a farsighted statesman. He saw what was happening in Europe. He called the shot. Only because of what he did, because he insisted on doing it, as devious as the ways may have been by which he did it, we were prepared when we finally got involved in the war. And . . . he saw that our involvement had to be inevitable. Because Europe just could not take them [the Germans] over.[40]

Immigrants of all kinds, then, coalesced around this national political figure, despite their reservations. Family, neighbor and neighborhood, voluntary associations, and religion had a more immediate influence, however. These institutions served as arenas of cohesion and division, unity and internecine disputes. The vitality of immigrant life was found in locality.

In the old country, places of residence differed markedly. Some of the immigrants who speak to us in this volume grew up in rural villages. The sod house pictured above, located in Ireland, was the original home for a family that later settled in Connecticut. Others came from urban areas, such as the Claus family, who emigrated from Germany to Manchester, Connecticut, about 1885. *Courtesy of Connecticut Historical Society, Hartford, and Manchester Historical Society*

After a lengthy journey across the Atlantic, immigrants disembarked and made their way to the Ellis Island processing center. Morris Kavitsky, a Jewish immigrant who arrived from Poland in 1914, remembered: "I had to go through what appeared to be an interminable examination at Ellis Island. Passports, baggage, and my physical condition were checked and rechecked. I was impatient to get to the great and humming city, which was so near to me now." *Courtesy of Ellis Island Immigration Museum/State Historical Society of Wisconsin*

Some immigrants remained only briefly in New York City. Many of the interviewees in this volume made their way to Connecticut shortly after arrival. Arthur Carlson arrived from Sweden in 1902. He did not remain in New York very long. "I really saw very little of New York because I was supposed to go on a boat to New Haven, where my brother was to meet me. The people on Ellis Island told me I could get to New Haven quicker by train so I took the first train out." *Courtesy of Ellis Island Immigration Museum/State Historical Society of Wisconsin*

As a Russian Jewish immigrant told a WPA interviewer in 1938, "To me this city appeared as a tremendous overstuffed roar, where people just burst with a desire to live." As the street photos of Hartford illustrate, not all city streets exploded with such density as seen in this Jacob Riis photograph of Mulberry Street on New York's Lower East Side. *Courtesy of Ellis Island Immigration Museum/Museum of the City of New York*

Patsy Petralle's Italian restaurant served as a neighborhood institution and reflects the mixing of commercial and residential property in a Hartford immigrant neighborhood. *Courtesy of Connecticut State Library*

Italians from Messina gather on the street in March 1909. They appear to be greeting the photographer with mixed enthusiasm. *Courtesy of Connecticut Historical Society, Hartford*

Immigrant mothers and their children are gracefully framed by a doorway arch in Hartford in the early part of the twentieth century. *Courtesy of Connecticut State Library*

Immigrant ingenuity in the face of meager economic circumstances is indicated by the well-crafted playwagon fashioned from a grape juice box for these Hartford children. *Courtesy of Connecticut State Library*

וווילים ענטיק
אר שולע 1931

The immigrant experience can appear contradictory, particularly during the first two generations. At this night school in Columbia, Connecticut, for eastern European immigrants, many of whom were Jewish, adults learned English. Their children and others attended a Yiddish school, operated by the local Workman's Circle in Willimantic, Connecticut, in an effort to maintain the old world language and culture. The Hebrew sign spells out "Willimantic School" in Yiddish and dates the year as 1931. *Courtesy of Columbia Historical Society and Sarah Axelrod*

Members of the McGrath family gather in an unidentified New Haven bar, where children accompany adults. Saloons served as social institutions where immigrants could congregate with friends, keep warm, find a toilet, and sometimes get a free lunch.
Courtesy of Connecticut Historical Society, Hartford

Religious institutions such as this Italian church in New Haven served an important and often a central role in immigrant neighborhoods. Within the Catholic church immigrant groups frequently formed their own parishes. *Courtesy of Connecticut State Library*

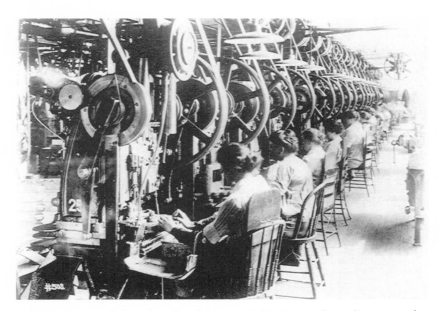

Immigrants frequently found work at Bridgeport's Remington Arms Company, where these women are dwarfed by the machinery. *Courtesy of Historical Collections, Bridgeport Public Library*

The Verdi Orchestra of South Manchester, Connecticut, about 1920. These Italian American musicians entertained audiences around the state. This orchestra is an example of the variety of voluntary associations that immigrants joined to perpetuate their cultural heritage. *Courtesy of Vera Andisio*

A Swedish float in Connecticut's Tercentenary Parade in 1935. Such celebrations helped maintain ethnic pride. *Courtesy of Connecticut Historical Society, Hartford*

Swearing in as U.S citizens, a landmark for many of the arrivals to America. While the large proportion of immigrants became citizens, many never did. Some stayed in the nation as aliens and others returned to their homelands. *Courtesy of Ellis Island Immigration Museum*

Pease in Newark News

That immigration problem again!

This cartoon reflects much of the anti-immigrant sentiment discussed in chapter 6, although it does not comment upon the tension between immigrant groups themselves. The increased nativism resulted in new restriction laws during the 1920s. *Courtesy of Ellis Island Immigration Museum/Newark News*

John Kluck with his family in 1925, 21 years after he arrived from Austria in 1904 and 55 years before his interview in 1980. Family and friendship networks assisted immigrants in finding work. Kluck recalled that his friend got him a job at the Cheney Brothers silk mill in Manchester, Connecticut. "It was mostly piece work and I made around $6 or $7 a week until afterwards, when you made $10." *Courtesy of George C. and Gertrude Kluck Stoneman*

Sando Bologna of Waterbury, Connecticut, rendered in a charcoal portrait by Robert C. Templeton of Woodbury, Connecticut. Bologna has written his own book about the Italians of Waterbury and was interviewed by the Peoples of Connecticut Project. *Courtesy of Sando Bologna*

Ignazio Ottone and his bride, Eleanora Spinoglio, on their wedding day in 1913, 10 years after he arrived in Manchester, Connecticut, from Italy. Ignazio Ottone in 1985, 6 years after his interview, and a year before his death. *Courtesy of Vera Andisio*

Lucy Addy Richardson on her wedding day in 1919, four years after she arrived in Manchester, Connecticut, from Portadown, Ireland; seated beside her is her husband Robert, standing are her brother William Addy and Robert's sister Christine. Lucy Richardson in 1980 at the time of her interview. *Courtesy of Robert E. Richardson, Jr.*

5

WOMEN AND MEN, LOVE AND MARRIAGE

The relationships of immigrant women and men—in love, marriage, and life in general—varied according to individual temperament, ethnic culture, and the accepted standards of the times. The economic atmosphere of the Great Depression also had an effect on attitudes about a "woman's place," as is reflected in the conversations that follow.

Repeatedly, those interviewed at the end of the 1930s contended that women, particularly married women, belonged at home. As might be expected, males primarily expressed this sentiment, but many women appeared not to question the point of view. Among some ethnic groups, such as the Italians, from the earliest period of immigration "homework" permitted a woman to assist the family financially while she looked after the home and the children. In some instances, taking in boarders offered women another means of enhancing the family coffers without entering the workforce.

Domestic service was not uncommon for the Irish and other groups that tolerated their females working in the home of a stranger. And by 1940, approximately 25 percent of women over age 14 worked in a wide variety of jobs; a little less than 33 percent of this female labor force was married, with a husband present in the family.[1]

If there appeared to be general acceptance of a "woman's place," economic conditions during the 1930s encouraged a different reality. Over the course of the decade, the number of female married wage-earners increased 50 percent, as male breadwinners lost jobs or saw their wages cut. Women supplemented meager salaries or substituted for lost incomes. To some, such as writer and editor Norman Cousins, they represented a threat to male workers. He simplistically suggested: "Simply fire the women, who shouldn't be working anyway, and hire the men. Presto! No unemployment. No relief rolls. No depression." Since the culture of the time divided work into men's and women's spheres, the decline in the male sector, such as heavy industry, did not mean less work for women. In fact clerical work, which had been feminized, grew dramatically. Few men, however, sought to wear the pink collar and overcome the era's chauvinism.[2]

The WPA interviewers heard over and over that women didn't work in the Old Country and shouldn't do so in the United States: "I believe that the woman's place is in the home after marriage. A woman can find plenty to do in her own home, if only to have meals ready on time." The hold of culture was simultaneously reinforced by tradition and loosened by the nation's economic plight. A complex combination of ethnicity, economics, and gender is at work in the pronounced attitudes expressed in this chapter.

The complexity grows as one recognizes that even when women remained at home, they played an active, sometimes dominant, role in their marital relationships. Marie Esposito was not alone in learning from her mother that "the papa is the boss and the smart woman lets him think he is getting away with it. So long as he feels that way, the woman can do anything with him." As Sydney Stahl Weinberg points out in her study of the lives of Jewish immigrant women, "men were the 'ceremonial leaders,' often assuming credit for decisions the women convinced them they had made on their own."[3] They usually assumed such "leadership" less by right than as a gift from wives who bestowed it on them out of respect and affection—and an acute understanding of the male ego. Esposito, whose narrative appears here, was Jewish; her husband was Italian Catholic. Their relationship hinged on her ability to let him have his way if she couldn't persuade him otherwise, which occurred infrequently. In that way, they never got into the "foolish arguments some couples have about who's boss in the house."

For some women, however, the family seemed less a place of influence and authority than one of conflict, exploitation, and tragedy. The tales told to WPA interviewers by Mrs. M., Mrs. N., and Mrs. S. attest to this. The tension between a younger native-born wife and her older and jealous Polish immigrant husband pervades the testimony of Mrs. M. Her belief that "all women have to be a little free" did not sit well with her mate, already badly buffeted by the Depression. The tale of woe told by Mrs. N. is a saga of drunkenness, poverty, and desperation that colored the life of a broken family in which child and wife abuse seemed the rule. Living with "an animal that was no man" spelled tragedy for a woman, who had the strength to survive. Mrs. S. also suffered from an alcoholic husband from whom she had separated. She was Swedish and he Norwegian, and the ethnic differences appear to be paramount in her assessment of a marriage gone bad.

While much of women's lives may have been spent in the private sphere of marriage and family, as the twentieth century progressed, the public role of women, including immigrant women, intensified. The Nineteenth Amendment was passed in 1920, but feminism extended into realms beyond the movement for the vote and women's rights. This chapter concludes with a brief consideration of the public role of women, as Ernie Demao tells about his mother's determina-

tion in the fight for suffrage. Mrs. W. discusses the social culture of political activity, and Eva Hudak, a union and political activist from the 1930s to the 1970s, is less than enthusiastic in her 1975 interview about newly emerging organizations such as the National Organization of Women. Although the "women libbers" may have given her a "royal pain," clearly America's female activists of the last quarter century have helped to reshape the relations between women and men,—and the world in which we live today.

A Woman's Place: "It Is a Disgrace for the Woman to Work"

At the time of the WPA interviews, during the late 1930s, the prevailing wisdom among many immigrants appeared to be that a woman's place was in the home. Men primarily propounded this attitude, but it was shared by women as well. Of course the intensity of such feelings differed among ethnic groups and among individual members of each group.

A 68-year-old Italian housewife remarked:

I told my husband that I wanted to go to work because a lot of Italian women they were working that time in Warner's Corset Shop, but my husband said that he didn't want to do this because it is a disgrace for the woman to work. He said that in Italy no women worked, and when the man could not support the family he was no man no more. This is the respect that Italians have for women.[4]

A similar sentiment was voiced by an unidentified interviewee, who regretted the changes wrought by life in this new country.

Now everything is different—the Italian women work just the same like the men in the shops. But the real Italians that have respect don't let the women work.[5]

Seventy-two-year-old Joseph Lazzaro arrived in Boston from Italy in 1920. By the time of his interview in 1939, he had moved to a four-room flat on the third floor of a three-story structure at 132 Willard Street in Bridgeport, Connecticut. He was the father of eight daughters and two sons; when interviewed, he was living with his youngest children, a 19-year-old son and a 22-year-old daughter. Lazzaro held strong views about a woman's place, often making comparisons to the Old Country and commenting on the wantonness of America's young women and the wildness of American culture:

The girls in this country are just like Gypsies—they paint like Indians and smoke like men. That's a shame. If I knew that my daughter touched a cigarette I would have her out of the house forever. The girls here are like crazy; they do everything that a man does, and the bad thing is that the men like this. In Italy you never hear of this; they always stay home and always go to places where the respectable people go. . . .

I go to the moving picture about once a year. The pictures are bad because they show a lot of crazy things: women smoking; stories that can't be true, how a rich boy marries a rich woman. I think that this is bad for the young people. My children don't believe these moving pictures. Sometimes they have a good Italian show, and that's good because the Italian *romanzo* is good, and is true. Sometimes they have Italian propaganda pictures; these are pretty good but sometimes they have too much propaganda.

The Italian people believe that the woman's place is in the house. Where I come from, the women are told by their families before they are married that when they are married that they should not speak to any other man unless they know him to be a friend of the family. If the woman want to go to a church on Sunday, no man can go with her; if she is engaged, then it is alright that her men could take her, but with the permission of the parents. In Italy only one man goes with one girl; in America one girl knows 100 men before she is married. This is not right. The Italian system is good and it is right. In America, it's a shame. The girls here go to dance halls and meet all kinds of bums; in Italy the only place a girl goes to dance is at the fiesta with her people. This the right way. I think the people here should try to act like the Italian people. They could learn very much of the way to act like decent people.[6]

John Burns, a 25-year-old second-generation Irish-American, who had married two years before the interview and had an 18-month-old son, recounted:

I married my wife two years ago. She is the same girl that I told you about that I met while at my first job. She continued work until the baby came and then she quit to take care of our son and the home. That is enough for any woman.[7]

Mr. P. S., who had come to Bridgeport about 45 years earlier from County Cork, added his support to the prevailing view of a woman's place:

I believe the husband should be the provider for the family. That was the case in my family. It seems a lot of young women today believe in working after they marry.

He went on to explain that this is done because living expenses are greater and young husbands don't make enough to cover them. Nevertheless,

I believe that the woman's place is in the home after marriage. A woman can find plenty to do in her own home, if only to have meals ready on time.[8]

Mr. M. concurred:

Personally I do not believe in women working day after day in offices. I think married women with children belong in the home. My wife is rather a boss, but I overlook this as she is such a thorough housewife, excellent cook, and above all a great saver. Jokingly I told her she must have some ancestors in the Prussian Army. She sure can give orders.

His and his wife's gender roles apparently were further differentiated through their choice of magazines:

143

My wife subscribes to *Colliers, Ladies' Home Journal,* and a book on knitting. I buy *Life* and get western stories from the library.[9]

Mr. R., a second-generation Irish-American who had been married for 32 years and was retired as a foreman from Bridgeport's Crane Company, also recognized household gender roles:

My wife say she does not know how any woman with a family ever gets time to go out to work. She finds plenty to do at our home between keeping the house clean and doing the cooking. We all like to eat and we keep her busy cooking for us. I even have to help out with the housecleaning when that time comes around. We have just finished—had all the upstairs papered and painted. That is some work and really is a man's job.[10]

Fear of race suicide—that women would not bear children—and blaming the media for permissiveness are nothing new, as another Irish-American, J. Hayes, illustrated:

I do not believe in women going to work after marriage. I think their place is in the home being homemakers, not breadwinners. I think it's nice to have a family, if possible. I don't see how this is possible if a woman works. I am much opposed to race suicide and the contraception measures now used and spoken of in every magazine. I think many of such magazines should be discontinued. They don't leave much to the imagination today.[11]

Also sounding the alarm of race suicide, Nancy M., who was born in Ireland and worked at the Eire pavilion at the New York World's Fair, remarked in no uncertain terms on the place of a married woman:

Another thing I can't understand is women marrying and maintaining positions. I have been taught and I firmly believe that marriage begets a home.

I can't see how it can lead to other than race suicide for a woman to marry and still work. I think if a woman wants a happy home she should stay at home and not seek a business career. If you want to be a career girl, stay single. Loom then as high as you are capable of looming. If marriage is your career, let marriage be your career. Make your home a happy one. Be there to greet your husband, be his pal, talk over financial affairs together. Don't think because he had to get a new suit for business you should spend money. Remember, he is the breadwinner and his appearance is an asset. Wait until next month—your dress will come. I have three sisters who are married, and all plan this way. They are happy and contented. I will arrange things the same way when I marry.[12]

Mr. D. was born in Galway, Ireland, and came to the United States in 1900. At the time of the interview he was approximately 63 years old, and was described by the interviewer as "full of blarney." He, too, discussed a married woman's place:

I detest the thought of married women in the business world. They work in offices or teaching and take the jobs of men and single girls. This, I believe, is the sure way to divorce. I always like my wife to be home to greet me. I like to sit around at night and discuss the topics of the day with her, and get her opinion. Today the husband belongs to a club. The wife has her bridge club, and they are out evenings separated. It is the ruination of the country. I believe in marriage for equality and companionship.[13]

Sean Ginty, who came to America from Tobercurry, in western Ireland, four years prior to his interview in 1939, shared similar views:

I do not think women should work after marriage. I think their place is in the home, not out in business. . . . We being from the same country, county and town, thoroughly understand each other. We live our lives very similarly to that we led in Ireland. . . . I like to see a husband and wife have at least one night a week to go together for enjoyment. I do not object to women smoking if they like to, but not for show. I think if they care to go out with their husbands and have a glass of beer it is all right, but I don't like to see women in taverns drinking and unescorted.[14]

Louis Goodwin, whose parents emigrated from Russia at the height of Jewish immigration, discussed during the mid-1970s the complexity of his parents' relationship:

My mother I think was a typically Jewish mother in many ways, in the sense that she ran the house. She was a helpmate to my father. She participated in the business. He was in the scrap business. We lived, so to speak, above the store. And she would substitute for him when he was away. She would buy, she would weigh scrap in, she would pay whoever might have been there to bring whatever it was. She was more a housewife and mother than a businesswoman, only because my father was a businessman. And his idea was that a woman's place was: "Okay, great, you're helpful, I appreciate it, but the house is your domain."

I mean it was in many ways an unspoken partnership without a corporate setup and no bylaws or rules, but each knew exactly what the other was to do, what each had to do, and nobody felt that the other was encroaching. I never remember my father saying, "Gee whiz, why don't you make a cooked meal?" or "Why don't you do this, that, or the other thing." On the other hand, I never remember my mother saying, "Well, why do you insist on dealing with that company or this company?" or "Why are you accumulating; why don't you sell or why don't you buy?" or anything like that.

She participated, but not to the point of making business judgments. At least if they did, it may have been part of the pillow talk when the children were asleep. By the same token I never remember him criticizing her.[15]

Seventy-three-year-old Teresa Falcigno offered another example of the woman's role in the family when she discussed her parents, who came from Italy at the turn of the century.

My mother never worked. Well, frankly, in those days women didn't get out to work. When I say my mother didn't . . . okay. My mother did know this tailor. You know how inside of the lapels in men's jackets there's a sort of stiffening material? That material in tailor-made suits, that stiffening, has to be sewn a certain way to the inner part, where it doesn't show. . . . My brothers would go to this tailor's shop and get the work, and my mother would do it at home. . . .

My father never really learned English. He would say a few words, "How are you" or something like that. My mother could understand most English, but she didn't talk it. If we were talking she would get the general gist. She never talked it. Because we were the only ones who talked English in the house. When she talked to any neighbors, they always talked Italian. I was born in this country, so I started school in America, and I learned English that way. . . . My mother was quite proud of the fact that she wanted us to talk Italian at home. She said, "It's your parent language. Sure, you're American. God bless America." She always used to say that. She said, "Thank God, America has been able to give me bread."

Yes, she was satisfied very easily. My mother's happiness was her family, and as long as she had her family with her it didn't matter. As long as her family was happy—that she wanted. Although she had some real old-fashioned ideas on lots of things. Like when the girls were growing up, my sister and I, we couldn't—until we were engaged—we couldn't go unescorted. She'd say, "Take your little brother with you." And then when I became 14, she said, "Fourteen years old—you've got to go to work." "Oh, but I want to continue school." She said, "No, when you get to be 17, 18 years old, you'll get married. What good is school to you?" Really, this was so. Well, I was made to leave school at 14, when I was in my first year in high school. I remember the dean came to my house and talked to my mother. She said, "No, no good school for girls." She'd say in her broken English, "No good school for girls. Girls don't have to know too much. As long as you know cook and sew. You know, 17 years old make a marry." She said she needed the help. Well, she did; she did need it. I was 14 in 1916. My father was making about $18 or $19 a week. There were five children at home, and my father and mother. Eighteen dollars even then didn't go very far. [My father], he was a pretty steady worker, but he always got a job down at the low end of the pole, because he didn't speak the language, because he wasn't skilled for anything. But he always worked in lumberyards. . . . He was always a pretty steady worker but never earned very much. My mother was very frugal and very careful. He turned all the money over to her, and she managed it. He would take money for maybe a drink or cigars, but that was it. She did all the handling. My mother was the one who ran the house, so to speak.[16]

Not all males shared the prevailing view of a woman's place. Andrew Porylo, a Ukrainian who came to the United States in 1911 and lived in New Haven, expressed this advanced opinion:

I don't believe in division of labor for men and women. I never did. . . . I always said that a husband and wife could do the same kind of work. I always felt that a man could do anything that a woman can, and that a wife can do anything a man can, as far as her physical condition let her. I don't believe a woman should slave in the house. I was always against it. My house is run like that. I am surprised when some woman says, "My husband is coming home. I got to give him something to eat." I couldn't see why he couldn't take the food himself. From the early days I used to help my mother in the house. Now I do everything in the house too. My wife used to work outside the home but she wasn't well, so she stopped.[17]

Apparently Porylo, an unemployed presser, practiced what he preached. His interviewer visited on several occasions, and quite frequently when she called, Porylo was helping his wife with the wash or ironing clothes; he often ironed while speaking. A presser by trade, he made little distinction between ironing his family's clothes and those of someone else. He did, however, ask his wife if she wished to iron her dresses. He explained to the interviewer, "She used to work as a presser in a woman's dress shop. She knows more about those."

Who's the Boss? "The Papa Is the Boss"

Clearly, the relations between male and female within a marriage involved power relationships that often were more subtle than surface investigation indicated. The testimonies of Marie Esposito and Mrs. M. attest to this.

Marie Esposito not only discussed how she related to her husband (in a manner not unlike the way her mother interacted with her father) but also touched on a number of other topics, including the participation of young girls in the gangs of New York's Lower East Side, the household responsibilities of a family's oldest daughter, dating and courting, attitudes toward intermarriage, and the role of the unemployed house-husband during the Depression.

Esposito was described by William J. Becker, who interviewed her for the WPA in 1940, as follows:

[The subject of this interview is a petite young lady who admits to being 25 years of age, although she could pass for 18 or 20 anywhere. She was

148

neatly attired, not flashy, and although somewhat reluctant to tell her story at first, talked freely enough after some encouragement. She is employed as a salesgirl in a five- and ten-cent store where she says she receives $12 for a six-day week. Her day begins at 9:30 a.m., and she is on duty until 6 o'clock on weekdays and 7 p.m. on Saturdays.

She seemed satisfied with her lot, the only fly in her ointment being that her husband is unable to find a steady job and they have a hard time making both ends meet with her weekly $12. She is of Jewish parentage, but both her parents were born in the U.S. Her husband is of Italian descent, both his parents having been born in Italy. They have been married five years, she said, and during that time the difference in their nationalities has never interfered with their happiness or that of their two children, a boy and a girl. In fact she seemed to think that their married life was without a flaw, excepting her husband's inability to obtain permanent employment.]

Becker then quoted Marie Esposito:

I don't know what this is all about but I have nothing to hide, so here goes. I don't get your reason for wanting the story of my life, but if it will help you out I'm willing to talk. I've always been on the level, so what [harm] can it do to tell you about myself, and if it will do anybody any good I'll consider the time well spent. Maybe I can't remember all the details, so you'll have to be satisfied with what I give you. Anyhow it is all the truth, without exaggeration, and I'm not looking for any undeserved credit.

I was born and raised in that part of New York City known as the Ghetto, on the East Side. You know there are mostly Jewish people living there, American-born, foreign-born, and some who can't tell you where they were born or why. My Ma and Pa were both born in that section and still live there. You couldn't drag them out of there with a team of mules or a dynamite blast. When they come up to visit us they can't wait until they get back, and I can't recall any inducement which could hold them up here. I thought at first if they could see how nice everything is up here, they would decide to make their home here, near me, but nothing doing. Pa said he'd die of lonesomeness up here, and as usual Ma agrees with him. She always does. If he said green was white, she'd agree. I guess that's the secret of their many years of happiness together.

She lets him think he is the boss, but when anything really important comes up she usually handles it without letting him know she is doing it. When it is disposed of, he pats himself on the back and claims all the credit. And she lets him get away with it, never contradicts him. She tipped me off to that system when I got married, and I guess that is why my husband and I get along so well.

"The papa is the boss," my mother always said, "and the smart woman lets him think he is getting away with it. So long as he feels that way, the woman can do anything with him." Well, it's just like pulling teeth to get them to come up here at all, and we make two or three trips down there to their one up here. I guess I feel the same way when I am down there as they do up here. We never stay there more than a day or over a weekend. It's a terrible place to live in, but I didn't think so when I was a kid running around down there. If anyone told me there were better places I would have called them liars or something. I thought New York was the only real place in the world and all the rest [was] just country. But I know better now, and I wouldn't live down there again at any price unless I had to.

My Pa and Ma were poor as churchmice when I was a kid. There were four children besides me, and the seven of us lived in one room on Delancey Street, which I now think is the worst of East Side streets. I remember my Pa paid $20 a month rent for that one cubbyhole, which was about 9 by 12. We cooked, ate, and slept in that one room. We had two beds and a cot, a stove, an alleged dresser with a cracked mirror, and we thought it was a palace.

My two sisters and I slept in one bed, Pa and Ma in the other, and the boys used the cot, sleeping end to end. Even at that I guess they were more comfortable than we girls sleeping three in a bed. Tough going, but we didn't seem to mind a lot. Raised that way, I guess I didn't know any better. Some of our neighbors were in worse quarters and didn't seem to mind either. I recall some not only squeezed their own large family into one room but rented out floor space to one or two boarders. Ain't that a laugh?

I love to go see the Dead End Kids in the movies because they remind me of my kid days. All the kids ran around kinda loose and I guess we did too. You know we never did anything really bad, just mischief. A gang of us would be walking along when suddenly one of us would suggest that it would be a wonderful idea to upset one of the many pushcarts that lined the curb and have the owner chase us. No sooner said than done, and the next minute you'd see a dozen or more kids running like mad with the owner of the upset pushcart after us lickety-split.

Sometimes the cops would get after us but that was just pie for us and just what we wanted most of all, to be chased by cops. We knew every nook and cranny in the neighborhood, and before the cops realized it we had all disappeared. But we had some bad moments while the cops were looking for us, for we never knew what minute one of us would be caught and maybe squeal on the others.

That did happen on one or two occasions but the cops in those days were good fellows, and aside from a good scare and a rap across our sitter with a nightstick or cane they didn't hurt us. Sometimes they thought it a good joke to upset a pushcart and they would laugh after they caught us. I must say that none of our gang ever squealed on the others when caught, but we were always afraid they might. There were some bad gangs in our neighborhood but our particular mob was not of that caliber. We never stole anything, except an apple or a banana once in a while, and none of us was ever arrested.

I came near it once but managed to convince the cop who had me that I had nothing to do with the theft and was turned loose. That scared me and I never roamed the streets with the gang anymore. I stayed at home nights and read magazines and books, love stories mostly, and about twice a week I'd see a movie if I could put the bee on Mama for the price. In those days you could see a good movie for a nickel. My Ma and Pa, too, wondered what had come over me, staying at home nights and all, but I never told them about the close call I had and they never found out. They caught the real thief later, and he proved to be one of another gang and I was happy because I always felt I was suspected even if I had never been prosecuted. If I had gone to jail that time there's no telling what might have happened to me.

You know, our gang was getting tougher all the time and we might have become real crooks. I always thank God for my escape and I will always believe He worked that all out to wake me up. And it worked for the rest of the gang, too, for they quit cutting up after I left them, and settled down to being good boys and girls. Some of them are among the leading citizens of the day and probably wouldn't care to be reminded of the good old days when they were what they thought was "tough."

My school days were nothing out of the ordinary. I attended fairly regular except when Ma kept me home when she wasn't feeling so good. You know I am the oldest girl and was looked up to, to take care of the house and the kids. You know, sort of take Ma's place when she was out of commission, which wasn't often. I never minded so much, but I liked school and hated to have to stay away. Every time I stayed away I would lose some of the things I had learned and was way behind the other kids in my studies.

No, I never played hooky, although I was tempted many times when my brothers took days off from school. My sisters always kept a good record for attendance at school. There was nothing to keep them away and they could go every day, and they did. Ma insisted on this, but Pa didn't seem to care so much. He always said if a person had a mind and wanted education he could learn by reading books and the newspapers. He thought school, after the first three or four years, was a waste of time for the average child. College he did not believe in at all.

He always said that he only went to school three years and picked up the rest of his education by himself later. And if I do say so myself, he is very well informed. He can talk intelligently on almost any current subject. Anyhow he has a nice business in New York and is making a good living with a novelty store. He knows how to buy and has a large clientele of customers who want the things he has to sell.

I told you we were raised in one room where we cooked, ate, and slept, but after I was 10 years old we were living in a comfortable five-room apartment and enjoyed all conveniences. Pa and Ma and one of my sisters are still there and they are doing fine. My other sister and my two brothers are married. Both the boys work in the store with Pa, and they too are getting a living out of it. Sis married a man who is the manager of one of New York's big department stores and she is well fixed, and maybe you do think she is high-hat. And how.

I don't mind her being that way for I know it has no foundation. I give her a piece of my mind every time we meet but it don't do any good; she tries that stuff every time all over again. You know what I mean about high-hat— she tries to lord it over the rest of us because her hubby's got a good job with a nice income. But if my pal was in the same boat I don't think I would feel above my own people or any of my friends. But some people are like that: when they're down, they're way down, and when they're up they think they are out of reach.

I guess I'm the only cluck in the family but I don't mind. I'm happy with my hubby and the two kids and I'm not asking any of my family for anything so far. And I hope I never will have to. As long as I have enough to eat and a comfortable place to sleep, there is nothing to it. Pa has several times offered Nick, that's my husband, money to go into business but he turned it down. He says if he can't get along without help from my people he will stay as he is. I've tried to talk him out of it, told him he was showing false pride, but I can't move him.

He even refused to accept a dowry from my father when we were married, and I admire him for that. Pa couldn't have afforded much of a dowry at that time anyhow, and it was just as well. Imagine a Jewish boy doing that? My sister cost Pa $2,000 when she married, so you can see the difference. And you can bet she isn't as happy as I am. Her husband is not the type Nick is, in no way. He is selfish and self-centered and if he has to choose between his own comfort and my sister's, he takes his own every time. They haven't any kids and they never will have, I guess. Well, they don't want any, so that's that. I wouldn't give up my two darlings for anything in the world. My brothers have two children apiece, which means they have happy families I guess.

Guess my other sister will be getting married one of these days and we will have a wedding on our hands, presents and all that bunk. Well, she won't get a heck of a lot from me because I haven't got the money to spend. I need it too badly for my own family and she won't be any happier if I gave her a $1,000 gift. But she won't mind for she knows my circumstances and won't expect much. Of course I'll give her some little thing even if she didn't give me anything when I got married. But it won't cost more than $5 you can bet, and maybe not that much. My hubby says to give her something, so I'll have to I guess. He is square.

I suppose you'd like to know how I met my husband, with me living in New York and he in Bridgeport? Well, it was like this. My girlfriend and I were taking a walk along Broadway—window-shopping, you know—when two boys walked up to us and we started talking. I thought one of them, my husband now, was just the thing. Love at first sight I guess, on my part anyhow. At first the boys just took the attitude that we were just a couple of pickups but it didn't take long to change their minds. The other guy got sore and wanted to drop us, but the boy I had said "nothing doing." He stuck around. The four of us walked around the streets all afternoon, and about 5 o'clock they asked us in for something to eat.

My girlfriend wanted to go but I declined. I told my boyfriend that I had to go home as my folks were expecting me for supper. Well, after asking my permission he took me home and we made a date for the following Sunday. He said he could come down on one of those railroad excursions. He came right to the house for me. That made a hit with my Pa. We walked around during the afternoon and saw some of the sights which were common to me but not to Nick. We stayed at my home for supper that night, and we spent a few hours together until he had to leave to catch his train for home. He kept coming down every Sunday after that, and we got better acquainted after each visit until I knew that here was the boy I wanted to marry regardless of the consequences.

I didn't know his nationality then. In fact I didn't find out he was Italian until a few days before the wedding day. But I didn't care. I was in love, I guess, and love is blind so they say, and I guess I wouldn't have cared if he was a coon at that time. I don't mean that, but just trying to be funny. My folks didn't like the idea of my marrying what they called a "wop," but I told them that it made no difference to me. I loved him and I was going to marry him even if I was disowned. Pa had no such idea, only he thought he could change my mind and have me marry a Jewish boy. But I never did like them; they are too selfish and get the idea that a woman is just a dishrag or a mop to wipe their feet on. I've heard that said about Italian boys, but not my husband. He is reliable and I am his every consideration no matter what comes up. Well, we were married in the city hall in New York by the Mayor then, I don't remember his name. We didn't bother with a honeymoon but came right to Bridgeport and started married life in a furnished room. Nick was working at the time at the Bassick factory and getting $35 a week. He worked there for four years and during that time our kiddies came to town. Since he lost his job he has held odd jobs here and there but he don't seem to be able to land one that is permanent. But he's awful—what do you call it—optimistic, and always tells me he'll land something soon. And I believe he will. I never nag him about it for I really believe he will come out on top in the end.

He's a good kid—he don't drink, don't fool around with other women, and spends his evenings at home with me. We both smoke cigarettes and I guess I smoke more than he does. He takes care of the housework and the kiddies, and when I come home nights he has the supper all ready. And he has developed into a darn good cook—at least I think so, for I enjoy the meals he prepares. I always get the Sunday meals when we eat at home. And I know he enjoys them too because he says he gets kind of sick of the food he prepares himself.

He does all the shopping too. You see, I'm tied up here in the store all day and can't get out. At the noon hour on Friday we go out together when I get out for lunch and we buy the supply for the coming week. You see, he depends a lot on my judgment for many things even though I let him think he is doing the selecting. It's fun to hear him say: "That's a nice piece of meat, honey, don't you think so?" And I say, "Sure, Nick, that's fine and dandy. But let's look at some more before we buy that."

Nine times out of 10 we buy the "some more" unless there's nothing better than his selection. That's the way I work it: always agree he's right, then casually make another suggestion, which is usually the prevailing one. Of course if he insists, which is seldom, I let him have his way. That way we never get into any foolish arguments some couples have about who's the boss of the house. I never make him feel inferior to me even when I know he is wrong in his contentions. Sometimes I just switch the subject, but in the end I usually win out without hurting his feelings or mine. I handle the children the same way, and as a result we are one happy family and I want to keep it that way. I've succeeded for five years so far and I hope to keep it up for 50 more. Don't you think my system is a good one? I do.

Of course we have arguments occasionally, who don't? But they are few and far between and are never serious enough to leave sore spots. Nick and I have never gone to sleep sore at each other. We always settle our arguments before we go to sleep. Nick is a good scout and he would do anything for me, as I would for him. He has made many sacrifices for me and the kids, and I know it hurts his pride to have me go to work. But what can we do? He is trying now for a job in the GE plant and he thinks he will land it soon. He has a friend on the inside who is pulling some strings for him and I believe it will work out. Even if he does I will keep on working for a while, but if he gets a decent pay I know he will want me to quit as soon as we get on our feet.

Yes, we have our recreation periods too. You know you can't die just because you are poor. You have to have some amusements. We go to the movies once or twice a week, and on Sundays and holidays we take trips in our car. Yes, we have a car. It is not so much as cars go, but it takes us where we want to go. A Packard and a Rolls-Royce can't do any more than that. If it gets out of order Nick can fix it because he is handy that way. The only time car trouble costs us money is when we have to buy new parts, but that ain't often.

I told you Nick don't drink, so taverns never bother us. I have no desire to sit in a smoke-filled room and listen to a lot of silly conversation and lap up a lot of sloppy beer. We like to dance, and we go occasionally and have a lot of fun. Nick goes to Mass every Sunday—he is a Catholic—but I don't bother. I may become a Catholic someday for him. I like the masses in the Catholic church. I have gone with Nick several times and I like it. I don't think it makes any difference what religion you adopt so long as you respect it and keep your belief in God and the Golden Rule. I can't stand these hypocrites who go to church and then violate every one of the Ten Commandments as soon as they hit the sidewalk. I seldom go to any church, never to my own, but I'll bet a cookie I've got a better chance to reach Heaven than many of those who live in the church.

I could tell a lot of stories about some of my friends who are supposed to be good church members, but why talk about my friends. They would about me, but I should worry.

I am living a clean normal life, take care of my family and husband. I try to do all the good I can with the limits of my resources, and I believe that is all that should be expected from a human being. Life is too short to talk about other people. We all have enough dirt in front of our own door without going to our neighbors. So the best way is to mind your own business and take care of it and no one can find fault with you.

Now I'm preaching and I don't want to. I am planning to give my kiddies a good education in spite of what my father thinks. I believe education is the foundation of success in life for anyone. I wish I had more of it and my husband too. But we both read a lot and maybe it will help us some of these days. No, I don't care for heavy stuff, but I don't like to read trash either, like *True Stories*, *True Romances*, and such junk. I think they're awful and people who read those are wacky. Nick and I get books from the lending library and sometimes from the public library. When we finish a book we take it back and get another after we have both read the one we had. I like a good love story but it must be of the sensible kind, stories of real life, not trash or a lot of mush. We pick our moving pictures the same way, something substantial which we can understand.

I guess I've told you about all I can about my life and hope it will help and has proved interesting. . . . That's all there is; there isn't any more. And thank you for coming to me. If you need any more and I can help you, let me know.[18]

Mrs. M., 35 years old when interviewed in 1940, was the daughter of Polish immigrants. Born in Bridgeport, Connecticut, at the time of the interview she lived with her husband and five children in a four-room flat of a six-flat tenement house occupied by five Polish families. Her husband, a Polish immigrant, worked as a street sweeper for the city. She volunteered that she would gladly seek work, but "the children are too young" and she was "suffering from nervous strain because of the tough life." Mrs. M. elaborated upon her husband's jealousy and her belief that "all women have to be a little free." The tension between the native-born wife and the foreign-born husband pervades her comments.

I was born in Bridgeport, so I'm not a real Polack. I don't know when my father came here, but it must be a long time because he was one of the first Polacks here, and that's a long time ago. He was a carpenter when he first come here and he had it good that time, and they were always hiring him. I remember how he always had work.

My mother died when I was a couple of months old, so I didn't know what a real mother was like. Then my father married again, and he died 15 years ago and then my stepmother married again, and I stayed with her until I got married. When I got married with my husband, we got married in New York by a justice of peace. People that I know said that it was no good and I should get married by the Church, but I don't mind what the people say, anyway.

When I was a small girl my father sent me to school in St. Michael's, but I didn't stay there long because the sisters were too fresh and they used to beat up the kids with a stick. That's when I quit—and my brother quit because the sister hit him so hard that he was sick from being nervous—and when we gave the case to the lawyer my father got money from the church because they were to blame. That's why I wouldn't send my children there to school—because they're too fresh and I love my children.

My husband, that I married, was always a molder and he was working in the Jenkins Valve Company, and he had a good job there making $35, $40 a week. That was good money in those times. Then the Depression came and he was laid off. From that time to this he never had a steady job, and he's always working for CWA, WPA, and all city jobs. That's lousy—a good man that wants to work can't even get a job!

I would like to get a job myself, because I'm 35 years old and he is 45 years old, but the children are too young, and the doctors says that I'm suffering from nervous strain because of the tough life. Sometimes I feel like I'm falling down. I went to see the doctor the other week and he made me get glasses, and I had to get them from the city because my husband has no money to spare. Yah. . . . It's too bad—no money. Everything that you have to get costs money and we haven't got it. When my husband was working he used to get everything. No money!

When I was younger I switched from the parochial school to the public school, and then I stayed there until the sixth grade and then left. At the time it was easy to get out of school, and I told them that I had to quit because I had to work and help to support the family. Then I went to work and I was getting cheap pay in some of the sweatshops. When I got older I got acquainted with my husband and then the first chance that I had, I married him. I figured that time that my father was dead and my mother was only my stepmother, so I wanted to live by myself. That's how it is when your own people die—the stepfathers and -mothers don't care. They treated me pretty good because they were religious people and they like me like their own, but I figured that my brothers and sisters got married so I wanted to get out too.

Well, I moved all over the city and here I am today, because when we had money we would get a good flat, and when my husband would lose a job then we had to go to a cheap place to live. That's how it is. Well, I would be satisfied if I was living better and my husband had a good job that paid. This way you have to live in the city and there's never enough for the kids to eat what is good. When my husband gets his check for five-sixty we have to pay the landlady—and she wants her rent on time. This week all I have left is 60¢ and the box of food that the city leaves us, and the kids get tired from that all the time.

My husband always looks for a job. He looks healthy and young but they won't give him a job because they say that he's too old. Yesterday the investigator come to my house and she was asking how I am getting along. I told her that she should try to get my husband a job on the outside because he don't want to work on a cheap job for the city—he wants to get a job he could make a good pay for the family. We get plenty of bread and I give the children plenty of toast out of it. Yes, they give us loaves of bread. See, I'm making it for the children now because they come from school. I want to give them everything good that I could get for them because I love my children. The first two that I had, they died right after they were born. The doctor told my husband that there was something wrong with this, so now I'm not taking any chances. That's why I want to give them the best.

I had another one too, and I was hanging curtains—you know how it is? I didn't know about these things then, and when I was hanging the curtains I think that the cord of the baby got around his neck and it strangled him. The doctor came to me in the hospital when I was brought down from the delivery room and he had a sad look on his face. Then I asked him how everything was and he didn't want to tell me because I was too weak. I wanted to know but he didn't tell me. Then my husband came to see me and then he told me the truth. That day to now I am afraid that my children will get hurt and I never let them get out of my sight. That's why I love my children. My husband likes them too because he is a home man and he never wants to go out for a good time.

My husband is terrible jealous because he knows that he is older than me. Sometimes I like to go to a tavern and we go to the Park City tavern and I drag him to go. If some of my lady friends come to the house, then he lets me go with them, but he wants to know where we go. I tell him that I'm not old and I want to have fun yet. Then he don't like this because he is more a family man. But I think that all women have to be free a little. The only time that I go to the tavern is when I have some small change—and that's only once in a long time, and so it's not a habit.

Now for the last year I don't feel so good; my eyes bother me and I see like a spot in front of me. My head starts to hurt me and I feel dizzy like I'm falling down. I know that it's a hard thing for my husband to get a job, so if I was feeling better I would go out to look for one. Sometimes I feel so weak that I'm afraid that if I get a job I won't be able to keep it. That's why I don't know if I should look for a job or stay home. When the investigator come to the house I told her that my husband was looking for a job with the slum clearance, you know where that is, on the East Side. He goes there when he don't work, and last week when he went there he was asking them for a job to do the wrecking. He heard that they wanted lots of men there, so he thought that he would get the job. Then they told him that he would have to join the union and pay them almost $100. He has relatives but they have their own troubles and they couldn't let him take the money so that he could get in the union, so this way he can't get the job. Why don't they give the men the jobs and take so much out of their pay every week? That's the only way that they could get the job, I think. That's what I told the investigator, but she said that she didn't know what I could do about it. And she said that if we could borrow the money someplace then it would be a good thing for all of us, and I told her that we can't even borrow a nickel because they won't loan money to people that are on relief. My husband is always looking for a job on the outside, and when he sent for this job in the slum clearance he saw that there was about 300–400 men waiting in line, and the boss there told them all that there was no job if they were not union men.

So that's why my husband come home. These investigators don't understand all these things; they think that it's easy to get a job. I find out how hard it is because I know that my husband always looks and he can't find any.

[At this point of the story Mrs. M. excuses herself, saying that she has to see what the children are doing in the bedroom. She leaves, and then begins to scold them for playing on the bed. "Didn't I tell you kids that you have to play in the kitchen?" she says. "You have all the room that you want if you stay in the kitchen. If your father comes home and sees the bed dirty he's going to give you all a beating!" The three children scurry to the kitchen in single file, followed by their mother, Mrs. M. Mrs. M.: "Now you kids better stay in the kitchen, and don't let me see you play in that bedroom again. It's getting to be a habit, and people think that we teach you bad manners." Mrs. M. then brings out some of the children's toys and lays them on the kitchen floor. "Florey, you show the man how you rock on your horse." This toy horse is about two feet high and is operated by a steel band. The youngest boy, three years old, gets on the horse and begins rocking back and forth. The other two now occupy themselves with a small rocking chair and metal toy alligator. "Alright, now you kids keep quiet if you know what's good for you, and don't talk so loud." Mrs. M. continues with her story:]

See the way that the kids play all by themselves? They're good kids, and the small one is crazy about that old wooden horse. I bought that from the Salvation Army store on Main Street about two years ago and I used it for the other kids, and now this one has it and he won't give it to the brothers and sisters. He likes that better than all the other toys. When my husband and me had money we always were buying the kids all the toys that they wanted, but now that he's on city relief it's different, we have to get the toys in the Salvation Army. Two of the children go to the Waltersville School; one is 12 and the other is 13 and they are nice girls. I never wanted them to go to the parochial school because about the things that they do there—I told you that before.

You ask me how I get along and my family life, and the only thing that I could tell you is that we are in poor conditions now and we're waiting maybe things get better somedays. The way they are going now, I think maybe it's going to take a long time before we have good times again. When my husband was making good money we were all the time invited to parties. . . . He never liked to go to them but I used to force him, and I told him that I felt young and when he'd hear that he would go with me. Now if I tell him, he won't go so much because he has too many things on his mind. He's always thinking about getting a job. When he had a good job we could afford to have a better home to raise the children up better. Now when we want to have a good time we have to go to the taverns and have a good time there. That's why my husband don't like it so much. He thinks that there are no gentlemen in these places, and so when we go there together he gets mad when he sees the men wanting to dance with women that they don't know. My husband says that if they would come with their wives then he wouldn't care, but the trouble is that these men are trying to get the women; that's what my husband says all the time when he goes to taverns. That's why he's afraid to let me go to the taverns—he thinks I want to go with the other men. The only thing that I want to do is dance with them once in a while. When I go to the tavern with my lady friends they dance together, and then some of the men, you know how they are, they see women dancing together and they want to separate them, and then when they ask us we can't. They're pretty sociable.

Of course there's some bad ones that want to get, but we don't have nothing to do with them. That's why my husband is jealous.

Well, you know how it is. The time when I had money, like some people, I belong to the Polish Club. They have entertainments there and all the Polish people go there all the time. These clubs are like benefit clubs and you have to pay dues, and when you die they give you some money because you have like insurance. Well, I used to belong to this, and all the Polish men and women they have good times there on Saturdays, they have dances and the better go there. I used to do this when I had money. Now that I haven't got it I don't belong to it and I had to drop the insurance. I could still go there, but I'm ashamed to go because I have got no money and I don't want to look like I'm asking for something. Some people they ask me why I don't go because they always used to see me there, one time. I always have to make excuses and tell them that I'm too busy to go there. The people in these clubs they act respectable because they are not like some of the people that are in the taverns to drink. They are a better class and they are respected by the women. That's why my husband never cared when I went to the club. . . .

I don't ask for much. All I want to do is to have a good time for a while, and my husband is jealous about this. . . . I think that my husband is like that sometimes because he's a little old-fashioned, because he wasn't born here. He comes from Poland. When he was in Poland, he said that he never went with other girls, and he's the kind that only want one woman.[19]

Two Sides of a Marriage: "This Animal That Was No Man"

The tale of the N. family is not a happy one. By the time of the interview, the couple had been separated for 10 years after a tumultuous marriage. The husband immigrated from Poland in 1901, when he was 17. He settled in Bridgeport after relatives helped him find a wood joiner's job at their place of employment. He moved to another employer and learned the molding trade. After 12 years in that position, and while making about $25 per week, he married a woman who came from a neighboring village in Poland. They produced 10 children. Then, in the words of the interviewer, "he later encountered marital difficulties and separated from his wife and family. Mr. N. says that he has never been the same since, and because of this he has lost his morale." He blamed the situation on his wife's infidelity.

The wife, on the other hand, told a story of terrible abuse in the marriage, which she blamed on her spouse's drunkenness. Shortly after coming to the United

States at age 15, she married Mr. N., who turned out to be her cousin. To some, this familial relationship helped explain her hard luck. She recounted her life with this "animal that was no man." Suffering, violence, child and wife abuse, colored their everyday life. According to the interviewer, "at the time of the interview Mrs. N. did not know that the interviewer had seen Mr. N. As a result, the information obtained was without any feeling of bias on either side. Rather, it is information based on authentic facts, verified by the children of these two informants."

Mr. N. told his story:

After I get married I have the family and I live good. I take care of the family all the time. I live happy. Then I have lots of trouble because get jealous because my wife have a man for the side. People they tell that he go out with somebody and that she is a bad woman, and I tell them to shut the mouth, because they don't mind their business. One time I catch my wife, she go out with this Ballas, Slavic-Czech man, and I beat him up and he almost was die. Well, my wife don't stop for this and after this man get better she do the same thing. I give her plenty time to think all about this and then she said that she likes this man, so I get out from the house. From that time I don't care about nothing. My children that time they don't know this kind monkey business and they don't like me because I leave. Now they are more older and four children they are married, and now they understand because they see how the mother is bad woman. I treat good my wife all the time but for this she don't like to be good, she wants to be bum all the time. My son catch one time this man and my wife and he almost make him go to the hospital, and mine son show me the leg from the chair that he broke on his head, and he said, "Papa, this I give you to remember that I almost kill that man that break up the family. Now I believe that it was not your business that the family was breaking." I tell my son, I say, "Teddy, you are a good boy. Now you understand Papa." My son now he comes to see me and he brings me whiskey and all the things that he could get from the house.

My wife is good for nothing. She goes in the saloon with all the other woman and they are all the same bums. I like the woman too, but I am not bad like some people, I like drink better.

You ask me how the Polish people live that time that I come from Poland on the East Side. I tell you. That time all the Polack people coming to Bridgeport they come on the East Side because they have all the relatives on this side of the city. Some people they live in the other parts of the city but they come to drink for the East Side because they have the saloons Polack just the same. All the people that time, they work in the shops on the East Side, and the rent was cheaper like other places in the city. Some people they make some money, then they move to Stratford and Fairfield, they buy the property there and they make house too for themselves. I like to make house too, one time, but after my wife she so bum I said no. No business for me to make house and spend the money for nothing.

Well, I don't have nothing now, anyway. I have the insurance for $1,000 and when I die my children could keep for themselves. I like all four boys, but I don't like Emil, he is the second one and he thinks that he is better like me. He thinks that he is smart fellow. He comes in this place sometime and he talks to me like he knows too much; he tries to tell me how to do this and how I should live. He drinks just the same so I don't bother him, why he wants to show me something I don't understand. The girls, they don't care for nothing and they mind their business and they don't come to see me. I don't care for this because I am like free man, if they don't come to see me.[20]

Mrs. N. offered a longer and significantly sadder and more compellingly powerful testimony:

I was a small girl, 15 years old, when I come to this country, to Hartford. My people they come to the town to work in the factory. My mother and father they come there. Just soon that I come to this country my husband that I marry come there and ask me to marry. So then we get marry in Bridgeport and I living with him on Hallett Street. I have now five boys, two girls. My story could make books from the floor to this high. [Mrs. N., with a broad sweep of her arm, first downward and then upward, indicated the stack of books to reach a pile of approximately five feet.] Yes, I have a bad life with this . . . uh . . . uh . . . uh . . . animal that was no man. We living on Hallett Street that time because all the Polish people living there and because the rent cheap that time, like $8 for one month.

My husband good to me for only five, six months and then he start to drink. He was spending all the time, and all the money he was spending for the drinks. He never take care of the house after that time. He always spend all the time in the saloons and sometimes I have to go get him, and all the times that I go to get him I see that he be playing cards and he talks with the other men just like him. After he don't have no work he want to go to Springfield, Massachusetts, and he get the job there in the foundry, and after in electric company. He had good job there for little while, but then he start to drink all over again and he was losing the job.

I already have Teddy that time, he was the oldest, and he was 22 months old. I now was having the other baby, and this baby was four days old. My husband, I expect him to come home about 5:00 that night. I wait, I wait, I wait. I wait all the time to 9:00 and still he don't come home. Then the baby start to cry and I go to the baby to see what's the trouble. I try to take off the diaper and the diaper it was froze on the baby. . . . I start to cry all for myself, and Teddy that time, only 22 months, he was waking because I was crying. He was crying, "Mama, eat . . . eat . . . I want to eat." I was crying, don't know what to do. I look for my dress. My dress that my husband buy me two weeks before. I take this dress and go for the rag-picker, and he give me 5¢ for the new dress that I buy not long ago.

I take the money and go to the Jew and I tell him give me one pint milk for 4¢ and I got one bun of bread for Teddy and the baby. Teddy eat this like he was never eating before, and when he finished he was crying for more because this was not enough, because young babies they always want to eat. I go to the Jew again and I was crying to him, I said, "Please, mister, give to me one more roll for my baby because he have nothing to eat." He said, "Yes, lady, I give to you for nothing." And he give to me two rolls instead. I take this to Teddy, poor baby, and he eat and then he falls asleep. The little baby, four days old, he was crying but I can't give to him the breast, because I am dry. You can't give to the baby the breast that is dry because what he is going to suck, blood? Because I don't eat for a long time and I don't have the right kind of food to eat, and I don't have nothing in the breast. So I try to boil some of the milk that I buy for 4¢ and give this to the baby. The baby falls asleep and I start to cry all over again. I cry like I want to break my heart out. I say to myself, "This is married life, for my husband to leave me like this!"

That time we was paying the high rent, $15. So I sit down and start to make the letters for some peoples that I know in Bridgeport. I tell them that I want to come to Bridgeport and all these things. I tell them all about my rotten life. I close this letter and then go out to the street and I tell this to the policeman that was standing for the corner, and I tell him that I need this money. I start to cry and then he tell me what's the trouble. And I tell him the story. He give to me 25¢ and he tells me that he come to the house to see what he could do. When he comes to the house he sees that everything is all upside-down. He sees that the babies are in the bed. He sees that there is no fire in the stove and then he says to me, "Where is this man that you call your husband?" And he tells me that he will take care of all this. He tells the woman in the next door something, and pretty soon she comes to me with the basket of woods and pail of coal. I take this and then I make the fire. After the fire she is started, this woman comes in the house again and she gives to me one pounds of frankfurts and I make these in the pot. I wake up Teddy and I tell him that there is something to eat. So he eats. This woman she sees me eating like mad and then she says to me, she says, "Why don't you talk about all the troubles that you got, why don't you say something?

You have the mouth to talk? Why don't you say something?" I tell her that I go to Bridgeport to the house of my friends.

My friends the next couple of days they send me $15 and they send somebody to take the clothes and the things that I have in the house. Then when I come to Bridgeport I went to live in the house of these people, and they were living on the East Side. My husband that time he come to see me when he finds that I come to this house of my friend. He tells me that he was going to get money so that we have some rooms. Then I go with him and somebody tells me that he was giving in the wedding, $15. This was the time that I was starving in Springfield. I was so mad that I tell him to get out from the house. But he tells to me all the excuses so he patch up everything. Then he be a good man for only two months and he starts to drink all the same like before. He was getting drunk in the saloon all the time.

When I see that he don't want to go to work steady, I go to work to help myself. I was getting job housework, then after this my husband was think to get a job. I have somebody take care of the children and this is how I have to do it. Yes, my husband was always good for somebody else but never good for the family. He was always treating the family like dogs. I was always working after this and I still do this same kind of work.

One time I was working for a Jew lady and I did all the housework for the family. I worked here for a long time, even when I have to get the baby. That time I have to work because my husband don't work steady because he drinks and walking around all the time. Well, I was working some days in the week and I do not get very much money but they treat me very good. When the time come that I have the baby one time, I was scrubbing for the kitchen floor and I start to feel dizzy. I was bending down and working, and the woman for the house said to me "Mary, I know that you are sick. Maybe you gonna have baby." "No," I tell to the lady, "I no sick, and I don't have baby." She said to me that I am sick, that I don't have to foolin' her. She said that she could see that I have baby pretty soon. So she tells the husband to get the Huckson [Hudson] car and to take me to my house. We get home and four hour after this I start to have the baby. That time my husband was not home, he was out for the drinks.

When I start to have the baby I tell to Teddy to go out and get the midwife. Teddy looks at me and says that he don't know what that is. So I tell him to ask the people outside and they will tell him. He say, "Alright Mama, I find." When Teddy goes out he meets some people and they tell him to go to see the midwife on the next street. Teddy goes like they say and he get the Italian midwife instead the Polish midwife. Well, anyway it is too late to change this and this woman she start to work on the baby. After it is born the wife takes it and put the pillow under the head. I see this after but I don't think nothing about it. After maybe three hours the baby starts to cry and I don't know what for. Then I see that the pillow is hurting the baby and take it away, and then the baby stops to cry. This is the difference with the Polish midwife and the Italian midwives. Well, the job is done that time, I can't pick it out myself so I have to take this Italian midwife because it is too late. Now all the peoples they go to the hospitals to have the babies and they have all the care all the time. That time you have to help yourself, because nobody wants to help. You see how bad it was my husband was not even there, and I had to work to the last day. Why? Because there was no money in the house. Four hours after I have the baby I tell Teddy to take the pot of hot water and to take the pail and bring to me. Then I take the baby and I make for him the bath. Oh yes, that was how it was. I always take care of the babies this way. Then Teddy help me to clean the house, and me, myself, I got up and clean all over the place. That time the people when they have the babies they always stand up right away, not like now all the people they are so delicate. Three days after I have the baby I have my husband come home drunk like animal and I was in the bed that time, and it was wintertime, too. My husband come with the rope and he starts to hit me on the backs. When I see this I start to holler and then Teddy gets up, but he can't do nothing because he is a young boy. Then I run for the other room and I jump out of the window one story to the ground. Teddy see me do this, and the father he was not care, so he goes to the other room in the kitchen. Teddy comes to the window and I tell him that he throw me down the baby.

That time the snow was like high and it was cold, but just the same he throws to me the baby. Then Teddy he jumps from the window, too. I go to my friend's house and then when the husband is drunk no more I tell him that I have to go to live in the house and he have to get out. Then he starts to pray to me that he wants to stay in the house. Yes, I know what I suffer myself. He spoils all my life. Three times I try to die that time. One time I take poison, one time gas, and another time gas. Yes, just because I am marry to this man. He never was thinking about the family. He was always thinking for hisself. Always drink, drink, drink.

Then we live on Goodwin Street one time and we have the boarders because I can't work that time, I have to make the living some way. Well, these two boarders they were eating fried potatoes and they come from work and they are hungry. I make the potatoes and I don't have enough for three peoples. Florian was youngest and he was three years old that time and he wants some potatoes. You know how the little children they are eating all the time. Well, Florian starts to take the potatoes from the plate from this boarder and then my husband comes in the house. When my husband sees this he takes the knife from the table and he throws it at Florian. The knife sticks right in the head. When the boarders see this, one got up and he is scared to take the knife out from the head. The other boarder gives one punch to my husband and knocks him on the floor. He said, "You are not a man, you are animal." Then the other boarder get the doctors and the Florian stay in the hospital for one months, just because this accidents. Sure, if you don't believe this you go see Florian sometimes and you see this on the head. He have scars.

Sure, I was separated from him for five times, and all the times I go back to him, but no more. He was always too jealous and that's the trouble. Now I have boyfriend that I like and I am satisfied because all my children they are big and they take care for themself. . . .

Now that my children they are older I work for myself. Teddy he is marry and he have the wife on the South End. Emil he is marry, too, and he have the wife on the East Side, and Lillian she is marry for one Polish boy in Yonkers, in New York. Yes, she have a good husband and he is working steady and she stay for the house. Yes, she have nice husband. The other two boys and the girl they are helping me out sometimes when they are working, and they are good for the mother. The girl goes to the high school. Sometimes she gets the small jobs to take care of the children for some people and she makes the few dollars. This is better than nothing. The boys they can't get steady jobs, they can't help this. Yes, I send the girl to the school because she can't get good work, anyway. They pay the young girl nothing for working now, so it's better that they go to school, better for to work for nothing. I come from the Poland and that time all the people they have no education, so it's better to learn something, maybe someday she gets better husband.

I don't want nobody support'n me so long that I have health and I could work all for myself. Maybe someday my children they be taking care of me, but I could work now, so I be like I am.

One thing that I want to say: I think that I have bad luck all the time because like I tell some people, and they tell me, I marry this man and he is my cousin. This is against the religion I think, and all the people they tell this to me, too. I don't believe this myself one time, but now I see that this maybe is truth. Yes, I have too much bad luck and I think that this is fault. Because why I have so much bad luck, you tell it to me? Us people we don't believe that the cousins marry, and then when I marry I don't think about this because my husband he wants to marry, he don't care. But you see what happen to me.

[At this point Mrs. O., a visitor who has been listening to a good part of the conversation, remarked that this was "a big surprise." Mrs. O.: "You marry cousin? Gee, this is big sin! This is no good for religion. Sure you have bad luck, because."]

"See, what I tell you about this? All the people that know this say the same things. Well, now I don't live with this man, so maybe I don't have such bad luck anymore."[21]

What Women Talk About

Mrs. S., the daughter of Swedish immigrants, married a Norwegian against her family's judgment. Like Mrs. N., she blamed her bad marriage on her husband's drinking. Initially she was reluctant to share her problems because "if you're Swedish, you get a habit of telling only the good things." Her comments, however, extended beyond marital problems and touched squarely on gender roles. She recognized that the girls of 1941 were learning to do more than care for a house, but women still talked "about things that all women discuss."

I've had bad breaks ever since I got married. I married a Norwegian and he never treated me right. He was always causing a disturbance in the house, and many times he would scare the life out of my children by beating me or threatening to do something worse. It wasn't that I was so afraid of him, but I didn't want anyone to know about our troubles, least of all my family. They had been opposed to my marrying him because they felt that he had no trade and probably couldn't ever do anything more than work at ordinary labor. I didn't feel this way about it; I thought that someday we would have better times. He had promised to be a good husband and we were expecting to live nicely together. But this didn't happen. When the usual hardships came he took to drink. First he began to feel that he was a failure, then he started to feel sorry for himself, and finally he began to threaten me with injury, saying that I had expected too much from him. I told him many times that this was not so. I told him that he should continue to accept things as they were, and someday we would enjoy better times. This only made him more resentful, and he resorted to many mean tricks. He began imagining things about me and to doubt my fidelity toward him. I was too taken up with the care of the children, and when things got worse I began to feel that life was not worth living. I began to neglect the children, and now they are showing it.

I have three children and they are all underweight. One of the boys is three, and he's very small for his age; the other is five and he's unruly because his health is bad; and the other is . . . eight, but you wouldn't know it—she's mentally defective, and the doctor says that she has a mind of a four-year-old. She never goes out because she is afraid to associate with other children. As far as her mental condition is concerned, she is falling back all the time. She is very small for her age and she looks more like a child of five. She is thin and pale, and the doctor says that we should have her taken away to the institution as soon as we could. All this is the result of my husband's quarrels—they used to be so bad at times that it frightened the children, and now they are suffering for it. If they had the proper nourishment they wouldn't be so bad off.

167

I have a bad heart condition, and this is the result of my hardships. I started to suffer this way five years after we were married. I don't care so much about myself; it's the children that I'm worried about all the time. If one isn't sick the other one is, and A—is always taking fits and going into convulsions. Lately she's been getting worse and she has me worried so that I don't know what to do with her.

I've been getting city relief now for quite a while. My husband lives some-where in the city, but he can't help me because he's working with WPA, and he doesn't make enough to support us. We get some aid from a Swedish aid group. It's small help but they do the best they can for us, and they've been very nice right along. I came to live here, in the village [Yellow Mill Village], since about a month ago, and I find it very nice here. It makes the children feel better that they are living in a nice place, and it helps me very much because I don't have to work as hard as I used to before coming here. When I lived on M. Street it was very hard because the children were always catching colds and they had no place to play. They were always getting hurt and would have a habit of going out in the street. Here we have none of that danger, and I'm glad I don't have to worry about that anymore.

When my husband first started to give me trouble I never told anyone. Our friends, most of them Swedish people, thought we were getting along very nicely. If you're Swedish you get a habit of telling only the good things. And this is the way I was until I couldn't stand it anymore. Then I told him to leave, and he's been out of the house ever since. If he could have fixed himself I would have taken him back, but he is so far with his drinking that he can't think of anything else. That's the one thing that drove him on the wrong path. He also felt strange because he married me, a Swede, who was used to better treatment.

My father and mother were born on the other side. They came here when they were in their thirties, but they didn't come directly to Bridgeport. They had been for some time in New Britain because there were a lot of Swedish friends there. My father was mechanically inclined and on the other side he has been working on machine work. When he came here he did the same thing. Later he heard about Bridgeport—that was about the time of the World War. Then he came here with some of his friends and found work in one of the places here. Since that time he worked in the same shop and never went any place else for work. He was satisfied to stay in the small shop. My father had my brothers take up his trade and they were successful at it. They have been working out of town for quite a few years.

My parents had always advised me to get married to someone who had established himself in some trade. The Swedes are that way, and they feel that their children should marry someone who won't have to worry about supporting the family. I had thought this all along, but then I met my husband and I fell for him. I forgot what I had been told, and the result was that six months later I married him. Norwegians have a habit of coming to the Swedish affairs. They feel that they have something in common with the Swedish people, and the Swedes don't seem to mind their company. But they are a different type of people. Most of them [Norwegians] seem to remain on the same type of jobs; they don't care about advancing themselves like the Swedes. Swedish people have the background and understanding that it takes to make successes of themselves. You very seldom see a Swedish person who doesn't know something about mechanics or some type of skilled work.

When I was a child my mother had all she could do in taking care of the family. We were many and she couldn't attend to us all. She meant well and she helped my brothers in their training. My mother still had the old idea of girls working out as cooks for different families. I worked out for a couple of years, and then I was in charge of the duties in my mother's house. The girls at that time weren't given too much attention. The family felt that the girl could marry some Swedish man who would be able to take care of her. This is the reason why the girl was only taught how to take care of the house. They had the feeling that she would be well taken care of when it came her time to get married. They still do this—the mothers and fathers now feel the same way. The difference is that the girls try to do something for themselves. There are many girls I know who are interested in office work, teaching, and other things. This is something new to the old Swedish parents. Years ago Swedish girls didn't know about these possibilities because she was never told and the family never discussed the possibilities of girls in the professions. The girls now get a lot of that from schools and they see it in movies, and they form their ideas in this way. In my day we either did housework or went to work in the factory. The young Swedish girls don't do that anymore. I know some who wouldn't take any job, except in business. Most of the young girls are now going to high school; I think almost every Swedish girl does the same, but the idea is still the same about Swedish girls marrying for security, and I don't blame them. These days you have to think ahead before you do anything.

The Swedish people are very close together. Everyone in the family tries to understand what the other does. They don't quarrel among each other, and you will never see them shouting or scolding. The parents have everything under control and when there is something that bothers the children, the family decides what to do best. The children usually confide their problems to the mother, and she takes things up with the father. The father has the last word about what is to be done. The father is not stern like some people of other groups, but he is so proud that he wants everybody to know that he is right in whatever he decides.

There is a difference between the old-type father and the parent who is born in this country. The real Swede still holds on to certain Swedish habits, while the American father will do things the American way. In the old days the father would have his children associate with the older people of his organization; you don't find much of this now. The young people go their way, and they very seldom attend the same affairs with the old crowd. In this way they are being separated from the rule of the parents, and they are mixing with people of other nationalities. They are beginning to marry people of all nationalities. You find that most of them strike good marriages, because they expect the husband to be a good provider.

There is another thing that they have to follow, according to the wishes of their family: if possible, they try to marry into the same religion. But there are many who disregard this and they marry Catholics. The older people don't like this, but at least they are open-minded enough to admit that the marriage is a good one if both get along alright, in spite of the differences of nationalities. I know I had the same thing happen in my family—my brother married a Catholic girl. At first my people didn't like the idea because they thought he would become a Catholic, but they realized later that she went to her church and he attended his, and there never was any discussion about this.

My husband was the same—he never let our differences in religion bother us. But that wasn't the trouble that separated us. His was drink, that was his weakness.

Most of the Swedes have the habit of going out to visit one another. Others prefer to associate with their society members. Most Swedish people belong to the lodges and societies and they attend them very often. They like to get together and talk everything there is to talk about. They are no "hotheads" like some people think. They think very hard before they come to any decision, and that's the reason why the Swedes never regret what they do. That's one thing you can give the old people credit for—they are always on their toes about anything and everything. If the young people could convince them about something, they are willing to listen and see if there is some good in it. But regardless of what it is, the parents always have the best answer.

No matter how little money the Swedes have, they are always thinking about providing something for their children's future. They don't actually give them money, but they feel they should provide for furthering their education. This is always the father's responsibility. The Swedish people feel proud when they could say that their child has entered into some kind of training, and some feel that it's a higher honor for them in having their son in a trade than in some profession. They really think it is better for their child to boast a trade. That's one thing I can't understand about them. I always thought that a profession was better than a trade.

When the Swedish men get together at the affairs, they are always talking shop. They talk about what they do and about what they have accomplished. The women talk about the things that all women discuss. When they visit in the house they will get together in card games—this is their favorite pastime. Most of the women either play cards with the men or they spend the time in quilting or crocheting different things. This is the kind of life they spend when they get together. They are always thinking of helping their friends; but even if a Swede needs help, he is too proud to say so. They only do it in extreme cases.

The Swedes like music and athletics. Some of the men join singing groups, others join athletic clubs. They like that very much. In fact, most Swedes feel it is a high honor for them should they join any one of these things. Almost all Swedish children take to studying some kind of musical instrument. Those that do pay a lot of attention to their studies, because they feel proud to demonstrate their abilities. I took up the study of the piano and I always liked it, and music was always appreciated in my people's home. Even now I hear some of the better music over the radio and I never miss the opera on Saturdays.

I like to read very much. My husband hated me for that; he used to think I was crazy—just because I had a love for reading books. I always like reading, and I used to explain to him that I wanted to gain more knowledge for myself, but he used to get mad about it and start to criticize me for it, saying that I was wasting my time. That's because he couldn't understand me, and he was a different type. He was rough, and he used to think that anyone having interests such as mine wasn't in their right mind. He felt that way since the first day we were married, and the only way he could express his resentment was to take it out on me by force and abuse. As I said before, I was never used to this treatment, and I took that sort of punishment for a number of years.

When things became unbearable I decided to put a stop to it. I couldn't tell my friends about my troubles because they wouldn't understand . . . and naturally, he gave them a different impression of what he was really like. Then it was also a question of pride. If nothing else, I always managed to keep my high ideas, and I never wanted to let on how I really felt. Before telling my friends about my intended separation I decided to discuss the matter with my people. They listened to what I had to say, and they were not surprised in the least. They said they had suspected the trouble right along, but they didn't want to say anything because they were afraid of hurting my feelings. They told me that the best thing for me to do would be to get a separation. I didn't want to air this in any court because I was afraid of such a thing, so the best thing I could do was to tell him to leave the house until such a time as he could see his mistakes. But he never got feeling that way, even after he left.

Almost all Norwegians act that way. They could live and enjoy themselves while there are good times to be had, but when they have to face something they lose their nerve. I have been told that he is just like many other Norwegian men. The women aren't so bad—at least they will admit their faults once in a while. The men are not as strong-willed. I tried to think of asking him back sometime, but I think I have lost all respect for him.[22]

A Place in Politics

For some women, their place was in politics. This certainly seemed to be the case for Ernie Demao's mother. Demao, born of Italian immigrant parents, himself became active in radical politics. His mother's influence is apparent. He told of his early contact with the suffrage movement.

They [the suffragists] used to parade down Main Street in Hartford. My mother would drag me along. Anyway, getting back to wearing these buttons at school . . . the young Catholic priest would tell the kids to pull that button off my shirt or jacket. . . . It seems, looking back now, I knew they were against the buttons, but I didn't realize that what they were really against was women voting. They were as adamant on that question then as they are on the question of abortion today—very backward.

Anyway, I would come home and my mother would say, "Ernest, where's your button?" "Aw, Ma, the kids took it." She'd put another button on me and say, "Ernest, you fight for that button." "Okay, Mom." I'd come home day after day, bloody nose, split lip, scratched face, dead black eye. It didn't bother her one bit. She'd wipe off my face, put another button on. She said, "There's plenty of buttons where that came from." And I'd say, "Aw, Ma, don't we suffer enough without having to fight for it?" I didn't know what the hell suffrage was at the time. So, you see, I come from the kind of working-class background [that has an] interest in social emancipation without being too clear as to what the hell it was about.[23]

More interested in the social culture of political activity and less in ideology, Mrs. W., of Bridgeport's Park Avenue, told a WPA interviewer:

I did have some fun a while ago. I entered politics as it were. That is, I was made chairlady of the Republican district over here. It is funny—I have always been a Democrat and always worked for the party, but something came up in the party that I did not like. That is, they did some talking I did not like so I just did not go to any more meetings and fell out of the activities of that club. I started to attend some of the card parties of the Republican Club and became very friendly with them and the first thing I knew I was very active in the party. I was elected chairlady of this district and worked very hard for the party, but the same thing happened there as in the other club so I just made up my mind that I would not have anything to do with any of them. I just could not get along with them, and those friends who claim to be friends are not so, and it took a few club meetings to find that out. I just washed my hands of the whole thing and so now I do not have anything to do with any of them. What I do is just sort of enjoy life. I go a lot with Mr. W. and we visit our friends and manage to have a good time.[24]

Eva Hudak, the daughter of Polish immigrant parents, married a Slovak, was a union activist, and became involved in politics. She recognized that "speaking up" was important, but she was not enthusiastic about the relatively new women's organizations that were developing when she spoke to an interviewer in 1975; she was 58 years old.

When I got active in the union I was with everyone. I think that . . . because I wanted to better my standard of living and [that of] other people like myself, I was willing to stand out there and be counted. Because I stood out, others stood behind me. They wouldn't stand out there in front, but they stood there behind me. Now don't ask me where I got that courage, because I often wonder myself: how did you ever do it? But today I'm a bail commissioner in the Court of Common Pleas. I love my job. I had to battle, number one, because this was a new job. The police had always set the bail before. If people didn't make the bail they stayed in jail. The police resented this; the prosecuters didn't like it. And number two, I was a woman. I was the only at first. Now there are two of us, out of 28 bail commissioners throughout the state. I think that I have helped women in this way.

You know, these women libbers give me a royal pain all right, especially this NOW organization. I went to their first meeting, and I wanted to see just what was involved. They handed out their so-called policies. One of them had to with bettering working conditions. I said, "Look, where you better the working conditions is in the places you work, and that's where you start getting into the organizations." You join the union; you get active in it. You don't do it from an organization like this; you get in there to do it. This makes me laugh when they say they are doing something. They are not doing anything.

When you think back 30 years ago, I was the president of a great big union here in town. I was a woman, and I was accepted, not because I was a woman but because I was doing the job. I think that in any place where a woman is doing the job she will be accepted unless you run into some real male chauvinist, and there you do have to sit on them. In other words, you have to speak up and let them know. Just like men. Men are very timid sometimes, and they will take a lot; in fact, they say men take a lot from their wives. But the thing is that those who speak up naturally, like they say, the squeaky wheel gets the grease.[25]

As women's roles shifted during the half century since the WPA interviews were made, it became clear that the hands that rocked the cradle, ladled the soup, or comforted others indeed could dominate the family, operate the business, or make the wheel squeak.

6

IMMIGRANTS UNITED AND DIVIDED

While the immigrant experience might have served as a unifying force for the millions of individuals who came to America's shores from Europe, such was not always the case. They brought with them the historical antagonisms of the old country, and they also found that the earlier settlers of the new frequently did not welcome those who followed. In fact, from colonial times on, newcomers did not find ready acceptance in the United States. Nativism (the policy of favoring native inhabitants over immigrants), xenophobia (the fear and hatred of foreigners or of anything that is strange or foreign), and racism (the belief that race is the primary determinant of human traits and capacities and that racial differences produce an inherent superiority of a particular race) characterized much of American society.[1]

As early as 1637, the Massachusetts Bay colony limited strangers to no more than three weeks within its territory unless special permission was obtained. Pennsylvania levied a duty on "foreigners and Irish servants." Germans, a large minority in Pennsylvania by the mid-eighteenth century, fared badly among the colony's non-Germans. The historian Roger Daniels has suggested that Benjamin Franklin was a "founding father of non-religious American nativism." The alter ego of Poor Richard disliked Germans because they bloc-voted against his interests. He only half facetiously advised his followers to learn the German language so they wouldn't be strangers in their own land. Franklin feared that Pennsylvania would become "a Colony of Aliens."

Other examples of nativism abounded during the next two centuries. Sometimes it coalesced around organizations such as the American, or "Know Nothing," Party during the 1850s or the American Protective Association in the 1880s, which was anti-Catholic as well as anti-immigrant. German-Americans became the objects of official and less formal repression during World War I; Italian-and Japanese-Americans were interned during World War II. During the interwar years, Father Charles E. Coughlin led a conservative religious and political movement that was vehemently anti-Semitic. Closer to our own time, immigrants from Asian and Latin nations have felt the sharp pains of prejudice.[2]

America and Americans, then, did not always welcome immigrants. In 1921, with the passage of the Emergency Quota Act, and in 1924, when the National Origins Act became law, the United States severely restricted immigration and tipped entry to the favor of northern and western Europeans and to the disadvantage of those from southern and eastern Europe. Non-Europeans were almost totally excluded. Changes in the nation's immigration laws in 1965, 1986, and 1990 shifted the balance, so that by 1991 there were twice as many Asians as in 1980 and 53 percent more Hispanics. Predictions for the year 2010 assert that the U.S. population will include 35 million foreign-born, the most ever. It is expected that they will come from Mexico, the Philippines, Vietnam, Korea, India, China, the Dominican Republic, Jamaica, El Salvador, Colombia, Iran, Laos, and Taiwan, as well as eastern Europe, Ireland, and Great Britain. Perhaps it was with this in mind that a New Yorker *magazine cartoon showed the Statue of Liberty speaking into a cellular phone, saying, "Well, it all depends. Where are these huddled masses coming from?"[3]*

Nativism has flourished in times of great tension, such as wars and economic depressions. Whether new calls for restrictions on immigration will be successful is uncertain, but given the history of the country it is certainly possible. Regardless, it is probable that internal tensions will continue. While it may not be as dismal as depicted by one immigrant, who told the WPA that "here in this country one nationality hates the other nationality," the sentiments of another seem appropriate: "Someday maybe we'll all say: 'What are we fighting about? We're all Americans.' But I don't think that day has come or will come in a long time."

This chapter begins with the immigrants' experiences in school—some kind, and some jarring. It explores the tensions resulting from intermarriage and from differences within ethnic groups. It reveals both "native" Yankee prejudices and the hostility between different immigrant nationalities.

Because so many of the interviews were conducted during the Depression and on the eve of World War II, they offer a snapshot of the isolationism and anti-European feelings common before the war, as well as the intense anti-Semitism evident on the eve of the Holocaust. Promoted by Father Coughlin, as well as other demagogues such as William Dudley Pelley and Gerald B. Winrod, this anti-Semitism affected America's willingness to accept Jewish war refugees. As suggested by the historian David S. Wyman, "the plain truth is that many Americans were prejudiced against Jews and were unlikely to support measures to help them." The interviews included here attest to the virulence of this prejudice, which cut across all classes within American society and reached into the highest levels of government.[4]

The final segment of the chapter is devoted to racism, the belief in white superiority and black inferiority, and to its many negative manifestations. Our interviews tell about housing and business practices that hurt African-Americans. They reflect on white flight and black existence. They reveal the patronizing racism of some, like the Irish saloonkeeper who would "rather trust

*a nigger any day than a Polack." In sum, the narrators discuss what Studs
Terkel has labeled "the American obsession." This country has dealt with that
"obsession," not always effectively, for four centuries, just as it has wrestled with
the "tired . . . poor . . . huddled masses yearning to breathe free." Freedom and
acceptance have not come easily.[5]*

*Throughout the history of the United States, forces of both unity and division
have affected the treatment and acceptance of immigrants to this nation. Economic conditions, the world situation, the background of the immigrants coming
to these shores, the role of demagogues and less significant (but equally opportunis-
tic) politicians, all have shaped the limits of tolerance, nativism, and racism.*

*Ethnic cleavages divided immigrants and were often played upon by employers,
who used such divisions to weaken working-class consciousness. Neighborhoods
owed their character to cultural traits, and groups separated from each other in
a ceaseless pattern of running away that formed America's cities and suburbs.*

*On the other hand, the experience of a Polish-Jewish immigrant, who escaped
the Holocaust in 1938 revealed that the forces of unity could be warm and
welcoming, despite the government's policy, influenced by anti-Semitism, which
did not welcome refugees. Louis Gerson, who went on to become a prominent
political scientist, described his first Christmas in America, and also recounted
how even a newcomer could share pride in the nation's forefathers.*

I stayed in Waterbury for a while, then came back to New York and enrolled
in De Witt Clinton High School, which is an all-boys school in New York. It
was, in my opinion, an excellent high school—excellent teachers. The principal was a man named Clark; I still remember his name. My important and
profound memories of my experiences that happened in high school relate to
the way I was accepted by the students as well as the teachers.

At that time my English was quite poor. . . . It came fast and about a few
months after, I enrolled in an English class taught by Miss Damon, Katherine
Damon, English Class 5A. She asked me—this was near Christmastime—
Miss Damon asked me, told me, that the principal of the high school wanted
to see me. I went to the principal's office. His secretary told me to wait. She
told me the principal was busy with someone else at that time, but about 5
or 10 minutes later she told me that the principal couldn't see me—I should
go back to my class. Well, when I went back to my class I realized the whole
thing was just a put-on job because when I entered my class everybody was
standing up. Around my desk were all kinds of gifts, and they wished me
happy Christmas. It was my first Christmas in the United States. Well, to me
that was a very important event in many ways. One because I could not help
contrasting the American Christmas to the Polish Christmas, because here

they were telling me that Christmas was really a secular event. It's everybody's Christmas. Not just one group, say a Christian's Christmas. But the way it was done . . . and the things they said made me feel welcome. Well, I should say made me feel very secure, and they welcomed me with such open arms. . . .

Once, I recall, during the class of American History when suddenly I said something to the fact about our forefathers, who fought in the American Revolution, and I stopped there. I asked myself . . . how could I say "our forefathers" of the American Revolution? Here I was saying it with a very heavy Polish accent. I just arrived from Poland and I'm identifying myself with the forefathers of America, but I looked around and nobody looked bothered by it and accepted it quite naturally. Then, of course, I learned a very important lesson about America. That is, that one can easily identify oneself with America's past and that the essence of America is the acceptance of the people, and people could become part of America's past as well as of the present, as well as of the future.[6]

The school experience had a lasting impact upon an immigrant child's self-confidence. Adeline Capucci, who came with her parents from Italy around the time of World War I, related the difference the attitude of a particular teacher made in her life.

I'm very nostalgic about [the school]. It brings tears to my eyes when I go by there and I see the school is gone. . . . When I was brought back from Italy, I couldn't speak much English, 'cause I was taught all in Italian. . . . And I didn't do too well in the fourth grade because the teacher used to say to me, "Sit down. You're so stupid." And I understand "stupid" because in Italian it's *stupido*, you know. And so I was very self-conscious and inhibited about it, and I did so well in Italian, and I thought to myself, well, I've got to do something about it. And I tried very hard to learn all I could, and finally, when I went into the fifth grade, there I found an angel. And I knew my work.

But I wouldn't put up my hand. She'd say, "Who knows the question? The answer to this question?" She kept me after school one day. She said, "I understand you very well. I've watched you. You have a lot of pride." I said, "What's pride?" She said, "You're embarrassed." I said, "I don't know what embarrassed means." She said, "You will not stand up because you don't speak very well in English." I said, "That's right." She said, "Don't do that. Stand up when you know something. I'll understand you."

She was my guiding angel. And with her—we worked together—and I

178

learned my English. Then I went to the sixth grade, and the teacher sent me downstairs with a note. And I thought I did something wrong. I wasn't arguing with her. She was a lovely teacher, and she never insulted the Italians or anything. She sent me down. This note stated that I was qualified to skip to the seventh grade. She thought I was ahead of the others.

Well, I advance myself because I had determination. And then I asked my mother, and she said, "Well, you can go if you get up at 6:00 and do all the work you're supposed to do," 'cause we had school at 8:00. And it was only half days. So I did the seventh grade beautifully. And this is how I graduated at 13 from the eighth grade. And then I got more aggressive and self-confident about it. But today I wish I had an accent.[7]

Not everyone, however, had as good an experience when beginning school. A Scottish immigrant told about his first days in class.

We, that is my brother, sister, and I, started to a public school that was only a few blocks from our home. They had some difficulty placing us, but I was finally put in the fourth grade. The first days of school, there was so much confusion among the children and teachers that I was completely overlooked, and I was certainly glad of the chance just to stand by and try and get my bearings. Unfortunately for me, when things began to settle down a bit and the regular school routine started, I got plenty of attention from my fellow students. My clothes probably were not bought from the same stores they had gotten theirs from, and I could see very little difference between my clothes and theirs, but everyone acted as if I had come to school dressed in kilts. And my speech left everyone within hearing distance openmouthed at first and then sent them into gales of laughter. So I closed my mouth firmly and opened it when I had to and then to say what I had to say in just as few words as possible.

After, I became used to the ways of schools in this country. I found the work very easy and I was a very bright pupil. I never could bring myself to the point of raising my hand and volunteering to answer as the other boys and girls did. I could write an answer but just could not stand up in front of the teacher and class and give it orally.[8]

The mother of a third-generation Italian-American had less choice when it came to participation in the classroom.

[Their parents] always spoke Italian in the home, to my parents—both sides, maternal and paternal. My mother did not know how to speak English until she went to grammar school at St. Patrick's. The Irish nuns, or Sister of Mercy, forced her to learn English. They said to her, "Now look here, you speak English, you don't speak Italian, or we will crack you one on the face." So my mother, that's how she learned English, from the schools, from the nuns, because they forced her. Otherwise at home it was always Italian.[9]

Knowledge of English played a crucial role in shaping the perception immigrants had of themselves fitting into the fabric of American society. A Swedish immigrant who came to the U.S. during the 1920s told how his mother only recently arrived in America, viewed the children of other immigrants as "foreigners." While emphasizing the importance of the English language, she maintained her Swedish lifestyle.

Frankly, when we did come over, my parents knowing English, the first order they gave us was that from here Swedish was out, English is in, in our household. So that's all we got from my parents, English—not Swedish, but English. You learn it the hard way. . . . [But my parents] maintained the Swedish way of life.

Oh, there's one thing. When we lived in the apartment over in Portland, I would say it was about the third day we'd been there, my brother and I had to go out, of course, and play with the children in the neighborhood. Now I don't remember anybody telling us that they were Italian or Polish or Irish or anything. We didn't know the difference. They're all kids to us, you know. We were rushing through dinner to get out and play. And I can see Mother standing on the rear door landing, shouting down at us, "Now watch out for those foreigners." Isn't that something? . . . That's what they were to her, foreigners. The fact that we'd only been there three days didn't enter into it.[10]

Alexander Karlonas, son of a Lithuanian father and a Polish mother, spoke English but felt a strong Lithuanian identity—and suffered for it at the hands of his Irish and Polish neighbors.

The only time we spoke English in the house was between us children. When I started school I didn't have any trouble with the language. Contacts outside the house when I was playing with other children enabled me to speak the language as well as Lithuanian.

My playmates before and for quite a long while after I went to school were Polish. There were some Irish in the neighborhood, but they played together most of the time. We used to fight with them for calling us names like "Hunkies" and "Polacks." I didn't get along very well with the Polish children either, because they were always adopting a superior attitude toward me, saying that I was a half-breed and in a lower class than they were.

I remember that after a rainstorm we used to build dams in the gutters, and they always broke mine and chased me away from theirs. If I sailed a stick of wood down the gutter, they always picked it up and threw it away on me. I hated them and I hated the Irish kids worse and used to join the Poles in fighting them.

When I was old enough, I went to St. Mary's parochial school. The classes were made up mostly of Irish, Polish, and Italians. The nuns favored the Irish children because they gave them the best marks and the prizes at the end of the year. They gave them the honorary jobs of passing out paper and writing on the blackboard. When Irish kids were late they were seldom punished, but when any of the rest of us were late for school the nuns used to whip us. . . .

I always felt that I belonged to the Lithuanian group. My mother always spoke to us in Lithuanian and we went to the Lithuanian church. Another thing was the attitude of the Polish children toward me. They always treated me different, so I began to feel that way. I have always wanted to go to the old country and visit the places that my father and mother told us about. I know I wouldn't want to live there.[11]

Maxwell Lear, a Russian Jew who emigrated to the United States with his parents in 1900 at the age of 19, described how his children were treated in school in New Haven. At the time of the interview in 1974, Lear, a medical doctor, was 93 years old.

We never discriminated against anyone. People came to our home—everybody. Larry Kelley, Yale's famous football player, frequently came to our house. He wanted to marry one of our daughters. Eddie Collins, Jr., whose father was Eddie Collins with the Boston Red Sox, he used to come here. All the kids congregated here, even when my girls weren't at home, because I always cultivated young people. . . .

Now the way I've lived, I feel I don't have an enemy in the world. I don't dislike a soul. But I've told you about my children. Pearl, my eldest daughter, came home one day from school and said, "Mother, Mother, the MacDonald girl called another girl 'a dirty Jew.'" And she asked, "Mother, what's a dirty Jew?" So Mother was stunned, and Pearl said, "And you know, Mother, that little girl that she called a dirty Jew is an awfully nice little girl. She's clean. She wears beautiful things, and she speaks very well, and she's a nice friend of mine. Why did she call her a dirty Jew?"

My second daughter came home from Edgewood School one day, and she was a fat little girl, and she said, "Mother . . . Jimmy Gilbert called me a big fat Jew." And Mother said, "Well, what did you say to him?" She said, "Called him a big fat Protestant." You see how the child's mind works, directly and honestly. . . . To her it is as much a crime to be a big fat Protestant as to be a big fat Jew. And my youngest daughter had a similar experience.

So the times are different. The temper of the time is different. Now it's easier and happier living because we are all in the same boat. We are all in the same trouble. We are all in the same difficulty, and we've got to help each other, at all times.[12]

In agreement with Dr. Lear's final sentiment, many shared the view of Mr. M., an Irish immigrant living in Bridgeport who had been in the United States for a quarter century. He contended that an individual had to be judged upon his or her own merits.

Our friends comprise people of all nationalities. Our downstairs neighbors are a young couple. The wife is Jewish, daughter of German Jews. Her husband is Italian. They are friendly with us. . . . I dislike no nationality. I think there is good and bad in all kinds. I think the individual alone is accountable, not the nationality.[13]

Another Irish immigrant expressed a similar point of view. Born in a small town outside of Tipperary in 1885, Edmond J. G. told an interviewer in 1939 how he became an apprentice in a dry-goods store in Tipperary. He stayed with that job for three years and then thought he would come to the United States to get some ideas that would help in business. He came to Bridgeport because he had relatives there and got a job at Howland's Department Store, where he became a buyer for seven departments, doing a great deal of business in New York City.

I was the first Catholic to become a shareholder when an old employee resigned and I took over his stock. There were about 40 percent of the employees who were Irish Catholic and the rest were Yankee. I always got along fine with all of them, and in New York I liked the Jews and Germans I did business with. The Jews are a fine people and many of my friends are Jews. There is good and bad in every race, and I don't see why the Jews should be so maligned. There are rotten Irish who make the Jews look like angels. I get along fine with every race. And I've met them all in Howland's. . . . The Germans are a fine race. That Hitler is doing them a great deal of harm and it'll take 50 years to erase the scars of intolerance. The poor people, I feel so sorry for them.[14]

For many immigrants, living in mixed neighborhoods was common, as totally homogeneous areas were the exception. Emma Reale, a 45-year-old second-generation Italian-American housewife interviewed in 1939, described her neighborhood in Bridgeport.

When we lived on South Main Street, there were very few Italian families in the vicinity. In fact we often called our neighborhood the League of Nations, for there was a German, Irish, French, and Italian family all within a short distance of each other. The German family lived across the way from us. From them we learned German expressions. There was one expression I remember so clearly: When the children wanted to come across the street to our house, they would say in German, "We are going across the street." The expression *über die Strasse* means across the way, and I still remember it. We used to say, "Mother, we are going *über die Strasse*." There were many sayings that we said at the time, but I have since forgotten them. We also learned to eat molasses and bread and tomato jelly from that German family.

At the French home, dances were held and we were allowed to attend. I remember one boy in that family who could not speak English to any great extent. One type of food that they ate, and which we children did not like, were acorns. They ate them with relish, but we children couldn't swallow them.

Then there was the Irish family close by. They had two or three children our age and we used to play with them most of the time.[15]

As a consequence of such group proximity and ethnic mixing, intermarriage was not uncommon, although it was more usual to marry within one's group. Strong feelings prevailed on both sides of the marriage issue. Mrs. G., who had come to the United States 32 years earlier from Roscommon County, Ireland, and subsequently resided in Bridgeport's North End, explained to a WPA interviewer:

My children live on a street where their playmates are German, Jewish, Swedish, et cetera. They play with children of all nationalities. In fact the tenant in my house is Swedish. I hope if they marry they will never marry secretly, without the consent of both sets of parents. But I suppose if they did we would have to forget and forgive. After all, they are our own flesh and blood.[16]

"People Like That Make me Sick"

Harold H., a Yankee from the Connecticut town of Thomaston, concurred, although his remarks about mongrelization, made in an attempt to support intermarriage, reflect some of the less positive aspects of racial thinking during his era. Moreover, his concerns about religion reveal the salience of that factor when considering its impact upon ethnic unity and division.

Intermarriage? You mean like a Yankee and a Lithuanian? Sure, why not? You see cases around here, don't you? They all seem to get along all right. What's the difference? It's good for both of them and good for their kids. Nothing any dumber, or harder to raise, than a thoroughbred dog. Give me a mongrel for brains and health every time. Same principle, isn't it? Seems reasonable to suppose that racial stocks peter out, like old families. New blood does 'em good. The only thing that makes trouble is the religious angle. I've seen that lots of times. A Protestant boy will marry a Catholic girl, or vice versa, and at the time they'll promise anything, but maybe six, seven years later, when there's a couple of kids and the question comes up what church to send 'em to, there's hell to pay.

That's one of the things about religion that always puzzled me. Why do so many people use it just as a means to start an argument? I mean, a man may go along for years not going to church at all, but the minute some religious question comes up, he remembers he's a Protestant, or a Catholic, and starts to slam the devil out of the other side. That's not Christianity.

No, I haven't any dislikes, if you mean do I hate the Polacks, or the Germans, or the Jews. I don't dislike any race of people. I try to be broad-minded. There's good and bad in all races, and anybody that says all members of a certain race are all bad is just ignorant. I know plenty of Yankees that you can't trust any farther'n you can see 'em, but just because they happen to be descendants of the old settlers they think they're better than average. People like that make me sick. I mean it, they make me sick.[17]

Others didn't share Harold H.'s acceptance of intermarriage. Mrs. O. a prosperous 59-year-old Irish-born widow of a tavernkeeper in Bridgeport, stressed her disapproval of marrying outside one's religion.

I firmly disapprove of Irish marrying people of other nationalities, and above all of other religions. The Irish are intellectual, thrifty, witty, and usually fair of looks. So why not marry and make a better race? I believe those of the same nationality understand each other's problems better. We'll be far happier by doing so.[18]

Sean Ginty, also a resident of Bridgeport, pointed out that even if a spouse of another ethnic background was a good mate, he or she wouldn't fit in when family and friends gathered together.

I don't believe in mixed marriages. My cousin in New York married a Hungarian. Poor fellow, when he gets with a bunch of Irish men he sure seems to be a misfit. My cousin is very happy with him. He is a good provider and treats her swell.[19]

An Irish foreman at Bridgeport Brass raised the issue of family reaction when two people of varied backgrounds married.

I do not believe in mixed marriage. If I could not find one of my own nationality and religion, I would stay single. You might as an individual get along with the girl, but in the family background a hitch arises. For instance, were I to marry a Jewess, what consolation would there be if her family disowned her? She sure would be a misfit with the Irish.[20]

Less abstract is the plight of 75-year-old Mrs. Murphy, who came to the U.S. when she was 18, and her daughter, Mrs. Benedetto. Mrs. Murphy complained:

My daughters are both married to Italian fellows. This fact I am sorry to admit. One daughter makes her home with me. Her husband doesn't seem able to make a decent home for her. She has not enjoyed good health since she lost twin boys a year ago, when both died at birth. Her husband is the meanest and most hateful man I ever knew. He is a very vile talker. But this is not uncommon in this class of Italian. He even calls an old lady like me vile names. My daughter has no kind of existence with him.

She then noted that her other daughter also married an Italian. She lived next door and was called in. The daughter, Mrs. Benedetto, told her story:

I was married 27 years ago. God forgive I ever got tangled up with a Wop. They are a bunch of peculiar people. [She goes on to tell how her husband was forced out of the gas business. He had to go into other work and is doing relatively well. She has seven children and wanted to get the oldest boy, 24, onto WPA.] I bet if I was a Wop like my husband, my son would be a water boy, at least, on WPA. The women who are Italian have nerve. They make believe they don't understand the language. I think the Irish get tough breaks. A Jew gets a little schooling, then thinks he is a wonder. You don't see them killing themselves. They bluff that learning and get soft jobs. I bet if we get into war, they will be scared if they have to go.

186

Mrs. Murphy then intervened.

It is a sad fate that befell my children. If they only married in their own nationality, I am sure there would be more understanding. But no, they would have these men.

I think it is a curse. I hope their children, in spite of the fact their father is a Wop, don't marry one. My daughter calls herself "Bennett," but I would say she ought to be ashamed before she married him, not now. I know this neighborhood where we live had all kinds of nationalities. This is how they met. I think one should move to better localities if they can afford to. Your children meet people of higher type. If one thinks there is happiness in this mixture, they are very wrong. I am a very old lady, and to think I see such unhappiness![21]

I Have Come to Like Italian Dishes ..."

After initial discontent, some families got used to intermarriage. John Burns, a young second-generation Irish-American, had been married for two years when he was interviewed.

My mother did object to my marriage—to an Italian for one thing, and also because I had been hurt. She thought it would be much better to wait and see if any complications set in as the years passed from my unfortunate accident. I will say that I don't like my mother-in-law, but I didn't marry her mother anyhow. I have come to like Italian dishes, but I also like meals cooked like my mother made them. I don't like garlic of any kind and I won't stand for any of those can and cold meat two-minute suppers, especially after coming home from a hard day's work. We both are Catholics, now go to St. Augustine's Church. Her whole family are converts to the Catholic religion. My mother and my brothers have got used to the idea that it is not a crime to marry anyone but a person of Irish ancestry and are frequent callers.[22]

Different tastes in food, as John Burns pointed out, could be overcome. An Italian housewife suggested, however, that even when that happened, regional differences fragmented her own group.

Some of the other nationality people, they cook more macaroni and greens like the Italians make. And some of the Italian people, they have the cooking like other nationalities. Why is this thing—well, because the people they are being like one now.

[However], in Italy all the people from one place they all do the same things, and if you see one Italian from one place it's just like you see all of them. That's why you see the difference from the Sicilian, the Abruzzese, the Romani, and all the rest of the people. When I come to this country all the people from one place were staying together and the other ones they lived in different places. I went to the East Side because the people from my place were living there.[23]

Regionalism among Italians was further elaborated upon by Mr. Paumi, who had come to the United States in 1910 from Messina, Sicily, and had worked at Bridgeport's Remington Arms plant for almost three decades.

All the Italian people that come to this country, they all went on the East Side or in the North End. The Sicilian people like myself, we all used to live like together on the East Main Street section of the East Side. That time these Sicilians, they were not liked too much by the Castelfranco, the Calabrese, and North Italian people because they think they were better people and they said that the Sicilian people they were bad because they used to kill a lot of people in Italy. That's why the Sicilian people, they live like all alone in one group on East Main Street and Howe Street. . . . Out of all the people the Sicilians they still have the habits like the mother and father. All the other Italian people . . . are not the same like we are.[24]

The Irish were sandwiched between their immigrant successors and those who preceded them. The sometimes hated, sometimes envied Yankees did not put out the welcome mat, and stories of "Irish Need Not Apply" are legion throughout New England. Like so many others escaping the potato famine, Mrs. Schread's grandfather emigrated to the United States during the 1850s. The 60-year-old widow explained about her family's relations with Yankees.

Bull's Head [a neighborhood] was filled with Irish families, who always seemed to gather together. The Yankees had nothing to do with them, and

I still think they resent us. When we children were growing up, Father bought a house on Lumber Street, a Yankee district. We saw very little of the Yankees when I was a child, and at school were pointed out as "Irish Paddies." All my parents' friends and mine were Irish, as they still are.

We had a happy life on Lumber Street. There was my brother and two sisters and my parents, and relatives from everywhere came to visit us. We used to sing and dance to all the old Irish songs and ballads and dance the Irish jig. We were always taught to be proud of being Irish and Catholic, and we knew all the history and legends of Ireland and followed the happenings in Ireland, as we did the local news. I often think that some of the Irish people who pretend not to be Irish and look down on their own kind are really ashamed of their background and ignorant of their heritage. [All of Mrs. Schread's brothers and sisters had become Protestant.]

The daughter of an old Irish family which was well-to-do and respected for many years, as they still are, scorns all the Irish though she went to an Irish preparatory school and married an Irishman. She is society editor on one of the newspapers and tried not to print notices about Irish . . . Catholic organizations, saying that weddings don't leave enough space. . . .

[Mrs. Schread goes on to tell how when married she moved to Washington and Park Avenues in Bridgeport, there were only Yankees nearby, no Irish.]

It was two years before our neighbors spoke to us, but when we had a big fire, our snootiest neighbors offered us rooms for the night. I enjoyed telling her we had several friends who would look after us.

We had a farm in Stepney for the summer when the children were small. There were no Irish families there then, and we saw only the Yankees, except on Sundays when our friends would come visiting. The Yankees were nice to us in that neighborhood, but they were never intimate with us. We used to visit back and forth, but they talked about us as if we were Negroes or Jews and the children overheard things that were unkind or prejudiced. I think they were polite to us because of my husband's business, but even the Hawleys, for whom he worked for so many years, always tried to keep him feeling inferior to them. Now, in that neighborhood there is a Catholic priest who has nearly eliminated the old prejudice. The Irish Catholics built him a nice church and community house where all the denominations like to hold their entertainments. They have clubs and teams of all kinds, and the children in Stepney and Long Hill would rather go to St. Theresa's than anywhere else.[25]

"Stick to Your Own Kind"

While Mrs. Schread may have resented being talked about "as if we were Negroes or Jews," the Irish, who had suffered the pangs of prejudice, often indulged in equal bouts of discrimination. The testimony of a Bridgeport appliance store owner offered an extreme example of such prejudice.

I've got an Irish partner and I sure am glad about that. I wouldn't trust an Italian as far as I could see, and I'd shoot myself before I linked up with a Jew. I have no use for those Slavic people, and niggers are only good for laborers. . . .

I don't like all these marriages with foreigners. I think the races should be kept separate. My sister married a Scotsman and that's bad enough, but if she ever married one of those southern Europeans, the family would disown her. My brother in New Haven—he's in the telephone company, an engineer—married an Irish girl, and my best girl is Irish. That's the way it should be. Stick to your own kind. . . . This mixing races is very unwise, I think. I'm an American and I think we should keep the foreigners out, except of course the educated and professional refugees.[26]

"Sticking to your own kind" frequently had roots in the Old Country. A Ukrainian-American, James Osochowsky, remarked upon the antagonisms transplanted from Europe to the ethnic neighborhoods of America's cities such as New Haven, where he lived.

Poles we did not like much at first because Poles had been our landlords. Italians we did not like because they fought against Austria. Russians we didn't like because they, too, fought Austria, and because our people didn't have liberty in Russia, although Ukrainians who came from the Russian Ukraine got along with Russians pretty well. We liked Austria better than Russia because Austria gave us more liberty, and during the war we liked Germans because we thought it was helping Austria and would help us.[27]

Frank Kovalauskas, a Lithuanian-American from New Britain, Connecticut, elaborated upon the ethnic tension not among the eastern and central

190

Europeans but between the eastern Europeans and the Irish. He had emigrated to the U.S. in 1902 at age 13, his father, a coal miner, having preceded him a few years earlier.

About 1905 I decided to go to Philadelphia and find different work for myself. By that time I could speak English a little and could understand it. My first job was dishwashing in a restaurant. Afterwards I worked as a short-order cook and counterman. Then I went to work in the kitchen of a big hotel. I worked there for about a year and was well satisfied with my work and my employer was satisfied with me. On this job was the first time that being a Lithuanian worked against me. The second chef's job was open in our kitchen and I tried to get it. The boss told me I was a good worker and he liked me but he couldn't give me the job because I was neither French or German. Those were the only kind of people he would have for the chefs in the kitchen.

A short time later my father bought a grocery store in New Philadelphia and asked me to come home and help him run it. I went back and went to work with him. Our business went fairly well. There were many Lithuanian families in the town and they traded with us; so did some of the Germans. The Irish would not come into the store. This was because they had been enemies of the Lithuanians and Poles . . . ever since they started coming in from the old country.

I remember when I was a boy and first came here, they used to throw stones at me when I walked in the street. Every time I went down to the store for my mother, I had a fight with them. The men that worked in the mines had trouble too. The Irish "Molly Maguires" would start fights with them when they were going to and from work. Some people were killed.

One time I remember in Shenandoah, the Lithuanians and Poles formed an army and went out to fight the "Molly Maguires." They beat up the Irish that time and didn't have much trouble with them later.

My father told me about one time when work was slack, he went to New Philadelphia with a friend of his to look for work there. They went into a saloon and asked the owner where they could find a place to live; he was Irish. When he heard them try to talk English, he started to yell, "Get out of here, you Hunkies. We don't want any of you in this town," and he chased them out without waiting for [them to] pay for the drinks they had.[28]

The anti-Catholicism of some New England Yankees left an indelible mark on the father of a Polish priest, and more emphatically on the priest himself.

Polish immigrants like my parents and others benefited tremendously by the existence of the parish. My father used to tell us, back in the days before we had electric lights, back there before World War I, no radio and no TV and that sort of thing. So these long winter nights, after we got through with our homework, he told all kinds of stories about life back there in Poland. The villages. But he also told us about his having arrived in South Hadley Falls, and the first Sunday—he was a stranger in a strange country—the only real time he had with anything in the area was the church. There was a church. There was a church bell ringing. It was Mass there. So he was on his way to Mass, and he had to pass through a barrage of stones tossed by the local hoodlums who resented the presence of these Hunkies, these Poles. . . . They were the local Yankees. He never went into that area. I don't think he could even identify them there. So we said, "Well, what happened?" Well, he looked at us kids and he said, "If you go to church now, if you've got the faith now, it's because I had to make a decision. I had to sit down after that barrage of stones and decide whether it was worth my while to be going to church and whether church was that important in my life. And I made my decision and you better keep to it." You know, that sort of thing. It was kind of interesting to us. The parish played a tremendous role, a great influence in our family, and I think that could be repeated by some of the other Polish immigrant families that came here.[29]

During the Great Depression, resentment shot out in many directions. An unemployed Polish-American laborer rooted his problems in the control of jobs by the Irish.

The people here got plenty to worry about, why the hell do they have to send money to the other side for? You know, I was talking about politicians before. I think that if all these groups like the Polacks, the Italians, and Slovaks got together, they would be able to get rid of the lousy Irish politicians. They're responsible for a good part of our bad time—they're always hogging all the jobs. Any boss that you see on any job is always a Harp. Goddam it, any job that you see, they're always in it or they have their foot in it. Around election time you see the Harps in all the clubs and they treat the [people] like a million dollars. Then after election they don't give a damn about [any] of the people, or the promises they made. Well someday, and it won't be long now, the Harps'll find themselves out on their can. The other people [Polish, Italians, Slovaks, etc.] are wise to the whole thing, and they're [sick] of holding the dirty end of the stick.[30]

"I Will Not Buy ... From a Jew"

The antipathy toward southern and eastern European immigrants, particularly Jews, grew during the Depression. The breakdown of the economy made immigrants especially vulnerable as scapegoats for the ills of the nation. Demagogues such as the famed radio priest Father Charles E. Coughlin blended anti-Semitism with simplistic economic nostrums and sympathy for fascist regimes. By 1930 Coughlin's "Golden Hour of the Little Flower" was attracting as many as 40 million listeners, and his following, if somewhat diminished, continued through the decade. Among them was Martin Brown, an Irish-American who was interviewed in Bridgeport in 1939, when Europe stood on the brink of the Holocaust.

I listen to [Father Coughlin] every chance I get. Occasionally I have sent a few dollars to help him carry on his good work. I think he is the only man who has the courage to tell about some of the things that the big man [FDR] has done. No one else would have the guts to talk about the things he does. If he was not telling the truth, he would not be on the air this long and perhaps he would have been behind bars by now. I buy his magazine *Social Justice* frequently and usually read most of its contents. I was active in the Union Party here. The only trouble I find with most of the followers of Father Coughlin is that they did not back him when they had a chance.

I think he is right in regard to the Jews—they are a bunch of bad eggs. They exploit everything without leaving anything for anyone else. There are, I suppose, some good Jews but they are in the minority. No matter where you find them in business, the factory or anyplace else, they are always out to skin you of everything you have. You never get a bargain from a Jew. You may think you are getting your money's worth, but you are not. To cheat you is their religion. I have had many dealings with Jews and I have never come out on top. The trouble with most Jews also is that they want to control everything. You never see them doing hard work. It is you and I who do the dirty work—while they make the profits. If I am going to buy anything, whether it be clothing, furniture, or food, I will not buy it from a Jew. I will always go to a store that has no Jewish connections. Occasionally I am fooled by the name such as Murphy or some such name. Why do they have to change their names? Because they want to get customers like myself who will not knowingly buy in a Jewish store.

They are always talking about the conditions of the Jews in Germany and other places. What do I care about it? They never say one word about the

Irish and their continued fight against the English. Why should I feel sorry for them when they never show sympathy for anyone but themselves? What did they ever do for the Catholics in Mexico—nothing. They have no one but themselves to blame for their condition in the world.[31]

Mary Knott, described by her interviewer as a 59-year-old spinster, was of English background but lived in an Irish neighborhood. She had been born in upper New York State and ran a rooming house on Bridgeport's Vine Street. Just as Martin Brown's comments reflected the influence of his time, Mary Knott's offer an excellent example of how the isolationism of the late 1930s affected many Americans' opinions regarding immigrants.

I have known many of the foreign families who swarmed into Bridgeport in the 1900s. Most of my friends are among the old families. Of course I see a lot of the neighbors. They are mostly of Irish descent, though many are now Episcopalians and Congregationalists. . . . I think the neighborhood has gone down in the type of the people it attracts. We have two Jewish families and a very ordinary Irish [family]. If the Poles and the Italians start coming in, it'll be a shame. But I think that most of the nice American and Irish families will be here for many years.

Being American, I think, is keeping out all low-class people, especially the Slovak races. I know there are many nice Italian and Scandinavian families, Germans too, but they shouldn't let them have a hand in the government. Americans should leave Europeans out of their lives and ignore their -isms. Europe never helped us. Why should we help them?[32]

Mr. D., a Connecticut Yankee and large property owner who lived in Stamford, was 71 years old when he was interviewed in 1939. He shared Mary Knott's opinion of foreigners and saw them taking the "bread out of American mouths." For him, immigration restriction offered an answer to the problems created by the newcomers and by the closing of the American frontier, which no longer could absorb them. (To many Americans at the time, including professional historians, the frontier offered an almost magical answer to many of the nation's problems.) Moreover, as far as Mr. D. was concerned, foreigners, especially in time of emergency, should have only limited constitutional rights.

194

You know, it's science that's wrecked this country and this city. Fellows inventin' this and inventin' that and other fellows coming from outside to set down here to manufacture. Why, this city and this town's got so many damn industries you can't go anywhere without running into their help. And all foreigners: Polacks, Wops, Czechs, Finns, Swedes, and lots I don't know the names of or where they come from. Why, you can walk from the corner of Broad down Atlantic Street to the railroad and hear more double-talk and see more foreign faces than you can in New York. . . .

This is a free country and we needed unlimited immigration to develop it. But when the frontier was gone and there wasn't no place to send foreigners out to, we ought to have cut it off clean. That was back about 1910. We had enough new blood right then. But no, they had to leave the gates wide open until the Depression almost. Result was we piled up a jam of non-English-speaking immigrants at our ports of entry along the Atlantic coastline with nothing for them to do but take bread out of American mouths to send back where they came from for Europe to rearm on. Christ! When you stop to look facts in the face, there wouldn't be no war in Europe now if we'd shut the foreigners out 30 years ago. And the money they made over here and sent back over there would still be in American banks, to the credit of us who made making it possible. . . .

These damn aliens have just about overrun Stamford. . . . What I've got against 'em is that they don't Americanize well. They settle in a section all side by side and carry on as though they were still back where they come from. That way they don't fit in like you or I would with the community's activities. What I mean is, what fitting in they do is all together, not individually. See what I'm driving at. . . .

And then there's another side. Sticking together the way they do and all speaking the same lingo besides English, they're still thinking and acting foreign. It shouldn't be allowed, to my mind. There's no telling what they're thinking and plotting against our institutions. And . . . when it comes to voting and organized pressure upon our town and city governments, there's no telling what they'll be able to put over for us native taxpayers to pay for. Take the Italians and the Poles: They're both Roman Catholic and mighty well organized, so that if we was to get into a war with either of those countries, there's no telling what they'd be able to do in way of undermining. . . .

In this country of ours, with Europe boiling over, we've got to figure that any man or woman who won't play the game our way or who tries to get something for himself he ain't entitled to by rights—well, they're little short of enemies to our cherished institutions. . . . I think there should be a national and state law passed forbidding any group of foreigners, who ain't full-fledged American citizens, to assemble for a meeting that's not conducted in the English language and open to anyone from the outside. Yes, and a steno-graphic report made of what goes on. . . . Foreigners who ain't citizens ain't got any rights, or shouldn't have, to my way of thinking. . . . I'll admit I sold some of my wife's Hope Street land to them Polish fellows. But they said they was going to take out their papers. Anyway, it's mighty poor land I never hoped to get rid of.[33]

In some instances, victims of prejudice were willing to accept some or all of the blame aimed at them by their detractors. William Winter, a Hungarian Jewish real estate and insurance businessman who lived in Bridgeport, arrived in the U.S. in 1888 and was interviewed half a century later.

Jews should learn the ways of others, and vice versa. The younger folks are doing this, but the older people are not. The mixing of groups should be cultivated, because each group now thinks that the other's method of living is awkward. They should get to know each other better. Open meetings like the United Forum, which I attend regularly, are good in overcoming this prejudice. It would be good for Jews to go to the churches since this would bring about a better understanding.

I think there will be a big change in the next 25 years. There will be much more intermarriage. I know an Irish woman who is married to a Polack. One of my daughters is married to a Gentile. Although I don't particularly encourage intermarriage, I don't think it hurts. I don't believe it should be carried quite to the extent that it was in Germany, but this will all work out in time. Jews are generally superior intellectually, and a mixture might be a good thing.

Much of the anti-Semitism is caused by jealousy. A man who has to work hard for a living might resent the fact that I do not have to work so hard. I have never felt any discrimination, however, probably because I have always had liberal views on such matters. I know of one case in which an Irishman refused to buy property from a Jew about 10 years ago. The sale was finally made by transferring the property to a mortgage company which resold it. There is little residential restriction on Jews. Years ago Jews had to buy their homes because they couldn't rent them. When Mr. J. bought his home in Lordship Park, there was objection because the deeds issued to the original purchasers were supposed to prevent the homes being sold to Jews. I don't know much about Bridgeport Housing Company's policy. Of course, agents have to follow the instructions of owners in this regard.

Round-table conferences between Jews and Christians, such as the one which was held here the other night, will help in the fight against anti-Semitism. Also, Jews should stop monopolizing the professions, such as law, medicine, dentistry, et cetera. The number of Jewish lawyers in Bridgeport is far out of proportion. Jews should go into fields like agriculture and others where the openings are unlimited. The trouble is that the sons of Jewish families have not been educated to this idea. My own sons, for instance, would not want to work at manual labor. If this sort of thing were done away with, in time the Jewish problem would be solved.[34]

If William Winter thought Jews might alleviate anti-Semitism by changing themselves, John Havas, a Magyar Hungarian who emigrated to the United States in 1901 at the age of 20, thought they might be helped by the demise of capitalism. This socialist plumber, however, did not appear to see very much wrong with Germany's treatment of "capitalist" Jews when he was interviewed at the end of the 1930's.

Well, yes, there's been more feeling against the Jews here in Bridgeport. Most Hungarians want to see Hungary become bigger and more powerful. The Jews are against Germany, because Germany has kicked them out. I don't know—from what I hear, maybe the Germans are right. The Jews are all capitalists. Well, the Hungarians feel that Germany is the best friend that Hungary got.

Well, Russia kicked out the capitalists and she's getting along all right. Germany is kicking out the Jews, because they're capitalists. Maybe that's the right thing. I don't know. But all I can say is, change the system and you got nothing to fear from the Jews. That's what the Russians did. A friend of mine, a Hungarian, was over in Russia and he says that you can't talk against the Jews there. They put you in prison if you do. They say, "The Jews are one of us. They're our brothers." Maybe that's what Germany should have done. I don't know. . . .

Then the Jews are getting away from the Hungarians. At one time they used to belong in the same lodges, because they used to talk the same language. But lately, the Jews are going off with their own kind. The Hungarians are sticking more with their own kind, too.

Me, I'm a socialist. The Jew is like me, except he has more money. But he's got a right to live just like me. Change the system so that people will get jobs and money, and you don't get these hatreds. The big fellows are the ones who start it. Well, I got to get back to work now. All I can say is, while you got capitalism, you're going to have trouble.[35]

"... When Things Go Bad, You See a Jew"

Stephen Kovath, another Magyar Hungarian, drew many of the same conclusions but displayed an even more virulent anti-Semitism. At the time of the interview in 1937, the 55-year-old Kovath ran a repair shop.

You want to know who is Magyar? Well, I tell you—there are mighty few Magyar. Most are Slovak, or Slovenian, and they call themselves Hungarian. They speak Hungarian and they feel Hungarian, that's why. The Jews? Well, those who speak Hungarian are Hungarian, but Hungarian Jews, don't forget that. Religion makes the difference. Like Slovak Lutherans. They're against Hungarians. Catholic Slovaks are like Hungarian Catholics.

There's been no difference between Hungarians and Jews in the last three years. They belong to the same lodges and societies and they're like brothers. The rest of this stuff is newspaper talk. Hungarians in this country . . . come from peasants. They know nothing of patriotism. Patriotism made by the big fellows—the big landlords—and they used to be part Jew. Hungarians come here to make money, then go back and buy farm. There ain't no patriotic societies here in this country. I belong to the singing society in the Pakocsi[?] lodge. We got Hungarians, Slovaks, Slovenians, and even Jews. They are Hungarians if they are of Hungarian descent, and Slovak if they are of Slovak descent. Being Magyar is like being American. Nigger can be American, so can dago and Jew and Irishman.

Jews and Hungarians get along pretty good. But I tell you, in Hungary we got a saying that when things go bad, you see a Jew. He can help you with money. When things no more bad, you forget about the Jew. In Hungary peasants work hard, times go bad, and then Jews take everything away. They charge 20 percent interest or more.

I think Germany did right in kicking out the Jew. Why? Well, you know, the Jews are not productive. How many Jews in Germany, you know? I tell you: 800,000. Where did they come from? I tell you: from Poland, Romania, Russia. They all come in after the war when Germany is poor and they take everything. I tell you, Jews don't go work on farm. They don't go work in factory. They just go in bank and loan money at 20, 30 percent interest. Jews are treated pretty good by the Germans—then when the Germans see that the Jews take everything, they get sore and they kick them out. You see, Hitler don't believe in making money out of the poor. He's for the little fellow. He believe in the state running factories for the people's benefit. The Jews don't care for the people's benefit. Just make money, that's all.

Hitler is going to make United States of Europe. He is going to do away with every little country having its own Maginot Line, its own money. He's going to say, "You've got a lot of wheat. All right, I got a lot of shoes. You give me wheat, I give you shoes. You over there, you ain't got no wheat or shoes? All right, I give you everything you need, so long you work for it." See? Hitler will make Europe more productive. No more poor. No more rich. He'll push Jews over in Russia where they belong, where there's plenty of room, where they can learn to work, where they don't spend their time exchanging, exchanging—just to make money. . . .

The big capitalists in England and America, they're scared of the Germans. They know that when Germany wins, there'll be no room for people who don't work, just collect profits. like the English upper class and the Jews. I tell you, my friend. I know the Jews, I ain't got nothing against them. I don't want to see none of them killed, but it's like weeding a garden—it's better to have the plants you can eat than the weeds. . . .

I tell you, Germany is the savior of Hungary. England cut Hungary into small pieces. All the trees in Transylvania she gave to Romania. All the trees in Slovakia she gave to Slovakia. Did anyone care Hungary was starving to death after the war [World War I]? No, all they could think of was to help such rotten countries like Romania, and Yugoslavia, and Czechoslovakia. . . . Germany and Russia together are going to run Europe on socialistic lines. That's the way I see it. People I talk to say the same thing. Everywhere I hear Hungarians talk this way. Once they change the capitalism, then they don't need to bother the Jews.[36]

Twenty-five-year-old Murray Braverman, a second-generation Jewish-American who had graduated from high school and was working as a lather at the time of his interview in 1938, expressed the doubts about his heritage that had been encouraged by the drive to Americanize all immigrants. Once he realized he "could be a Jew and still be a good American," he began to take pride in his heritage. The experience of Murray Braverman offers a fine example of what has become known as Hansen's Law popularly stated by the pioneer immigrant historian Marcus Lee Hansen. He suggested that many second generation children try to reject their immigrant past, while the third generation tries to recapture it.

My playmates during my preschool and school days were practically of all colors, races, creeds, and religions. All spoke English but all belonged to different groups. There were Irish, Polish, Jews, Italians, Greeks, Negroes, Russians, and even a few Americans. We children were too young to have any differing attitudes to the various groups. Once in a while we would have some irate mother tell her boy not to play with "that dirty nigger" or "that dirty Jew" or "Wop" or whatever the nationality of the child . . . happened to be. But this kind of outburst would not cause a split in the ranks of my playmates. As soon as the angry woman would leave the scene, everything was forgotten and play resumed as before.

Of course every boy has a fight at some time or other. I was no exception, except for the fact that I had one or two fights a day. Quarrels would begin over minor things, and a fight would start if one or the other began calling names reflecting on one's nationality. I remember distinctly that when I fought with boys of different nationalities I did not mind their calling me "dirty Jew" or similar names, but if the fight happened to be with an American boy, then I would almost burst with anger and anguish, trying to justify myself as being as good an American as my opponent was. My one ambition as a child was to have people think of me only as an American. I would have given my right arm to have them forget that I was a Jew. This was probably due to the fact that in school a teacher would at some time or another make what appeared to me a rather nasty joke about a "Mr. Cohen" or a "Mr. Levy." Gentile children would snicker on hearing these names, and I would just bristle with hatred and belligerence. I went so far as to chide and ridicule children with names that gave their nationality away. In this way I thought that I could divert the attention to other Jewish children and that I would be considered only as an American.

There were a few things—privileges, opportunities, et cetera—that my American friends had but which were denied me, that caused me to become embittered against my parents. My friends had dogs, cats, canaries, and all kinds of pets, which were not allowed in my home. As a child I figured that the reason that my folks did not allow animals in the house was because they were Jewish. And how about the delicious smell of bacon? I believe that I would have sold my soul at that time for bacon and eggs or ham and eggs. My folks did not keep a kosher house, but they claimed that they actually hated the very smell of either bacon or ham. Of course I didn't stop to consider this at all. Another thing which caused me as a child to regret that I was born a Jew was the fact that my American friends would dress up on Sundays and go to church. I couldn't figure out why I couldn't do the same. I thought that if I could only do this one thing, then I would be considered a full-fledged American.

I even went so far as to feel ashamed of my parents. I never wanted to invite my friends to my home because my parents spoke a broken English, did not serve bacon and egg sandwiches, never went to church, didn't know a baseball player from a racehorse, and didn't even know who Tom Mix was. How I wished that my parents were more like the parents of my American friends! After a while I gave up trying to Americanize them in the manner that my friends' parents were Americanized. The best I could do was to deny that I was Jewish and spend all my time in the company of my American friends. Once in a while I would think of the country from which my parents migrated and wish that I could go there and see what makes a country with such terrible un-Americanized people click. All I knew about Poland was told me by my parents or relatives. I hated that country very much, for I considered that it was its fault that my parents were so different. If someone went so far as to suggest that I go and live there, I found it very hard to restrain myself from killing him.

Both my parents had come from across, my mother from Russia and my father from Poland. I did not notice any clashes between them because of their different national groups. Either my father became a full-fledged Russian Jew or my mother a full-fledged Polish Jew. I felt that I belonged to neither group and that I was a real American and nothing else. I ardently wished that my parents had never seen the old country or that I had been born of American parents.

Such were my ideas until about my second year in high school. With the help of adult acquaintances and teachers, I began to realize that I had nothing to be ashamed of because I was Jew. It was explained that one could be a Jew and still be a good American. I was told that America was made up of a conglomeration of nationalities and that the Jews were just another one of these groups. Slowly I became reconciled to my parents and my nationality. I began to read more and my eyes were opened. Gone were my childhood ideas and hopes. I became fully proud of being a Jew and even went so far as to study the Jewish language. My entire outlook on life was changed and I began to take a real interest in what was going on in the world.[37]

A 24-year-old Jewish housewife in New Haven told her WPA interviewer that, in true social Darwinistic fashion, only the strongest survive. Her ruminations about the Jewish character offer insight into such thinking on the part of some American Jews as World War II and the Holocaust dawned.

I don't know why some people are against the Jews. I think they don't know any Jews. They say Jews speak very loud in the street, but for that matter some Italians do too. Most likely I can't say what's wrong with the Jews because I'm Jewish. Probably a Gentile would see their faults better than I.

Some Gentiles say that Jews are too aggressive. But you have to be. Gentiles are too, those that want to get ahead. If you go to work someplace and you know what you are selling, where it comes from, and how to sell, then you get ahead. Jews would never get anywhere if they didn't fight to get ahead. Anybody has to fight to get ahead. Some people say only the strongest survive, and I think that it's true. You hear people say Jews are the honored race, but all they ever got for their honor is being chased from one country to another. So if they didn't fight they would never survive.

Many Jews have gotten ahead. Morgenthau is a Jew, and Melville [sic] Douglass, and Eddie Cantor. Some great people don't advertise it, though, and some even change, but I don't see how anyone can change. I think in your heart of hearts you are still a Jew. How can you change what's born and bred in you for a generation? One Italian girl I know married a Jew and changed. She lights candles and everything, but I think still in her heart she is Italian. You can't change so quickly.

Anyway, I don't see how anybody who wants to get along, Jew or Gentile, can be unaggressive. And you know some people say Jews are dirty. But there are dirty Gentiles too. You see some Italians, you hate to get near them— and some Italians, you'd be proud to have them speak to you. It depends upon ignorance and a person. You see some American girls that are so clean and neat, it's a pleasure to look at them. The same with the Jewish girls. I don't think that it's religion that makes you clean; it's what you are.

I met some Yankee girls at my cousin's once. They were so nice, and gay, and happy. It's good to see once in a while how the other side lives. These girls were nice. They helped my cousin to get a job, and they don't think it's below them to visit her even though she is Jewish.

But you know what I think? Jews know how to live better than Gentiles. Even the poorest Jews live better. Take chicken, for example. For Gentiles, even not such poor ones, to have a chicken is a feast. But take the poorest Jew, he will try to get a chicken for Friday night no matter what happens. They'll go without things and get a nice supper for Friday night.

One thing, though, I like very much about Gentile religion and that's Christmas. It's such a cheery holiday. People buying things, exchanging gifts and everything. Even the way they talk on Christmas is different. They are pleasant and cheerful.

But Jews, though, they think more of education, I think. My grandfather was a very poor man, a poor tailor, yet he saw that his children graduated from high school, and one son went to college to be an engineer. Lots of people can't afford it, and they suffer and give their children education. Take Italians—there are more Italian boys and girls working in factories than Jewish girls. I saw some young Italian girls coming from work in the bus once. They were so young and they worked in factories. Jewish girls that age would still be in high school, but some Italians don't believe in education. They are stricter with their children, too. You got to be at home at a certain hour. If the girls go out with a fellow, somebody goes with them. I know one Italian family, the girls could never go out alone with a fellow. Jewish children get more what they want. Jewish parents seem to be more loving. Gentile parents love their children too, I guess as much as we do, but they don't show it so much.

I am glad I know all those Italian people. I can understand them better. That's what I mean about people knowing each other better. Let them come together, and then the Gentiles will know that we aren't bad. And we too would know Gentiles are not bad. For every Father Coughlin there are thousands of others who are real nice and don't like what he is doing. Take the lady downstairs. She is descended from German people, and she says she can't see why Hitler is acting the way he does. Hitler says that Jews made the war, but how can that be true when all the governments were Gentile? That's why I think all people should come together and see how they work and how they live. The lady downstairs asked me once what it was I had on my door. I told her it was mezuzah, and I explained to her why I did it. You know, since Hitler came to power, so many Gentile girls go around wearing crosses. They never wore them so much before. I think that's alright, but I think we should wear Jewish stars too. We are just as proud of being Jewish as they are of being Gentiles. But if everyone knew why we do such things or why they do such things, there wouldn't be so much misunderstanding. I remember in school, children would eat ham sandwiches for lunch. I wouldn't eat them, but I never felt any different from them. They'd ask questions about our holidays, and I asked them about Easter or the name day. That's the way it should be, I think.[38]

"There are Not Many Yankees Who Can Afford to Rest in These Days"

As the comments of a New Haven Yankee seed store owner reveal, the Jews weren't the only group subject to stereotype. Nor were the Yankees able to rest comfortably on their laurels.

The Italians are responsible for most of the holdups and accidents in New Haven. It's because of unemployment. The young fellows are hotheaded; they are going to get what they want; they take a chance and many times get away with it. I think we will have trouble with them for years until they become Americanized. The majority of Italians here are not of the bright class; there are a few fine ones. I've often thought how musical they are; there are lots of good singers among them. Most of them play a guitar, a harmonica, or some instrument; it's in them. I can't help but feel the Italians as a group are an asset to Connecticut. The Italian women are thrifty; they will see a picture of a flower in the window and will buy one or two bulbs. All the groups buy flowers; the Jews are very fond of them.

The Irish are good people; they are great politicians. I know there is a feeling against the Irish teachers in the schools. I think the teachers are kept on too long. They should resign when they are 40 or 45; they do not keep up-to-date; different tactics should be used in the schools. The Irish like the whiskey, and it doesn't do them any good. I saw a chap the other night in a hotel, he was drinking and bragging about what a good time he had the night before; he looked like an Italian. I know he wasn't a Jew; the Jews don't perform like that. I think all this drinking among the Yale boys is a very bad thing. I never touch it.

We have quite a few German customers. I've talked with them; they like this country; they wouldn't want to go back. A lot of them have spent money here on homes, and they have grown right into the American way. They are nice to deal with. Quite a few of them are farmers whose custom we have had for a long time.

The Polish have money for what they want and pay cash for it. They are good quiet people; they mind their own business.

We have scarcely any French customers. The Swedish are nice people— progressive and clean. They purchase and pay for everything; they never try to lower the price.

The Jews are great people for poultry; they have good-sized places. We bought our Barred Rocks from one of them; he has a huge place. He has made a great success of it; he wins most of the blue ribbons at the shows. We had to stop buying from him. We didn't want to, but we couldn't depend on deliveries—never know if they'd be on time. I don't know why; perhaps he had more business than he could handle. The Jews are very nice customers. There are a lot of them in the poultry supply business. The only trouble with them is they do try to grind you down to the last drop. They are much worse about it than the Italians; but the Italians have the same notion. The Jews are more persistent.

The Jews are great gamblers; they are bankrupt one day and at it again the next. They will never give up; they will try all kinds of things. The Jews stick together; they will help one another. There are lots of nice Jewish boys; I visited one at the shore and he couldn't do enough for me.

One Jewish businessman I know never could make a go of his business until he started a part-payment system, 50¢ down and $1 a week. That was never a custom with the Yankees, but the foreign crowd bite on a thing like that. When his partner died he was worth $100,000, and his business has branches all over the country. It's surprising he has never lost on an account.

The young American has no desire for farming as a rule. There are a lot of Yankee farmers, of course. We have customers among them all up through Cheshire, Guilford, and up through Killingly. They keep up-to-date; they get modern equipment if they have any capital at all. I think the Yankees don't push themselves forward the way the other groups do; they are apt to hold back, wait for the other fellow. There are not many Yankees who can afford to rest in these days.[39]

Stereotypes permeated institutions and sometimes influenced institutional policy. Louis Sachs, an 81-year-old attorney at the time of his interview in New Haven, reminisced about his days at Yale. In this instance, one man's prejudice was offset by another's humanity.

The [Yale] Law School—absolutely [no discrimination]. In the college, yes. And I'll give you an example. My freshman year in college . . .

I might, before giving you that example, because it's important so that you won't draw the wrong conclusions. My older brother took the entrance examinations for Yale College in 1909. He had taken some in the previous year, in 1908, when he was a junior in high school. But in [1909] he thought he would try out for the William Henry something, a prize [given] to a freshman entering Yale College who passed the highest marks in Latin composition, Latin grammar, Caesar, Cicero, and Virgil. My brother took all those exams in his senior year, and he won the prize; he was the highest man on all the exams, and Yale gave him the prize without any qualifications or any hesitation.

I entered college the next year, 1910. By the way, my brother William was on a scholarship and I was on a scholarship; otherwise we couldn't have gone to college. In my freshman year, school began in September, and I would not go to school on either New Year—Rosh Hashanah, if you know what that means, the Jewish New Year—or on Yom Kippur, the Day of Atonement.

At that time we were allowed eight cuts a semester. First semester eight cuts, and the second semester. And if you took eight cuts and you took one more, you were put on probation, and if you were a scholarship student you lost your scholarship. It so happened that Rosh Hoshanah and Yom Kippur came, as they always do, close together, and during the first two weeks of college, I had eight recitations on those three days and I took eight cuts, because I wasn't going to go to school on Rosh Hashanah or Yom Kippur, come hell or high water.

So, after the first day after Yom Kippur I got scared. I didn't know—maybe I would get sick. So I went in to see the dean, Henry Sheets Jones, and I told him what my problem was. I said, "Professor Jones, I am here on scholarship. I've taken eight cuts for three Jewish holidays, and I'm just an ordinary human being, I might take sick, and I want you to know that I didn't take these eight cuts because I wanted to be truant or anything, or cut classes. I had to take them, and in case I have to take another cut I hope you won't hold these eight cuts against me." And the answer I got from the dean of Yale College was "I'm sorry, young man. This is not a Hindu, Chinese, or Afghanistan college. Nor is it a Jewish college. This is a Christian college, and if you take another cut you'll have to suffer the consequences." I was a kid of 17, and I nearly died when he told me that. And he said it in a very mean and determined way which scared the daylights out of me.

I started to walk out of his office, and I had to walk through a room in Connecticut Hall, where the dean's office was, a room which was occupied by a man by the name of Thomas Tully, whom I didn't know from a hole in the ground. And as he saw me walking out—I must have looked ghastly— he said, "Just a moment, young man." And he called me over to his desk. "Something bothering you?" And I told him what happened in Dean Jones's office. Tom Tully, by the way, was an Irishman. And he looked at me and said, "Don't pay any attention to that. If you get into any problems, come and see me and I'll take care of you." Now, that's why I tell you, don't jump to conclusions. Here was the dean saying no, you can jump into the lake, and here was his assistant saying don't pay any attention, I'll take good care of you. He never had to, because I was a young man and I never took sick during the rest of the term. So that was the only evidence of anti-Semitism that I personally ran into. There were others, however—my classmates, Jewish classmates—who did run into problems.[40]

"A White Man's Country"

Yankees, however, were more likely to hold views similar to the dean's rather than his Irish assistant's. Mr. K., a New Haven inventor, believed in "Anglo-Saxon intelligence, integrity, and ability" and contended that "this is a white man's country and, God willing, it will continue to be." His notions of white supremacy, however, were aimed less at race than at the European immigrants who came at the end of the nineteenth and during the early twentieth century.

I was taught by my parents to be tolerant of those whose religious and political preferences were different from mine. Different brands of religion or politics do not interest me. But the monumental assurance of certain groups that they alone are right do not invite my tolerance. This is a white man's country and, God willing, it will continue to be. The insidious and vicious proselytizing of alien groups must be met with an iron fist.

Two nationalities have spread over this country like a nauseous disease. One, without a country of its own, is a nuisance wherever it obtains a foothold. The other furnishes 80 percent of our convicted criminals, whose activities before and after their incarceration cost untold millions. Deportation of all those who are not, and never will become, citizens of this country constitutes a major problem whose solution will mean much to those American citizens who wish only to live, work, to do—to live decently and bring up their families in comfort and security.

The Hungarians, Poles, Lithuanians, and Italians came in when cheap labor was needed; the bars were let down and the country was flooded with them, mostly Italians. That is the reason for the terrible mess we are in now. The Italians, Poles, and Hungarians have added nothing to the wealth of this country except as cheap laborers. They are not pioneers or builders like the Norwegians, Swedes, and Danes. They excel as market gardeners, but they have never opened up the country, the ranches or great grain farms. The Italians don't like to get away from city life; they like to be in the midst of noise and confusion. It seems as though the more ignorant people are, the more they like noise.

The Italians are a great expense to this country; they are in all branches of crime and are responsible for most of the crime in this country. The older generation were better; they had parental authority that amounted to something. I met 200 to 300 jailbirds and placed them in jobs. I have an intimate knowledge of their family life; it was terrible. The young ones mix freedom with license. They get inflated when they find they can walk up and down the street without a soldier putting his hand on their shoulder. The state will have to take care of these criminals. There is too much indifference. They should be put on farms under supervision. It is of vital importance to the welfare of the state. The Italian idea is to get something for nothing. They don't consider ethics. Prohibition is responsible for a lot of it.

I know some very fine Jews, families with parental authority who lead clean lives. The present-day kikes are a long way removed from that. I don't like them; everywhere you go you have to buy from them. They should have a country of their own. There are 15 varieties of them in Palestine and all fighting among themselves. There are some very fine representatives; every race has produced men and women of character. I dislike their assurance and their attempt to patronize white people in their conduct with them. Some of the fine Jews deplore the tendency of the younger ones to give up the old customs and traditions of the race, the customs of family life and deportment. I am prejudiced against them. I don't want any part of them; I want to get away from them as far as possible.

I have no personal grievance against the Irish. I do think they have over-stepped the bounds when they assume an "holier than thou" attitude. They use the public high school hall for Monday night meetings; the hall is jammed full of Catholics. The Protestants are up in arms, but they can't do anything about it; that's not legal, American, nor decent. We can't object to anybody worshiping God the way they want to. I respect the religion of the natives in the Amazon jungle. But these birds under the guise of religion try to force their religion on everybody. I have no use for the Catholic religion; it was bred in license, vice, corruption, and violence. It has done good—there have been brainy men in it. The priests flourish; they have great monstrous buildings. They sweat and bleed the poor laborers to death so they haven't enough money to buy food or shoes for their children.

The Poles are good citizens; they are pioneers. There are a good many of them in agriculture in Norwich. I met a good many of them. They were intelligent and had nice families. I went to their homes in the hills. They were courteous and decorous; their children were taught to mind their own business. The children ranged from 5 years old to 16 in one family I visited. At dinner they were helpful, well-mannered, and didn't speak unless they were spoken to. The Italian children are harum-scarum. They play with guns and wear gangster hats. That's bad—that's where the criminals are made. We don't get many of the fine type Italians; we get mostly the trash.

I don't know many Swedes or Danes. They are clean-minded. They don't figure in the criminal history of Connecticut. They mind their own business like the Chinese. They are very good citizens.

I have good friends among the older Germans. They are responsible, intelligent citizens. I haven't much use for those on the other side; they are taught from the cradle to take a gun and kill someone. I hope they will get rid of their crazy madman; conditions are terrible.

I have good English friends. The English are inclined to be over-assertive. They have stolen everything they could lay their hands on. They have no use for the Americans; they just want their cash. I do hope they will clean up over there—get rid of Hitler and his mob.

The trouble with the Yankees is they are living on the record of what their ancestors have done. It doesn't amount to much. It's nice to know you have good blood, but if most people traced back they wouldn't find anyone of any special importance in the family. The only thing ancestry does is that clean living and thinking of two or three generations will produce a good line. You can study that in this country and in England.

I believe in the Anglo-Saxon intelligence, integrity, and ability. Now if a man expresses a viewpoint, he is said to be intolerant. But look at all the

-isms and cults that are striving to undermine all that is respectable and clean in American life. Anybody can be tolerant; you can be tolerant of a skunk if he leaves you alone; it's a negative intolerance.

I was brought up by my father and mother to believe that one got out of life in proportion to what one put into it. One should have an object in life, ideals. Be clean-minded—clean living brought its reward. There is no substitute for hard work.[41]

The French-Canadians came to this country years ago to work in the mills. The older generation were very respectable and peace-loving. They are gregarious; don't like to be alone; they still keep to the coast.

Miss K., also from a New Haven Yankee background, believed her office had become so inundated by Italians and Jews that she didn't know "whether I am in the Empire of Mussolini or the Kingdom of Moses!"

I have been in contact with a great many Polish people. I can't tolerate these animals. If you look them up, in proportion to the number that come here in a list of 20 countries, you will find they top the number who don't become citizens. They are at the bottom in bank deposits.

We get few of the very high class Polish, like Majeska, and others who are outstanding. Immigration has been carried too far. The Polish have large families. Among the Polish children in the Connecticut Valley a high percent are criminals. It is not surprising when you realize that for centuries Poland has been fought over; the country has been overrun with soldiery; they have intermarried. How could the results be otherwise? When some of the Polish men become citizens they will say, "Now I can go fishing—they wouldn't let me go before." That's all they took out their papers for.

The first Irish who came over were the pick of the village; they came on family funds, or their own initiative, to a new country. They had to be resourceful and self-reliant in all their contacts. The first to come in each group seem to be higher class. In the second and third generation all this is bred out. I don't like the Catholics; but I have to be civil to them; I have no love for them. I admire the Catholic Church; it is strong, rich, and wise.

In my formative years I knew no Catholics. I first saw foreigners in Lawrence, Massachusetts. In the factory mills there were many Portuguese; some of the mill owners were Portuguese and got their own people to work for them. There are a lot in mill towns. And there are a lot of Italians too.

The Italians have awful voices; they are jealous and flighty. Look at the morale of the Italian army. There aren't many high-class Italians here; the ones we have are just a cut above a bandit. They are awful creatures, a menace to the country. They are too much in business; they have too much control. They aren't American; they have their fiestas on Sunday afternoons; I think that is shocking.

I am not allowed to express any opinion. City employees are requested not to; the lid blows off if they do.

There are quite a few Jews on the staff. I feel that the Jews today don't keep to their traditions. If they employ Gentiles in their stores, it is not because they like them; they do it because it is good business. In the office where I work there is often not within reach of my voice anyone of my own kind; they are all Italians or Jews. They are so patronizing. One of them asked me what I was going to do when I retired. I said, "I am going back to New England." One of the girls very condescendingly said, "But Miss K., you are in New England now." I said: "Oh no, I'm not. I don't know whether I am in the Empire of Mussolini or the Kingdom of Moses!"

The Swedes and Germans are all right. They are steady—good workers and basically sound. The Canadians start with a common language; they seem to be like us; they belong.

I am prejudiced. These feelings of mine are just prejudices; that's all they will be called. . . . People say these foreign groups contribute this or that and compensate for their undesirable qualities. I can't see it, no matter how I try, or the more I study them. I am constantly in contact with a great many in the foreign groups. I can't see any good in most of them. I don't meet the higher class, the cultured ones; there are few in New Haven.[42]

Calvin R., another New Haven Yankee, had faith that despite his group's becoming a minority, it could hold its own in craftiness and "could skin a mosquito for his hide and tallow." He feared, however, that with the younger generation, decadence might be setting in.

I don't object to the foreigners. I wouldn't want a nigger next to me. We have Polacks living next to us. They are all right. I wouldn't want them to sit down to the table with me, although they'd probably have better table manners than I have. The Hungarians, Slovaks, and Polish don't enter into the scheme of things much. They are clannish, but as a whole they aren't scrappy.

The Irish assimilate well and make good citizens. Of course they've always been in politics, usually in the Democratic party. I'm not interested in politics. I haven't anything against the Irish.

I don't think much of the Italians. We judge them by the Sicilians we have here; half of them are cutthroats. We have more poor-quality Italians; 90 percent of the white slavers, gangsters, and criminals are Italians. All you've got to do is look at the names in the papers. They never make good citizens. A lot of them have been here 30 to 35 years and haven't bothered to take out their papers. I think everyone should be a citizen or get out; they have got to take root. Not all of the Italians are a bad lot; there are many good ones among them. Our criminals are mostly Sicilians. I never saw a good Sicilian yet. The Wops are great for knives.

The French-Canadians are a no-good lot; they are sly, crafty, and undependable.

I've had varied experiences with the Jews, some detrimental and some nice. I don't think the Jews are so smart; they are persistent and take advantage of opportunities. I think they're overrated; there are just as many nitwits among the Jews as any other race. It doesn't seem to matter if they are educated or not—when they are smart, they are very smart. I think it's due to the persecution they've undergone for centuries; it's made them crafty. Jews will stoop to a lot of tricks. You can't insult them; throw them bodily out the door and they'll be back next day.

An English Jew I bought my rugs from was a decent sort of a chap. He bought my store and went out of his way to be helpful. I've been to his house and I've never seen anything about him that was crafty or tricky. I don't have the hatred for the Jews that some have. I don't class them the way some do. It's a peculiar fact—people will see others making a success and will run them down. It seems to be human nature. The Jews certainly have control of the financial system.

The Jews don't like to work with their hands. The few Jewish farms in the Colebrook colony are woebegone. They aren't tillers of the soil. I'm not particularly fond of the Jews, but they have made a place in the history of the world that few races have, and that from time immortal. There are some awful nice Jews in the upper and lower brackets. Look at Governor Lehman and men like that.

I think the Swedish, Germans, and some of the real Polish (not the Lithuanians) make good citizens when they come here with that intention; the Danes too. A great many of the Italians, English, and some of the Germans never give up the idea of allegiance to the old country. That is permissible to a certain extent; they should concede that we have something here or we wouldn't have gotten as far as we have. The English are steeped in traditions; that's what is the matter with them. The English and the Americans have got to stand together. The German nation is the most highly organized nation in the world today. The English run down the Americans because they meet the rough type of American. They are stiff shirts; hundreds of years of rule has made them so.

The Yankees are more clannish than any of the others. If you're not a member of the First Congregational Church, you're a nobody. I've seen it. If the *Mayflower* carried as many people as they claim, it must have been as big as the *Queen Elizabeth*. The Yankee is an Englishman; you can't get away from that. They still have the money; you can't tackle their pocketbook; you can't pry them loose from a nickel. They never give something for nothing. They'd rather hold on to something forever, if it represents money, than to give it away. A Jew will give something away, considers it good policy.

The Yankees still hold the whip hand in spite of being a minority. I don't know anyone craftier or trickier than a Connecticut Yankee; they could skin a mosquito for his hide and tallow. A Connecticut Yankee can trim a Jew anytime. And *lazy*—why, some of these college graduates are so lazy they won't walk a few feet to drop a towel in the basket. They'll drop it on the floor. I've seen it many times in the washroom at the library. The Yankees are getting decadent; they ought to get in a little new blood. They are still at the top in politics, along with the Irish. I think they always will be.

The future? I wouldn't want to venture an opinion; it's a big question. No one can foresee it. I'd like to see us come out on top. We have a wonderful country; we have everything here.[43]

"Marry Young ... Breed Early ... Breed Like Rabitts"

In a complaint about birthrates commonly made about new immigrant groups, Dr. S., a 62-year-old New Haven WASP, feared that while Yankees "don't multiply like others ... Jews and Italians breed like rabbits."

In my class at college I don't remember any Italians. The few Jews we had always sat in the front row, always had their noses in everything; you had to look around them to see what was going on. They were smart, most of them. One half of the class flunked the first year and had to be weeded out. The boys in my class were mostly Americans; Pennsylvania and New Jersey stock and two or three Pennsylvania Dutchmen.

Of course the real American doctors are gone; they are dying out all the time, and their patients too. My patients are mostly Americans and they are dying off rapidly. I don't see so many of the young people.

As far as the Italians are concerned, we used to have and do now have them.

The Italians stick together; the Irish stick together; so do the Poles and the Jews; that's the trouble. I have no feeling against any of them.

The consulting staff at G——— hospital is mostly Jewish. The Jews infest the place; there are more of them than there are Italians. The Jews are smart and get there. I've never had any Polish patients. I believe they are good citizens. There are plenty of Italian and Jewish nurses; they are all right, as far as I know.

The difference the influx has made is already here. The Yankees are dead or dying; they don't multiply like the others. The Jews and Italians marry young and start to breed early; they breed like rabbits. The American Yankee fellow doesn't get married until he can support a wife; the others don't wait. You can't tell which race will get the hold; they'll fight it out among themselves. The American is dwindling out; this country has allowed all these different nationalities to come in.[44]

To C. W., a 54-year-old custom tailor, the new immigrants represented a threat to democracy because the "cross-fusion of racial bloods . . . are not competent to govern themselves." Such beliefs had guided American foreign policy during the late nineteenth century.

The foreign groups? I try to be broad-minded, but it doesn't pay; it's very difficult to be. I hate to be elbowed off my own sidewalks. I don't think the Latins will ever assimilate. There is no place in our colony for the Latins. They are hot-blooded; they can't adjust to the cool Yankee ways.

The best stocks are the northern. We don't get the high-class Italians. The better class don't leave their country; only the down-and-outers come over. The others are a fine breed. In the last five years an Italian has taken $60,000 out of my pocket on property, along with a Yankee. The Yankee was the meanest, the shadiest. The Italians are a greasy lot. I put $5,000 in a gymnasium in the Italian section; got four Baptist church field-workers and an Italian minister to help. The gym was set on fire. Perhaps it was my own fault. I shouldn't have done it. I'd like to live out in Minnesota with the Swedes and the Finns. You can't judge the country by Connecticut. The Italians stay by the seacoast. In a cross-section of New York State, Michigan, and Indiana, conditions are very different. I did Americanization work for a while, so I saw a good deal of the Italians.

The Germans and Scandinavians are the best type we get. If they'd only kept that blood instead of getting in the Latins. The Pilgrim fathers would have been wiser if they'd built a higher stockade.

213

In 1901, when I was in the spotlight, the tailors were Germans and Swedes. Now they are all Jews. The Jews will drown you out if they can outmaneuver anybody. The Jews are very close-knit. I often wonder what they are cooking up when I see a group of them sitting around a table. They don't get out to the shore with a keg of beer and have fun the way our family does. As treasurer of the symphony, I met a good many of them. I don't like them much as a race. They do compete with me in business because people are more money-minded than they used to be.

There are many good citizens among the Jews. I don't consider them generous. They'll give for show—buy a $20 ticket for the symphony concerts and give $2 toward the fund. It's the Yankees who get out and raise the $6,000 we need to keep it going. The musicians have no idea what we are doing for them. We have, from the first, paid them all we took in and raised their pay when we could and still they want more. And we have raised the attendance from 100 to 2,300. They are artists, but in the final analysis the long green is what counts. The Yankees are putting in the money and these people are putting in the art.

The Jews predominate in the wickedest strip-tease shows—the Minsky's. The Americans by a great majority don't see these shows, but they are all over the country, and the young people go. I think it is very bad; anyone knows candy isn't good for a child.

The Irish? I was on the fire board for six years and believe me, I know the Irish from Dan to Bathsheba. I love the Irish; they are a wonderful race—volatile, not venal, as far as their public path is concerned. Not as venal as the Yankees in Wall Street. Why shouldn't the Irish get their thousands; the Yankees have gotten millions.

The Irish are honest as the day is long. They are clannish; they'll hang together until they hang separately. We are all of us out for the feathers of our own nest, but some are shadier than others.

The Hungarians are phlegmatic. I don't know much about the Poles and the French. The English don't know there is a Connecticut or Rhode Island. They are so self-sufficient they can't comprehend how the German machine could be built.

I have almost come to the conclusion that democracy doesn't work. I say this guardedly. The cross-fusion of racial bloods of all kinds we have here are not competent to govern themselves. They need someone with organizing ability.[45]

R. W., a 41-year-old Yankee sales manager in New Haven, had married a Ukrainian and was proud of it. It was his feeling that the Yankees had to bring in new blood "or they'll all die out." While he may not have liked all new immigrants, he expected them to assimilate, because "if the American race can absorb the Negroes it can absorb anything else."

I married a girl of foreign-born parentage—a Ukrainian and a Catholic. I have two boys. I'm glad I married a Slav. After 16 years of being married to one, I'm glad when I see other people's wives. I like the Slavs; they're swell people. My wife's folks had six girls; five of them married Yankees. My brothers all married Yankees that could trace their families way back. They'd all intermarried with Yankees. Their children are always having their tonsils out or have something the matter with them. My kids are never sick. The Yankees are inbred. We need these European bloods. I believe all these people here will assimilate—they've got to. If the American race can absorb the Negroes, it can absorb anything else.

I admire the Finns and all the Scandinavians. The Poles are good people; the ones here have gotten away from the Catholic Church. I haven't any use for the French—they are the scum of the earth. I've been to France. The Romanians are the same; the men wear corsets.

The English, Dutch, and Scotch have overpowered and subdued every race in the world. In the long run the Germans haven't a chance. The basic Anglo blood has settled the earth. And the Yankees have invented everything. They have years of background.

I like the Italians. We have a salesman here, a third-generation Italian. He is very charming, pleasing and cultivated. I never think of him as anything but an American.

The Yankees pass the plate on Sunday and rob the widows and orphans on Monday. The ruling English class think what is good enough for them is good enough for the masses. The Yankees are the same breed of cats. It was a good Yankee—Sargent—who brought in a lot of Sicilians to work in the factory to throw good Americans out of business.

The Germans are *dumb*. Good mechanics? They are if they have a blueprint made for them—then they are. They are pigheaded; once they get an idea you can't get it out.

I don't like the Jews; they run the company I'm in. They are the only ones who can compete with the other fellows. The factories don't care how many they slaughter to get theirs.

I don't think the Jews are overrated. A Harvard professor has written a book about that. He says out of 100,000 Jews and 100,000 of other races, the Jews have more brilliant minds among them than our kind. We've slaughtered the weak Jews for centuries. We've given them selective breeding. Their average mentality in every department is superior to ours, there is no question about it. If we can't lick 'em we might as well join 'em. The scientists and leaders in Germany are throwing the Jews out. Spain drove them out and has never been the same since. They are awfully grippy but we have to have 'em.

I go back to my old ideas that we are evolving a new race and that we've got to assimilate them all. The Yankees have got to intermarry—bring in more phlegmatic blood or they'll all die out.

The Irish? I've never seen an Irishman whose word I could trust. If truth and a lie had equal value, he'd lie. They are tricky. They break the Ten Commandments every day, then go to a priest and it's all wiped out. He'll raise hell all his life and then be absolved on his deathbed and go straight to heaven when he dies. I think the Catholic religion is the worst racket ever perpetrated on the people. It has no right to exist. I married a Catholic and the more I've investigated, the more I condemn it. The Catholic Church owns 95 percent of the fertile land in the Philippines. The church has tremendous power for good, but it prostitutes it for material gain. Any country where the Catholics are in power, the poor are the poorest and the rich are the richest.

I believe young people should be segregated by their mental ability. Those with a high IQ should have every educational advantage, free. Let the others be the laborers. Boys and girls of 16 or 17 all should work hard for their elders. It would be a good thing to put all the Ph.D's in the army for four years to get some theory out of them. Everyone should render service to the community. The carpenters should build a home for every couple that gets married, and they in turn should get their clothes and food. And so on in other walks of life.[46]

"Two Standards of Ethics"

The WPA interviewer described Grenville Griswold as a "delightful man to meet." The 70-year-old genealogist came from a prominent Connecticut Yankee family and lived with his brother and sister-in-law in an impressive colonial house on the green in Branford, Connecticut. His opinions about Yankees and immigrants reflected the self-assuredness of his status—and the extreme prejudices of his era.

There is no question in my mind about the superiority of the Yankees. The initiative which they possessed and the fundamentals of uprighteousness and freedom of thought and action they brought to this country have never been equaled by any other race of people.

I am always ready to give any man his due, and I am cognizant of the contribution other races have made to our business and cultural life. But history has not been able to show that in any part of the world has a race built a lasting civilization or a form of government like ours. And the foundation of all that we possess today is the result of Yankee precepts.

I will acknowledge that the Christian religion was in its early years more bigoted and vicious than any religion ever made by man (and incidentally, we know that all religions are man-made). It has taken centuries to eradicate the blighting bigotry and unnatural rules of conduct laid down by the early Christians.

Thank God that education has enlightened each generation and permitted Christians and others to see the folly of early teachings. Customs change, modes of conduct vary, as our nation grows, and a religion to be helpful must keep in constant accord with changing conditions. The Protestant Church has been able to do this in a large measure. The Catholic Church has been adamant against making any concessions to meet natural decent reforms. But the Catholic Church is not a religion in the strict sense of the word. It is a method—iron-fisted, unbending, heartless, and dominant beyond any power built by man. And today when the very world is trembling in terror at the monstrous acts of an altruistic [sic] maniac, neither Protestants, Catholics, Jews, nor any other group have been able to halt the ruthless stream of mechanized murderers who have laid half of Europe in waste and are today attempting to destroy the only stronghold of democracy left on that side of the globe. . . .

The question of competition with other races, especially the Jews and Italians, in business means a clashing of two standards of ethics. The viewpoints of races differ and always will. Geographical environment, racial traits, and characteristics produce varied mental traits and customs. While physical traits ofttimes seem to be similar in several different races, yet there is always a distinctive element in each race.

The Jews have been a problem for 2,000 years. They have only themselves to blame for what they call oppression. Many of the prominent Jewish writers are aware of this fact and so state in their writings. The Jewish people are not a race; [they] have never and will never discard their deep-seated conviction of oppression. They won't make the effort to live like white people. They constitute a nuisance in any country where they live. Their greed, unfair methods of meeting business competition, and their constant assurance of equality if not superiority disgusts those with whom they come in contact.

I don't wish to convey the idea that I am an isolationist on racial questions, but you have asked my views and I am giving them to you.

I think the Italians in this country have been and are today definitely a liability instead of an asset. While there are many of their race who contributed in different ways to the growth of our civilization, their contributions have been more than balanced by their criminal record. A majority of our gangsters, crooks of all types, and lawbreakers are Italians. Personally I have no use for them. They are unreliable at best. Our best type of immigrants have been those from Norway, Sweden, Holland, Denmark, and Scotland and Wales. They have been pioneers in the truest sense of the word and built up the Northwest and Central West.

The Latin races were pioneers in the fifteenth and sixteenth centuries and planted their flags in remote parts of the world. The Portuguese and Spaniards, especially, were of the adventurous type. But these countries seemed to have lost this early characteristic by the eighteenth century and are today far behind in civilized growth.

There have never been any facts brought to view that have discredited the superiority of the English-speaking people. Their growth to prominence and power in the world has been based on substantial standards of decent living, wholesome family life, compulsory education of the young, and unlimited opportunities for personal accomplishments in all lines of human endeavor. Recognition and help for those whose ideas make for the welfare and happiness of the masses have been prominent factors in our business and artistic growth.[47]

Liberato Dattolo was a 40-year-old task laborer on a New Haven Railroad repair crew when he was interviewed by the WPA. Dattolo had come to America 25 years earlier and had settled in Bridgeport, where he boarded with an Italian family and then married one of their daughters. When interviewed, he and his wife and 11 children, ranging in age from 2 to 18, occupied two three-room apartments on the first floor of a 12-family house. All other tenants—and the landlord—of the very dilapidated structure were Slovak. Liberato Dattolo had strong feelings about other ethnic groups and remarked, "Here in this country, one nationality hates the other nationality." While taking a dim view of all, perhaps his sharpest prejudices targeted blacks. His support of Mussolini, who had attacked Ethiopia, intensified the racism.

Everybody in this country got the idea that if you could beat the other man, then you're smart; don't make no difference how you beat him. When I come to this country I tried to treat the people the same way like I treat them in Italy, but it's no use because all the people here when I first see them they make me feel like they don't want to talk with me. When I first see the

218

Polacks and the Irish, they looked at me like I was a ghost. I wanted to be friends with these people when I first meet them, but they don't give me a chance because they always want to make fun with Italians when they first come here. When these people find out that a man come from the other side, they make a lots of fun with him and they call him all kinds of names. I know this because they treated me the same way when I first come to this country. After when I started to learn the language, they stopped to bother me anymore.

In Italy when a man is a little poor, not much, the people have respect for him. Here in this country, one nationality hates the other nationality. I don't know why. I know that my friends used to talk with me about the same thing, why the other nationalities don't like the Italians. The Polacks are not smarter than the Italians, but why do they think that they are smarter? I can't understand this. In America when the Italians have a holiday, the other nationalities make fun of them and they are jealous.

I remember that one time I went to the Feast of Santo Rocco on Pembroke Street, and I was in the crowd with all the people, and three men—they looked like Polack people—they were talking. One man said to the other man, that looked like a bum, he said, "What do the Italians waste all this money just to make a good time, and why do they make fireworks for the holiday? I think they're crazy." The other man said, "That's right what you say, the Polish people and the Slovaks never do anything like these people. These people just want to waste money." When I heard this I was mad and if I had something to do the job with, I don't care for my liberty that time. I felt like I show them what I mean. The Italian people don't have these fiestas because they want to make show-off. They have them because they want to honor the saints just like they do in the old country.

The Italian people are different than the other people. When somebody dies in the family the Italian people feel like they lose somebody, and that's the right way. When the people in the other nationalities die, they don't care so much. The Polacks, when they die, the people in the family and all the friends have whiskey and beer, and they have a good time just like a party. The Americans and the Slovak people, they do the same thing. I was to a Slovak funeral one time and the people there they talk about everything, and they talk like no dead person was in the house. All the women get in one room and all the men get in the other room. The women talk and the men drink.

One man that I know one time told me that the Irish people have the worst thing. They make all kinds of fun when the Irish die. They take the dead man and they try to make him stand up. If they do that in an Italian place they would get killed for making such a disgrace. The Italian people, when somebody dies in the house, they never forget who they lose. I can't understand these other people how they do it. I don't think that they're civilized.

The Italian people don't go to the show or no place when somebody dies in the family. When somebody dies in the other nationalities, the people go to shows and they go to the dance in one or two weeks. That shows that they have got no respect for dead people.

I am in America most of my life and I make my living here and I raised my family here. I am a citizen of this country and I like it here, but everybody thinks about the place that he was born in. If you went to Germany or Italy you would like America just the same like I like Italy. I am interested in America and what they do here, but just the same I can't understand everything how they run it here. That's why I am interested in Italy, because I came from there and I like to read in the papers what they do there. The Irish talk about the Irish country and I like to talk about my country. I read *Il Progresso*. I don't get it every day like I want to, but I get it twice a week. I read in there everything that the people do on the other side and how the government is getting along.

When I came here Italy was in a bad condition, and all the people knew that something was going to happen right away. After I came to this country Mussolini was made the head of the Italian nation, and from that day to now everything there is all right. Mussolini fixed everything in Italy now, and today Italy is more powerful than it was before. Sometimes I have a talk with some Polack or some Irish people, and they say that Mussolini is no good, and for this sometimes we have a fight. They say that if I like him so much why don't I go to Italy. I tell them that I have my family here and this country is all right for me because I spend most of my life here, but I tell them that just the same, things in this country could be better if we had a man like Mussolini to tell all these big shots not to bother the people.

The trouble with this country is that all the Jewish people they are running it now, and the working people have no chance to make a living. Look all the factories that the Jewish people have. They are people just the same, but they should only have some money, not all of it. Look! The Jewish people when they have their sons and daughters, and they are young, they tell them that they're going to be smart and they're going to the colleges when they grow up. The other people haven't got a chance like this. When the poor people want to get a better education, they have to work hard and to do everything to go. The Jewish people don't do this. They have plenty of money. And when they have a good job they all stick like glue one to the other. If the Italian people were like this they would be smarter than anybody else, because the Italian people are smart anyway.

Mussolini is doing a good thing for the Italian people now. Before, the Italian people didn't have no schools and most of the Italian people that you see now, they can't read and they can't write. But now in Italy, Mussolini is letting them learn everything that they want to learn. That's why a lot of the people here in Bridgeport like the way that Mussolini is taking care of the

Italian people. That's why I am interested in what they do there because now it is a government for the people. Before it was different; it was for the big shots. All my friends that stay on East Main Street, on the corner even now, they say the same thing.

About what Mussolini done in Ethiopia, I think that he done a good thing because that country belonged to him, and he want to make the people there civilized like they should be. [Haile] Selassie didn't care to civilize the people, so Mussolini is doing it now. He is making schools for these people and he is making them like Christians. Yes, they can't say nothing about Italy, because Italy is doing the right thing. . . .

There's too much Polack and Slovaks in this place. The street is all full of them and the kids in this section are bad. I teach my children to be good and not to answer the father and the mother when they say something, but in this section it's no good to teach them these things because they always learn bad anyway. Sometimes the children come home and they start to say bad words. When I ask them where they hear this, they say that they say it on the street. Sometimes I even hit them so that they could talk with respect. Then they're good for one week and the next week they start all over to swear again.

Then the other kids, they always bother the small babies. The children that don't go to school, they play in the yard and they don't go anyplace. The kids in the same house, those lousy Slovaks, they come out and fight with the little babies. Then my wife hears them cry and she's got to go outside and start to fight with the other kids. When the bigger boys come from the school they start to play with all the roughnecks on this block, and lots of times they come home crying and with the shirts all torn. My boys are not for fighting; they are been brought up the different way to be good and not make trouble. Sometimes I get so mad that I tell them to hit them when they got a chance to fight. What are you going to do when you can't do nothing with these kids in this section.

The older children, when they come from school, get together and lots of times they play with the colored children. Well, I don't like to see this because you know that after a little while the kids get used to this and it's no good. I tell my kids to stay away from them because they learn the habits of the black people and that's no good. Most of the black people are not civilized, and they should not be together with us people. In this section it's bad with the Slavic people, and with the black people it's worse. When the black people talk, they start to laugh just like a jackass and they are like crazy. Sometimes I pass by the black people's house, and I hear them laugh and make all kinds of noise just like they be in Africa. Well, someday Mussolini will fix them up, and maybe they get to be like people someday, and not like animals.

Since Mussolini tried to make the black people civilized in Ethiopia, the colored people in this country don't like this very much. I don't see why they be like this. Mussolini wants to make better people out of them. What do they want to do, be ignorant all their life? Sometimes these black people in this section talk to me when I sit outside. They say that I stick with Mussolini. I tell them all about what Mussolini tries to do and they say that I make a mistake. These people don't understand anyway. They don't read what Mussolini has to say, so how could they know the true thing like Mussolini writes in the papers. This is all I have to say about the bad section in the East Side. One time it was good and now it's bad because there are too many people that have no respect for themselves that live in this section now.[48]

"A Scholar and a Gentleman"

While the racism expressed by Liberato Dattolo was common and reflected the time, the experience of Edna Mary Purtell, an Irish-American political and labor activist born in 1899 of an Irish immigrant mother and a native-born father, demonstrated that racial tolerance could be taught.

I want to say something right now, that my life as far as participating in society was made very easy by both my father and my mother. Because I remember when we were kiddies down on Portland Street, there were black people in the neighborhood. I remember my mother getting us five kiddies around her and saying, "Now, look, here is the dictionary. I don't want to hear one of you children ever use the word "nigger." " She said, "Here is the dictionary, and in the dictionary a 'nigger' is a niggardly, a mean person, scrimy person." Always I remember that you could be a "nigger." She said, "I don't like to say this, but I don't want you to play with anybody who uses that."

I remember my sister Eileen crying because she couldn't play with this little girl because she used the word "nigger." That's my mother.

I remember my father when we lived on Mather Street, setting up on the hill. I can always remember that. Mr. Horace James was our janitor. And he was black. I remember that even some of the other kids, too—the effect that Mr. Horace James must have had on us kids, because we didn't mind if Mr. Merson called us down, but we used to say, "Oh, not Mr. James."

I remember . . . [Mr. James] was going by, and I was only about five or six. My father, I can remember him looking down and saying, "There goes a scholar and a gentleman." So whenever I heard the words "scholar and gentleman," all I saw was Mr. Horace James. "There goes a scholar and a gentleman."[49]

The lesson learned by Edna Purtell, however, did not spread far enough to prevent discrimination in housing. Race often meant paying a special housing or rental "tax" if you happened to be black. William Winter of Bridgeport explained this in his 1939 interview with the WPA.

In my building I don't make a point of doing business with Jews or with any particular group. I try to reciprocate, dealing with those who buy from me and where I can do best. It happens that there aren't any Jewish building contractors and most of the building workers, especially masons, are Italians. I don't employ a contractor but hire my own plumbers, carpenters, masons, et cetera. One Polish plumber, whom I keep employed continuously, has worked for me for five years. My workers are not union men.

Regarding Negroes, they are oppressed worse than the Jews. It is true that Negroes have to pay more rent than the places are worth, because many of the houses they occupy are so bad that a decent white man won't live there. At one time I had to refuse a flat to a Negro because of the objections of the other tenants. I did sell a house on Cleveland Avenue some years ago to a Negro whose mother was a white German woman. There wasn't any fuss made about it and he is still living there. His house is one of the cleanest on the street.[50]

A third-generation Irish saloonkeeper commented to the WPA about the blacks who frequented his tavern. While he disliked foreigners, particularly "Polacks," his comments about blacks displayed a grudging respect.

I find the Negroes are OK. They come in here and don't bother anybody and nobody bothers them. We have quite a number of old-timers here among the white customers and they never bother the Negroes. If a young fellow makes any cracks about the coons I always go over to him and in a nice way, so the coon can't hear, tell him to cut it out.

You know I went in the sock for a lot of money in them days and I still have a lot of it out. There are businessmen today pretty well fixed who owe me dough and won't pay it, druggists that I sold alky to. Do you know the only ones that paid anything on their bills have been the veterans and the coons. When the vets got their bonus they gave me something, and when I saw they were OK I always settled for half the amount. I did the same for the coons. Not many of them were veterans, but they come in even now and give me a buck or two when they can afford it. I rather trust a nigger any day than a Polack.

I don't like the idea of women drinking in taverns. They ought to be barred from places like this. But there is one thing, though—when you get nigger women in here, they behave like ladies. I never had trouble with a single nigger woman, but some of these damned foreign white women get a smell of the bar rag and act like damned fools.

The coons have a club down the street—well, it's like a speakeasy—and it is a good thing. It brings them together where they can talk and not be bothered by white folks. But I don't chase any of them down there. It hasn't hurt my trade any, but it gave Johnston a rub because he was scaring the niggers out of his tavern.

These coons around here are pretty well fixed, some of them. They own their own houses and have pretty good jobs. They are a quiet bunch and we don't have any trouble here like in the South End.[51]

Sometimes children departed from their parents' views and instructions regarding race. Clyde Trudeau, a second-generation American of Irish and French Canadian descent, who was interviewed in 1987, described how he crossed urban geographic and racial boundaries as a child.

In my case my father was too proud to get a city box. It came off the back of a truck that made the rounds. The guy would go out and your name would be on the list, and they would drop off basics—potatoes, powdered milk, and everything. I certainly remember the powdered milk and cocoa because my next-door neighbors, who were also somewhat poor but who weren't too proud to get a basket, used to help feed me and help feed, as a matter of fact, the rest of the family by sharing some of their food—this wonderful, wonderful Italian immigrant woman—with my mother.

My father didn't know that. I think he might have known it, but he certainly wouldn't admit to it, because he was much too proud for all that sort of thing. He was a well-educated man himself, as a matter of fact. Here was that strange contradiction between the neighborhoods that I was brought up in—on the east side of Bridgeport at that time, but prior to that my earlier years were on Roosevelt Street. As you proceed down Roosevelt Street, there is a small bridge there that crosses the Pequonnock River. On the other side of it is Island Brook Avenue, where the black ghetto existed and where I was not allowed to go, for fear that I would get mixed up with the blacks that were over there.

Little did my parents know that my very best meals came from the city dump at that time, thanks to the help of some wonderful, wonderful black guys that I knew. I still remember their names—especially one, Moses, who came to tragedy at the hands of Bridgeport police, who shot him down in the dump over a scuffle. It was said that he had lost his mind or something and went on a rampage.

But this big, wonderful black man saw me come over there for the first time. I crossed the bridge and went over to the dump on Saturday and waited for the trucks that had collected fruits and vegetables that were to be dumped from the major markets in town—Mohegan Market, some of the old markets that were in town. They would dump them. But what they would do is they would also dump out apples and oranges and things that had a little rotten spot on them, but of course the rest of the fruit was good.

And so I went over because I saw some of these black chaps on the bridge when I used to go down there to fish. I'd see them at the other end eating good fruit, and I got into conversations and developed strong friendships with some of these black kids, unbeknownst to my parents. There I went, over to the dump to watch, and there were all the men. There were some, oh, at least 30 or 40 men with varying sizes of hooks.

As soon as the trucks pulled up, they would rush toward the back of the truck and the hooks would start to fly, to reach out and grab the cases to pull them over to make claim on them. And Moses was the biggest, strongest of all the people there. There were whites, also. But he took me under his wing. I was off to the side. I looked and I went in, naive as I was, with my bare hands and I went to grab one. Some fellow reached out and hooked onto it and was pulling it away from me, and Moses reached over with his great big hook, spiked into it, pulled it over, and the guy said, "That's mine!" Moses said, "Where Moses' hooks is, that's Moses'!" He pulled it over and he come over here and he said, "Come here, little fellow." And from that day on, he had taken me under his wing and I went home with full bellies all the time.[52]

"Trust Everybody, Niggers Too"

Michael Califi, an Italian immigrant who came to the United States in 1905 at the age of 25, explained how he moved from Bridgeport, Connecticut, to Atlanta, Georgia, where he earned a better living by trading with blacks, first in a grocery store and then in a meat market. This illiterate immigrant's business sense was based upon a cynical view of his African-American customers. His story about posting a sign, "Trust Everybody, Niggers Too," is a classic in its testimony both to immigrant business practices and to the racism of the era.

225

A few months after we got married, we went back to Bridgeport. I went to work in a factory for a little time, and then I start open up some stores. I was happy now, because I was married and I was all settled. I had a few dollars, and worked in the shop a short time and saved some more money because my wife she knows how to save money. We had a nice little home, four rooms all furnished good. After a few years I make up my mind I want to go down south in Atlanta, Georgia, and start business over there just like my brother. My brother was making good money, and I want to do just the same.

Now I make up my mind and I told my wife all about my idea to go down south, and she said "Well, Mike, if you think you like it better down there, write your brother and ask him if it be alright." Then she say: "I stay in Brooklyn with my brother for a little while until you get all settled to see what you going to do down there." So right away I told her to write a letter to my brother because I can no write, and she write him a long letter, just the way I like. Then my brother answer me, and I see he say business pretty good down there, and I went. I sold all my furniture here, my wife go back with her brother, and I go down south to my brother—to see if I can make more money, that's why.

Now I am in Atlanta, Georgia. This is a nice place to live. The weather is warm pretty near all the year. In wintertime it is just little bit chilly, just like April in the North here. So I meet my brother and I live with him. He owned his own house, and he had a hot dog stand, and he sell coffee and sodas and hamburgers, and nothing else. He was making good money. Even now he's got the same business. Now he owns lots property. He buys cheap property from the Home Owners Loan. He fix 'em up, paint 'em little bit, clean 'em up, and then he rents them for good money. Sometime the property is in a cheap spot, and so he rents it to the niggers.

Down there you no call the black people 'color folks,' you just call them 'niggers.' If you call them 'color people,' that's too good and take advantage of you. You got treat them rough and tough because they are dumbbells. No sir, I find out for myself you can't be nice to them, no sir, not down Atlanta or anyplace down in the South. You can no trust this kind of people. They cross you any time, and they stab you if you give 'em a chance.

Now I stay there a few weeks and I do nothing, nothing at all, see? I just go from one street to another and look around for some kind of business. My brother tell me lots of things, and he put me wise about many things. Sometime he go around with me and look at this business and that business, and then we go home and talk things over and over.

Finally, one day my brother find out that a grocery store was for sale, and he told me to go and look right away because that was a good spot, and lots of nigger customers go there. See, the niggers spend money like hell, not like white people. The white people down south save money, but the niggers, the son-of-a-guns they spend every penny they make, and the next day, after payday, they are broke. So I go down and see this store—this was a grocery store and meat market, and they carry cigars and cigarettes, too. I think that time this store was taking in more than $400 of business every week. Anyway, I look at this store and see it was doing pretty good business; all niggers go there. I go back and told my brother that the business was all niggers, and he said: "That's what you want, Mike. That's the people that spend the money." The white people no spend much money, see?

So a couple of days after, I go over the owner of this store, together with my brother, and we ask him how much he wants for the store, the whole shooting match. And he said, "Give me $1,000 and the place is all yours." I talk things over with my brother, and I asked him what he think of the idea and the price, and he said "Pretty good, Mike." "Alright, if you say pretty good, I give you the money and you buy it for me."

So, I give my brother all the money and he give this man a deposit on the store. Well, when I took it over it was making pretty good business, but I push it up a little at a time. And I do it this way. I got some niggers and I told 'em if they bring me business I give free drinks. The moonshine whiskey cost not much—it was all corn whiskey, anyway, all cheap stuff. So the niggers start to bring me lots of business. Then I see when they come in the store and they bring a $5 bill or a $10 bill, you could give 'em any kind of change. Some of them niggers are just like dumbbells, but I never cheat 'em with short change, no sir, I won't do that to a cat or a dog.

But I tell what I do one time. They all want to trust from one week to another. Well, I cannot do that because it cost lot of money. Anyway I figure out how I could do that. So one day I make up my mind to put a sign and say "Trust Everybody, Niggers Too." Then you should see my business go up. I got lots of trade. Now I started to figure maybe these damn niggers no pay me like white people, so what the hell I am going to do. Well, I think about another trick. When the niggers come in and buy, I charge 5¢ more on each piece they buy. When they come in to pay, I figure out how much extra I charged them and I take all that extra money and put it on one side, with the name from each one of the niggers. So when they no pay me one week or two weeks, I say nothing to them. I say, "That's all right, come in just the same." Then I take the extra money I charged them (those that didn't pay me) and I pay out of that money. This way I never was back with my cash, and push my business way up, and I make more business than anybody in Atlanta, Georgia.

Then my brother told me if I want to make more money I got to start to sell fish because the niggers go for fish. So, what I do was to order some fish. The fish you got to buy by the barrel, because that's the way they sell 'em down there. The first day I buy one barrel, maybe about 200 or 300 pounds, I forgot now how much it weighed. Well, I sell it very cheap and it go like hell. I see that it go quick. The next day I buy three barrels. My wife say to me that she was going to cook, and fry it and sell it already cooked. She made more money with the cooked fish than I did. Anyhow the fish sale was getting bigger and bigger, and pretty soon I was selling about $100 of fish every day. Altogether I was taking in about $200 a day. I made lots of profit because fish was cheap and the price was good.

One time I got a big bargain on cigarettes. I buy 300 cartons of cigarettes at half price, and I sell them on retail and made lots of money. Down there you always get a chance to get bargains; sometime on the fruit, like bananas or watermelons, sometimes on groceries, and sometime on fish or meat. I was selling everything because my store was a big place. I had a butcher, a delivery boy, my wife cooking, and me selling fish outside the door. Yes sir, those niggers give me some damn good business. They spend money just like water, they throw it away, but the next day after payday they are broke.

I kept this business up for about three years. Then my wife got sick and she could no help me much more. I was tired myself because I work long hours.[53]

One might do business with African-Americans but, according to one second-generation Slovak resident of Bridgeport, "Niggers shouldn't be allowed to live with white people."

Since nobody wanted to take the rents on the lower part of the street where the tanks are located, the niggers started to come in. The niggers came in about eight years ago and have multiplied like worms. Another reason why the niggers came in this section is that the Stanley Works took over the American Tube and Stamping Company. The Stanley Works hired more niggers than the former company, and in this way it encouraged them to come to the East Side. Anybody knows that the blacks have been on the East Side not more than 10 years.

Well, I personally don't hold anything against them, but some of them are real lousy. Take the case of some of the niggers that live two houses away from here. There's some real good ones there—they mind their own business and never make noise. Then you take over in the other house, and you find that the niggers there fight like hell among themselves and keep all hours of the night. Some of them play the radio up to 4:00 in the morning. Sometimes five or six cars pull up to the houses here and they bring a couple loads of other niggers from the South End. These people start dancing, singing, hollering, and cursing to all hours of the morning. As far as I'm concerned I don't give a damn, but what gets me is that they have helped to lower the conditions of this section, and no decent people would want to come to live here.

In a way the landlords in this section are responsible for the coming of the niggers. They shouldn't have rented their flats to them. I'm sure that in time, even if the white people did like to move in this section, that they would because it's so hard to get rents in the other parts of the East Side. Instead the landlords started crowding in the niggers in their flats, and in time more niggers came in because they learned that anybody could raise hell in these parts.

No sir, I'd rather have my house empty than to have any niggers in it. Once they get in a flat, you start seeing all kinds of insects and bugs. They wreck the walls and everything else in the house, and if you give them half a chance they'll rip the house apart with their wild parties. Well, it's a good thing that I don't live right next to them.

One thing that puzzles me is that when they start building the housing units here, what are they going to do about the niggers? I always believe that niggers shouldn't be allowed to live with white people, and that they should have a section of their own in some part of the city where they will be a good distance from our own kind. When the housing project takes form in this section, the niggers could find a place in the houses that are empty in other sections of the city. I think that this ought to take care of them. They shouldn't be allowed in the new apartments because they'll wreck the place before it's built. The Slovaks in this section have all been asking me this question.

The colored kids in this section seem to be all right. I know that a lot of the people here, both Slovaks and Italians, don't like the idea of the colored kids playing around with their own children. In spite of this the kids play together, and they don't seem to mind what the parents have to say. I personally don't like this playing around among the different kids [because] somehow they might get mixed in a scrap someday [and] it might mean that the older niggers will get in it. That's the only thing that I have against them—that they should live apart from the white people and have a section of their own.

As far as bothering me, I can't say that they have because I never talk to them. The other nationalities on this block aren't too anxious to associate with these people. They feel that it's bad enough to get along with some of their own race. Well, why talk about it. There's no use talking about spilled milk.[54]

When neighborhoods changed demographically—particularly when they "tipped"—white flight occurred. In the case of one Italian-American's grandfather, however, change was indeed difficult.

I think my grandparents lived on Windsor Street for six months. They didn't want to live there too long. They didn't move as much as my paternal grandparents. Their second house was on Bedford Street. I have pictures of the Bedford Street houses. Their third apartment was on the same street. They lived in both houses for a total of 10 years. Then they moved to Williams Street, where my other grandparents lived, only the opposite side, and they lived on Williams Street up until, I would say the late '50s.

When my maternal grandmother saw the area was getting and becoming more black, she wanted to move. Though we had black neighbors on that street many years before the increase, we were happy with them and they were happy with us, no doubt, as long as I can remember. I've lived on Williams Street since I was born, which was September 23, 1948. We moved out of there in 1960. There were always black people there as far as I can remember, and I think they were there before I was even born, but my grandmother saw the neighborhood was becoming *too* bad, and she said to my grandfather we should sell the house and move. But my grandfather didn't want to sell; he was content where he was! He was older, and when you're older, you know, it's hard to make a change.[55]

In his discussion of race relations in Connecticut's Ansonia-Derby area, Joseph Dulka's comment that "we never thought of them [African-Americans] as having any problems until now" is most telling. Dulka, a 53-year-old factory worker at the time of his interview, was the son of Polish immigrants.

The blacks had their section just like the other ethnic groups. They lived all around us. As a matter of fact, a block away, which was Tremont Street, where I lived, they called it Little Harlem. It was mostly Negroes. Most were block buildings, and there were a couple of Spanish families that lived there. The rest of them were Negroes. Across the street, towards the back, were Negroes in black homes. You also had a Negro church, right across from where we lived.

Now with the Negroes, there wasn't too much conflict as far as ethnic groups. As a matter of fact, they stayed by themselves. Some of the kids mingled with us, played with us, but we never thought of them as having any problems until now. Problems like they weren't able to go anywhere they pleased because if they did they couldn't get a motel, hotel, or anybody who would accept them. Of course, we've had some conflicts amongst the blacks, but it wasn't because they were black. It was just because of an argument or so. A kid had an argument with anybody, you have differences.

Living amongst so many blacks at that time, there was very little dope that I know of. Maybe a little marijuana, I know a couple of kids had. There were no muggings that I know, outside of a couple of kids, white, that tell me they tried to roll a drunk. As far as the dangers that you read about in big cities, where your Italian groups and your Negro groups had your muggings and fear of having unlocked doors, why, in the same block that we lived in there were two or three families, Negroes. Nobody has conflict or trouble. . . . You've got to know people personally, and as far as robbing somebody's home, or anything like that, hell! You can leave your door open 24 hours a day and have no fear of someone coming in or being robbed. The people were all around; doors were very seldom locked. Now in the big city you have three or four different locks, chain locks, and you have to change your lock every so often. You've had the same ethnic groups in Ansonia where I lived, but none of that was going on.

You did have some conflict between the Negro and the police. You've always had; it was not known, but you knew yourself that there was police brutality, especially amongst the Negroes. They abused that race quite often, and the only way the Negroes won out is through big numbers. Where I remember some police being backed against the wall, club drawing, gun drawing, club in their hand with 50 being surrounded, about a big group of Negroes. Nothing ever come out of it. No arrests or anything, but it was one of those big conflict groups that I think the blacks would rise through being pushed around too often.[56]

"I Don't Think Most Colored People Want to Be White"

Mrs. E., an African-American woman, was 32 at the time of her interview by the WPA. She had emigrated from the South at the age of 12 and was a day worker and part-time practical nurse. Her husband worked as a chauffeur and janitor. They resided in Stamford, Connecticut. Her assessment of race relations might be found in Mrs. E.'s remark that she didn't think "most colored people want to be white. They'd just like the same treatment white people get."

After my homesickness wore off, I was quite happy up north. I didn't have any work to do except my lessons, so I had plenty of time to play. Maybe too much time, for we used to run the streets a lot. I don't think I ever did anything very bad, but some of the others used to steal things from the counters in stores, just to be smart. I don't remember any ever getting caught. Yes, I played with white children, about as much as I did with colored. The white children in the neighborhood treated us about the same as they did each other. The only difference was that when we had fights, they called us different names—different, but not any worse than what they called the white children they fought with.

I don't think I felt any real slights till I got into high school. . . . I didn't have many good times at high school. There were only a few colored pupils there then, though a lot go to high school now, and we didn't have a big enough group to make our own fun. The white boys and girls didn't have anything to do with us—even the ones I'd played with in grade school just spoke when we met in the halls, and hurried past. I never tried for any of the clubs, because I knew I wouldn't be wanted.

What did I do for pleasure as a young girl? Well, I've always like the movies, and I enjoy sewing and cooking, too. And I went to church regularly—I still do. I've never been much of a reader. I guess I take after Pa in that.

I didn't finish high school, because I got married when I was in my junior year. I've been happier than I was as a girl. Ed has steady work the year around, which is more than most colored men have; and I work, too, and help out. We have friends—other married couples—that we go around with. We belong to the Baptist Church. Ed is an Elk, and I joined the Daughter Elks, and also belong to a sewing club that we call The Thimble, after the one in "Vic and Sade"—on the radio, you know.

I don't think most colored people want to be white. They'd just like the same treatment white people get. My mother's sister was white enough to "pass" anywhere, and so is my second sister, Bess. But neither of them ever tried to "pass." Of course some light Negroes do, but I think it's mostly because they can get things easier that way—respect, and better jobs. For myself, I always think colored men are much handsomer than white men; and I've never seen any white child that looked as pretty to me as a really pretty colored child.[57]

Anthony Tapogna had emigrated with his parents to the United States in 1920, when he was 10 years old. At the time of his interview in 1975, the Italian-American attorney contemplated discrimination in American life. We conclude this chapter with his remark that "Some day maybe we'll all say: What are we fighting about? We're all Americans. But I don't think that day has come or will come in a long time." Almost two decades have passed since his comment. Are we any closer to that day?

I didn't feel it [discrimination] that much, and I don't know that it bothered me that much. . . . I didn't run home and say, "Look, I was discriminated against today. Somebody got a prize that I should have gotten." As a matter of fact, I thought that I was treated pretty well. On graduation they awarded me the first prize for oratory, for delivering the best address. I was made . . . editor of the *Outlet*, the newspaper in high school. I was in the inter-high orchestra. I think I mingled, and I associated myself with Jewish friends. To this day one of my dearest friends is Maurice Hertzmark, who was in high school with me, and lot of others—Irish and others. We didn't have occasion to feel bitterly about discrimination or bias—at least I had no such experience.

[As to my father] if there was a job available and it was between him and an Irishman who could speak the language and who had been here before him, I think the Irishman would get it in preference to my father. There's no question about that. There's no question about it. And as a matter of fact you find that even to this day, that there is an undercurrent and a subtle discrimination and bias among whites and whites. We don't see it on the surface, we don't see it so flagrantly as it might have been the case 50 or 75 years ago. But even to this day it is subtle and more sophisticated, but I'm sure that it's there.

Now, you take some of our banks today—and I had occasion one time to talk to one of my banker friends. I said, "How many people of Italian origin or extraction or descent do business with your bank?" "Oh, a great percentage of them." I said, "How many are there on the board of trustees of your bank?" Not one. *Not one*!! Now, from selfish interest you think they might want to put one of them for show purposes on their board of trustees, but we don't have one. We don't have one. In many, many such institutions— banks, insurance companies and so forth. I'm sure such institutions . . . do business with a great percentage of Italians, but we haven't reached that plateau yet. You see, we hear a lot about the discrimination against blacks and against the Hispanic surnames and about the American Indian. But there is a lot of discrimination against the Italians. There's a lot of discrimination.

They say "minorities." Who are the minorities? According to some defini- tion, even in the laws today, it's the blacks, the Spanish surnames, but what about the other minorities? Of course the Italians have risen a notch above the low plateau that they enjoyed 50 years ago, but still they haven't reached their potential and recognition in the business world, in the professional world, and other areas. It's only because of the political significance of the Italians in this state that we . . . finally see an Italian [Ella Grasso] as governor of Connecticut. But that should have happened 15 years ago, because the Italians are the biggest numerically—in politics today, we have maybe a half million Democrats in the state of Connecticut. And that alone is a sizable block of people if they were to associate themselves as a group in political affairs. But we haven't realized our fullest potential. We don't seem to scream as much as the other minorities do. And we don't threaten and we don't do this and that. But we still have a lot to gain, a lot to realize, that should be rightfully theirs. Unless we've come to the point now where we are assimilated into the mainstream so that we don't distinguish ourselves as an ethnic group any more.

[On Italian ethnic identity.] There is, there is, but I don't know that it's as vocal, [that] it's as vociferous, as some other minorities. Now, when the blacks don't get what they want, they rush and they scream and they yell, and people yield to them because they're yelling and screaming. Now, I don't think you'd find that among the Italians. They won't yell and scream, they won't threaten, they won't threaten to burn and loot and this and that. . . . I don't know whether they've become overly civilized about those things, but maybe so. Maybe it's the thing to do. But they haven't asserted themselves in the business world or even in the political world to the extent that I think their numerical strength entitles them to do. But, I don't know whether it's a sign of the times or what.

Someday perhaps things will turn around. Someday maybe we'll all say: "What are we fighting about? We're all Americans." But I don't think that day has come or will come in a long time.[58]

Conclusion: Talking about *From the Old Country*: A Conversation Among the Authors

SUTHERLAND

What are we trying to do in this book? I think what I was hoping we would accomplish is to really personify and give flesh and blood to what is a standard discipline in history—that is, the study of immigration. It's easy to look at immigration with statistics, data, and perhaps ignore the fact that these millions of people represent real-life stories, real successes and tragedies. The best people, it seems to me, to talk about those experiences are the immigrants themselves. I think that's a good reason to collect between two covers people's recollections of what probably was one of the major, if not *the* major, experiences of their lifetime.

STAVE

One of the things that I think is important to keep in mind in light of what John was just saying is that we're really trying to reach an audience that includes both scholars and students and a general audience. That what we're trying to do in the book is to bring forward material that deals with the important issues of immigration, a history of immigration, but do it in such a way that it has an appeal to the reader as well as a sound scholarly premise. Each one of the issues and each one of the excerpts and the interviews, the way the chapters are set up, is based on issues that historians have dealt with for a long time, but that should be of general understanding and interest to people who are not academic historians.

SUTHERLAND

Yes. For example, in our first chapter the interviewees were asked to describe their homeland—their villages, their communities, their living conditions. That is, I think, worthy in and of itself, but there also has been a tension in historiography between the argument that immigrants were mostly poor, uprooted, disoriented, huddled masses and a challenging view that the immigrants were not alone, but were sustained by family and friends. Well, when you read these interviews (and we've got a lot, including many that are not in this book), you see that overwhelmingly the people whom we or others have talked to had strong family orientation—that the immigrant experience, whether or not they undertook it alone, was usually undertaken, if not with help, [at least] with consultation with other family members or with family members who had preceded them, or kinfolk, or fellow townspeople who were assisting or were in some way involved. In other words, these people were not "wretched refuse," to use another phrase from Emma Lazarus's poem. Now, that's a historiographical debate, but it is expressed—or one argument in the debate is expressed—very clearly by most of these immigrants. That is that they were not as uprooted as we might tend to think.

STAVE

It seems to me that we're really dealing with the question of individuals in history and broad social and economic forces. Often when we talk about immigration, we have the idea of this faceless mass of people who are being pushed or pulled to a place, without looking at . . . the individual as a single being who is making the decision of whether to stay in a place or whether to leave a place. Sometimes they have no choice. On occasion you may have a situation where it's life or death—you cannot remain behind. Such was the case with Jews who had faced pogroms. Frequently, however, there is a choice, even if economic conditions are very bad. One of the things that we hope that the interviews in this book do is to show that individual decisions were very important and that these people are living their lives on an everyday basis and have some self-determination and control over what is happening to them. This appears in just a variety of contexts: in family decisions, in work decisions, in whether to leave their homeland, where they live once they come over to America, how they perceive and deal with other individuals. This does not denigrate the factors of culture—ethnocultural issues, in other words, questions that affect groups. There certainly are these issues that affect groups, which will shape how a person thinks, but you also have to note that the person, him- or herself, is an actor in this.

236

SUTHERLAND

What you have here is a collection of decisions. Most of these people made individual choices, and some who did not come with them also made the choice to remain, but there were choices.

SALERNO

Most of these interviews do show that these people weren't helpless or up-rooted—I think that's true. Yet when I finished reading the interviews, I wondered whether or not the old image of the immigrant success story was true for most European immigrants. Because when I started looking at individual cases, I saw a lot of pain, a lot of loneliness, and a lot of conflict, not just between native-born Americans and immigrants, but between different immigrant groups. My optimism about the immigrant experience was not as strong when I was finished.

STAVE

Al, I think that's an excellent point because a number of the interviews that we have in the book deal with pain. It was a hard life and you see this in the workplace, but some that struck me the most were in the family, where the chapter that we had put together on women and men show some of the struggles within the family and the terrible conditions that had occurred, particularly in the broken families. Families affected by alcohol, families affected by the Depression and the economy. And there's a great deal of suffering that occurred. Also when we talk about the issues of nativism and racism, it's quite clear that there was tension and that there was dislike and sometimes hatred among individuals and among groups, and this is not necessarily part of the American Dream. It's part of the tension that existed in the society.

SUTHERLAND

Yes, a good many of these people reflect that, including some of the successful ones who say that they're glad they came and that they wouldn't want to go back. Nevertheless, as we said, these are choices, and usually a choice means giving something up as well as gaining something. There are people in here who do not enter into the occupations that their parents would have had them enter into.

STAVE

For good or for bad, John? Moving upward or downward, how do you mean?

SUTHERLAND

I don't know that it matters [whether it is] for good or for bad in this context. We have one individual who does not go into his father's bakery shop; instead he makes a decision to go to school and learn a trade. He knows, and his father knows, that he's not carrying on the family business. You see the poignancy come through there. But perhaps a more basic one is when you make the choice to come and leave people behind. These individuals are leaving people behind. Sometimes they go back to visit, or many times they never see them again. So I agree, I don't think it is an unambiguous success story. It's a cost/benefit situation, and I suppose in the individual cases they have to decide for themselves whether the costs did outweigh the benefits, or the benefits outweighed the costs.

SALERNO

After reading the interviews, I think that Handlin's thesis is still partly valid. There's still a lot of truth to it. What I saw in these interviews was many broken hearts, some broken dreams—especially in the way the parents talked about their children, about how they were losing control over them, seeing them adopt American ways that they just weren't comfortable with. Although America may have given them some kind of economic stability, much of their culture disappeared with their children. I don't want to exaggerate the idea of family breakdown, but maybe there was more of it than most historians are willing to admit.

STAVE

You're talking about the Handlin thesis. For our readers, I think there are two books that had some impact on our own thinking, although I hope we go much beyond that. Oscar Handlin wrote a book that was published in 1951 and won the Pulitzer Prize, called *The Uprooted*. It talks about the alienation of immigrants, and [states that] that immigration to a great extent is a process of alienation and then finding new roots in the society. In 1985 a book by John Bodnar, with a name that takes off from *The Uprooted*, called *The Transplanted*, tries to emphasize the idea of transplanting culture from the old country to the new. In a sense, these two shape or reflect the thinking that goes on with respect to immigration. Now, in recent years, historians such as Roger Daniels have pointed out that both of them, in a sense, are looking at the immigrant as the mass and [that] we have to make certain that this idea of the individual is considered and given due consideration. But there has been a lot written about the American immigrant and ethnic history that looks at alienation and the carryover of culture. These are some of the questions that influenced our own thinking when putting together some of our chapters and [deciding how to divide] them. I think if you look at the chapters in this book and you look at *The Uprooted*, to a great extent they are similar.

SALERNO

Perhaps my thinking is colored because many of the interviews I read were WPA interviews done during the Depression. We're looking at people living during one of the worst times in American history. The later interviews were more positive. So that might have colored my thinking, but I think the truth is somewhere in the middle. It's neither the Bodnar thesis nor the Handlin thesis; it's a little bit of both.

STAVE

Yes, Al, and when you're talking about the WPA interviews, we should note that when we started this project, we were really thinking of using materials from collections that John or myself have undertaken in our own interviews, such as the Cheney Mill Project in Manchester, Connecticut, that John has done and the Peoples of Connecticut ethnic group project that we did at the

Center for Oral History at the University of Connecticut. However, we came upon the WPA collection. It is part of the ethnic group survey done by the WPA in the 1930s. When we set up the Peoples of Connecticut Project in the 1970s, we collected this material, copied it, brought it to the university from the State Library, [and] indexed it in very good form for use. John and I, when we first started this, identified the boxes that had interviews in them, and this is the material that we used. We found them so rich and useful that they make up a large body of the book, and they perhaps explain some of what you're saying because they were done in the Depression. Much of the volume will reflect the 1930s. We hope, however, [that] the addition of materials that were done in the 1970s and '80s gives another dimension to the book and helps us span a long period of history. To my knowledge, I think the earliest memories in the book go back to the time of the American Civil War. Someone recollects what happened to his father.

SUTHERLAND

Yes, that's one of the advantages of the WPA interviews. They reflect a different time. These people were being interviewed, not during that great postwar spurt of the economy in the '50s, and '60s and the '70s, but when the economic future of this country was not at all certain, and as Al points out, that is reflected. I think there is an ambiguity about the American experience in many of those interviews. Another thing that I like about them is that they push back the frontiers of memory for us. These people, after all, were interviewed 50 years ago, so that, for example, you have a gentleman talking about his experiences fighting in the Russo-Japanese War. You couldn't interview anyone today who had had that experience. We have some people talking about coming to this country in the 1880s and in the 1890s. I would also point out that there is some similarity between the WPA interviews done in the '30s and the interviews done in the '70s. Again, I think the biggest advantage is the fact that most of the interviewees, whether they were interviewed more recently or 50 years ago, do remember the immigrant experience as being within a family or kinship context. The decision to leave, the assistance in getting a job once they get over here—no matter which ones you are talking to—that seems to have been the experience of most of them. There was assistance, there was help, although some of the immigrants were very much alone. But that doesn't appear to be the case with most of them.

STAVE

With the WPA interviews, the fact is that these were not tape-recorded, as we do today with oral history. People took notes, and in some of the interviews we have, I was impressed by the fact that they seem to be verbatim. Some tried to pick up dialect. In some instances I think the picking up of the dialect may have been patronizing, but they picked up the dialect. Others were in very perfect English, almost reading like a deposition or something where obviously the interviewer put it into his or her own words—but they, like the WPA slave narratives that come out of the same time and the same project, offer us sources which are really extremely useful. Now in one instance, with respect to the interviewers, I had asked Al to find the names of some people who did the interviewing to see if we could contact them, and many of them were lost to time—had died, moved and couldn't be found. But I remember talking to one man who was from the town of New Britain, Connecticut, who was Polish and he did the Polish interviews for the WPA. I spoke to him on the telephone because he refused to be interviewed with a tape recorder on site, which I thought was a little ironical. What did he do when he interviewed? Well, he wrote them up when he went out and interviewed. He said, "Because I was Polish, I took information about the Polish community," and then he wrote them and gave them to Dr. Samuel Koenig, who was the head of this whole project. He gave the material to him once a week, and then he said, "The doctor told us what he wanted. There were some others working with me. He talked to us all at the same time," and he pointed out he had no idea what the doctor was going to do with them. It was interesting to discover that he really didn't have a sense of how this material was going to be used. Later, he said he thought it was for a history. The interviewers themselves were not always the most skilled people, but they were people who were put on the Work Relief Program, who obviously had some education and ability to do this. How much background work they did is hard to say, but it's not the same as doing an oral history today, where you're going to build it into a background where the good interviewer will sometimes know more than the interviewee about the subject, and then be able to ask intelligent questions.

SUTHERLAND

Yes, there are some methodological problems with the WPA material that result in our sometimes treading on thin ice in using them. There is a sobering reminder to those of us who have had students go out and do oral history interviews. I wonder if 30 years from now, when talked to about that experience, some students will say, "I really wasn't quite sure what I was doing," although I think I very carefully prepared them and explained and instructed. So I think it's useful for us to hear that from one of the interviewers. Also, there are cases there where you will come across a series of interviews where it's pretty clear that there is an effort to elicit a particular response.

STAVE

Obviously, an example is in the chapter on women where they ask about a woman's place. You know, "How do you feel about women working?" A lot of the material we find in that chapter talking about "a woman's place is in the home," well, there's a leading question involved. The information that's given offers different views of the attitudes of the time, but it was solicited. Another example is when we talk about the anti-Semitism during this particular period. This is an era when Hitler is on the rise, when there is a good deal of anti-Semitism in America itself. The WPA interviews asked about the place of Jews in society. So again, it is a question where the interviewees are responding, and it's not necessarily spontaneous. I think in some of the interviews it may well be spontaneous. But there are certain topics that are being asked about, and this obviously comes out in the interviews.

SUTHERLAND

You reminded me of another methodological problem, which I think reflects the fact that we are doing a better job nowadays. That is, with only a few exceptions, we don't have the questions that are being asked in the WPA interviews. Now, in our transcriptions—and again, as you mentioned, the WPA interviews are not tape-recorded—we always transcribe the questions with the answers. In a couple of occasions in the WPA interviews, you do have questions, but often you don't.

STAVE

You just have the testimony of the individual.

SUTHERLAND

The testimony of the individual. We would probably have a better understanding of that testimony if we also had the questions that were being asked.

STAVE

I think of the Peoples of Connecticut Project, where we had guidelines for questions and we went out and asked about ethnic issues. The POC probably was not that different from the WPA work, although the tape recorder deals with the whole issue of memory. Memory raises some fascinating questions for us. The tape recorder removes one filter in the whole interviewing process, where if you are taking notes, the person who is taking the notes is serving as a filter on what someone else is saying. Depending on how you write it down, you're going to capture some of the ideas, you're going to leave some material out. The tape recorder will include everything the person says. However, it is transcribed, and sometimes the way it's transcribed will make a difference as to how it comes out. But memory is a very important issue—how the filters of memory work. As we were saying before, when Al was talking about the alienation and pessimism of the time, people are influenced by their own time. So in the 1930s they're going to remember something that may have happened in 1910 in a way that's influenced by the Depression, the situation in Europe. If an Italian is looking at an African-American, is he looking at the African-American in terms of what's happening in Ethiopia when Mussolini is invading? These questions are important. We have to be careful as readers of this material to avoid nostalgia regarding the immigrant experience. We must realize that we're dealing with perceptions.

SALERNO

I think that's the big difference between the WPA interviews and the People of Connecticut interviews from the 1970s. There is nothing nostalgic about

243

the WPA interviews. Most of the interviewees were in their thirties, forties, and fifties. Their answers were very frank, and the bitterness that they felt was still very close to them. But with the people interviewed in the 1970s, events that might have angered them in the 1930s, by the 1970s perhaps they had come to terms with them. They could even laugh at them. I've noticed that the interviews in the 1970s were much more optimistic. In some ways these are the success stories of immigration; they had come to terms with the immigrant experience.

SUTHERLAND

Exactly, Al, and more than come to terms with it. We need to remember that the people in the seventies and eighties are survivors, and the fact that they've lived through the Depression notwithstanding, they have a much better life now. Those early interviewees were going through the Depression, while these individuals are older. Even those who are perhaps not as well off as some others are living in an America of a whole host of public services which did not exist, and indeed came about because of the Depression, Social Security being the most obvious. We don't know how many of the people who were interviewed during the WPA did not go on to be survivors, and as you said, it would have been nice if we could have traced some of those interviewees. So when we interview immigrants in the '70s and '80s, in that sense we have a rather select group and we don't know how representative they are.

STAVE

You mentioned success stories. That's an interesting question because when we did the Peoples of Connecticut project, the way those individuals were chosen was through advisory committees of various ethnic groups. I think John remembers, because he was working with the project on the advisory board at the time. What we did was to go to the various ethnic communities and say, "Could you recommend some people from your ethnic group to talk to about the immigrant experience?" Of course, what they'd always do, as we learned as we went on, was they'd recommend the most successful people— or tried to. We tried to have a mid-course correction with respect to that, to go out and find people who were not "successful" in terms of occupations or wealth. We realized after a while that, yes, we were being pointed to the leaders of the community because the community wanted to put its best foot forward and wanted to have the people who were the most successful represent it. What we did try to do was to go out and find individuals in positions that might be considered menial, unsuccessful in society, to reflect on their experiences. That was one of the biases built into some of those interviews, and it may help explain part of the thing that you are seeing in the difference between the '30s and now. I don't think you're going to have the same American Dream concept, although the interviews that were done with the Yankees, the Connecticut Yankees, many of them I think were sort of the old-line successes. Yes, I think that is so. They looked at the new immigrants with a certain questioning, a certain condescension.

SUTHERLAND

Yes, and one of the other differences we've commented on in the WPA project is that there was a lot of division. We've seen a good deal of very frank hostility among members of some ethnic groups toward members of other ethnic groups. Again, part of that is exacerbated by the fact that this is a time of economic crisis and that's when you see increased ethnic tension. These interviews were done in the '30s and we should not be surprised, when there's a great deal of competition for jobs, to see that kind of divisiveness. But I also think there is another aspect to this, and that is what is permissible to talk about publicly. Here there's a great difference. You see the use of language, epithets, in the 1930s interviews that you don't see in the later interviews. As we all know, that doesn't mean that there are still not ethnic tensions. They're more subtly expressed, perhaps, in the later interviews than they were 50 years ago. So I think that's another advantage of having such a wide time frame in the interviews.

STAVE

With respect to the immigrants that we're looking at, this book really deals almost totally with European immigrants. To a great extent it deals with immigrants who came in the period from the 1880s through the 1920s or so, although we certainly have people who came earlier and we have people who came later. We have to keep in mind—the reader has to keep in mind—that the immigration process continues. That is, if the Irish were looked upon as the old immigrants from northwestern Europe, who came in in the 1840s, '50s and perhaps '60s, certainly also the Irish are coming through the twentieth century. In fact, if you go to Boston today, you'll see many immigrants who have recently arrived, some of them not legal immigrants, but illegal. We recognize that this is just one facet of the kinds of people who have come to the United States and that immigration today in the 1990s has certainly changed. We have to consider that the immigration laws in America that were passed in 1921 and 1924 and in 1965 and 1986 and 1990, all of them shift the kinds of people who can come. Today we have a different kind of immigrant in terms of their national backgrounds, people who could not come in [earlier]. People who were closed out early in the century, to a great extent now enter. A recent newspaper accounting that was based on information from the Immigration and Naturalization Service talks about who came in 1991. People from the Soviet Union are the largest immigrant group, close to 57,000 of them—probably Jewish immigrants, I imagine. Then you go to Philippine immigrants (55,000) and Vietnamese and Mexican, from mainland China (I expect a lot of students), India, the Dominican Republic, Korea, Jamaica, and Iran. These are not the countries that were sending the immigrants to America's shores, the people whom we're talking about here. These are people, in some instances people of color, people from Asia, and we recognize that our immigrants do not include many of those, and we understand this. We think that there are certain generalities in the immigrant experience. On the other hand, each group is different and as we were stressing before, each individual is different.

SUTHERLAND

And one other thing, too, to muddy the water a little bit more. We have to remember that the America that the immigrants are coming to today is also different. That probably is one of the greatest contrasts between the period under consideration and today. The immigrants then were coming to an America with a radically expanding industrial growth economy. Today's immigrants are coming to an America in a post-industrial era in which the decline in entry-level manufacturing jobs has been continuing for several decades. Nevertheless we remain an immigrant nation and probably always will remain an immigrant nation. People will continue to come here for basically the same reasons that they came 80, 90, and 100 years ago, and that's because they envision greater opportunity. It's also a cost-benefit situation, such as you raised earlier. I'm thinking now of the book by the Mexican-American author Richard Rodriguez, in which he describes much of the same poignancy of the break with culture that you were talking about earlier, Al, growing up in California as a second-generation Mexican American. So I think there's a good deal of continuity to the immigrant experience, in spite of the great differences. I think we also should remember that people were pessimistic about the immigrant experience early in the 20th century, just as they are today. They question America's capacity to absorb the newcomers. That certainly is not a new emotion among Americans, and [it] was very much a fear in the first couple of decades of this century. It continued to be a fear in the remarks of several of the people interviewed for the WPA project. I guess I would be very hesitant to question whether America's assimilative powers are not as strong as they have been before. History indicates that this country has an enormous capacity to absorb.

STAVE

Yes, but we also know, as historians, that history never repeats itself and we have to keep that in mind. The experiences are always different because of different factors—for instance, the idea of post-industrialism. We've used that term—it may be an overused term and a poor term—but essentially the kind of economy . . . into which the latest immigrants are coming makes a very big difference as to how they can be expected to adapt to or succeed in the society. Of course you have all sorts of cultural issues, too. Something in the book that we see so strongly is the idea of family kinship groups, friendships. All of these have an impact and I can't help thinking about Asian immigrants—Koreans as an example, Vietnamese as an example—and the impact of family structure that perpetuates success in business because once someone develops capital, then that capital is used to help out the whole family. If, for instance, you own a greengrocery store in New York City or in South Central LA that had so much trouble during the riots after the Rodney King incident, those were built on the fact of family savings. In 1992 we heard a lot in the presidential campaign about family values. Well, for immigrants family values seem to make—at least as I read some of the interviews we've done in this book—a very important impact on what happens to the future of some of these people.

SUTHERLAND

Absolutely. That was my whole point at the beginning. For many of these people, it was family and kinship networks which got them over here and which helped them to survive in the early going. Even the loners in our interviews—I'm thinking of one fellow who is all alone and he's Russian Jewish, but fortunately he meets a Russian Jewish policeman who helps him out and steers him to the right boardinghouse or whatever. I guess the only thing I would say is that there appeared to me to be a trivialization of family values in the 1992 campaign. If there's one thing that we have seen in these interviews, it's that among these people, (a) there were real family values and (b) they really mattered.

STAVE

Yes, they created a great deal of tension, and maybe comfort, but their effect was extremely great, and that seemed to appear in many of the chapters. Another element is cultural background. What kind of culture and what kinds of attitudes do you have as foundations of institutions in society, as the basis of intermarriage, of education? Are you shaped by some of these values, even though you're making individual decisions? You carry cultural baggage with you.

SUTHERLAND

Could we not leave that for a minute?

STAVE

Yes, sure.

SUTHERLAND

Not the cultural baggage, but getting back again to the family situation. What I'm referring back to is Al's original remark about the costs of coming over here and the fact that we ought to modify the idea of the traditional success story. A contradiction in these interviews is that these people come over, most of them in any event, for economic betterment, but the way in which America forces them to achieve that economic betterment causes some of this poignant disruption. I'm thinking of the people who come over here with skills and find that they cannot use those skills because what has caused the great industrial expansion in America has been mechanization, which placed its emphasis upon semiskilled labor rather than skilled labor. Thus we have people remarking about that, whose immigrant experience is separated by several decades. We have cabinetmakers in the 1930s talking about the fact they came over here and couldn't use their skills as cabinetmakers. We have a fellow trained in a French Peugeot plant immediately after World War II, who comes over here and finds that many of the skills that he came over with, hand skills, are no longer necessary because America is so far more advanced that many of those processes are being done by machines. I think, if I recollect, that many of the people who went through that experience are still, when they're being interviewed, economically fairly well off, but they feel that they have lost something. They had to give up something, nevertheless. I guess what I'm saying is success in America still cost them.

SALERNO

That's the danger of talking about success stories. Even if immigrants became successful, you have to ask what was the cultural cost. I'm thinking of a book I just read, John Ibson's *Will the World Break Your Heart?*, about Irish immigrants, whom we usually consider the most assimilated American immigrants. His argument is that, yes, they did assimilate, and many became success stories, but they paid a high price for it. Some stereotypes that people had about Irish people, like drunkenness, may actually be proof that they didn't assimilate all that well. Maybe drunkenness was a real problem, caused by their inability to adjust. Perhaps family breakdown was quite real. Even today, when we talk about Asian immigrants, we say their children do well in school, or that they are the success stories. But do we ask what the price is when you're labeled a success story? When Asian families use all their savings to open a small business, when the entire family works in the store, what does that do to them when they are all trying to get ahead? What will happen 20 or 30 years from now when they're economic success stories but they haven't really lived? They've lost leisure time and much more. That is what I think about.

STAVE

What about the issue of race, which we deal with to some extent in the book, but not a huge amount?

SUTHERLAND

Because our book is about European immigrants, the issue of race comes across only from the European perspective. Sure, in these interviews we see some reflection of racist attitudes in America. I don't think we should be surprised at that.

SALERNO

One question I have is why, among oppressed groups, there was so much hatred towards other groups, especially blacks. I mean, that never fails to surprise me. You would think there would be more brotherhood between groups at the bottom of the social ladder. Obviously some oppressed immigrants were able to think better of themselves by knowing they could think less of blacks, and even [of] other immigrants.

SUTHERLAND

That's an age-old question going back at least to the Populist era, when you had efforts to encourage cooperation between poor whites and poor blacks.

STAVE

Why do you get these tensions? Is it a social reason that the groups that are oppressed are always looking for a group that may be even more oppressed so that they could feel more status in society than they have? Some of these antagonisms come out for that reason and perhaps for reasons of economic competition, particularly when jobs were scarce, when many of these interviews were done in the 1930s. But you're right, there's an intensity there that we demonstrate in the final chapter of the book, where there's some evidence in one interview where a woman is talking about how her parents tried to show her the value of all people, whether they were white or black, but then many of the other interviews showed interracial tension and the anger or dislike or hatred that appears. That's a rather sad commentary on the society.

With respect to the book itself, before we conclude: Looking back at it now, do you think we had any special problems in trying to put it together and how it came together? I recently did another book of historical photographs and our problem came to be [the] selection of the photos we were to use, not finding them. It seems to me some of the same problems occurred in this book. We had such a wide array of materials.

SUTHERLAND

Absolutely. I suspect we could start all over again and come up with an entirely different set of interviews because each of us discarded so many. When I was reading the interviews, I had three piles, and those were "Yes, absolutely," "Maybe," and "No." The discouraging thing was, after the first pass through, I had a very tiny "Yes" pile and a very tiny "No" pile and a very huge "Maybe" pile. We ought to be honest with the reader when we talk about perception, when we talk about subjectivity on the part of interviewees. The selection of these interviews, obviously, has been to an extent subjective itself, and we hope we selected a representative sampling of the interviews we had to choose from.

STAVE

John, on what basis would you choose an interview? Why would you choose one? What kinds of things were you looking for?

SUTHERLAND

Well, first, I was looking for the topics that were my responsibility in the book. That was done for me in an initial reading, of course, as it was for you, by Al. So I did have a group of interviews for the homeland, the crossing and arrival, and for work. I tried to pay some attention to representation. It's a book about European immigration, so I tried to have a number of nationality groups represented in the interviews. I tried to have interviews that went on at some length about the topic. I didn't reject out of hand someone whose discussion of crossing and arrival only took up one paragraph, but on the other hand I felt that the greater detail that one went into discussing his or her crossing, the more beneficial it was to the reader. So I looked for people who went on at some length about either finding a job, or the crossing and arrival, or their homeland, depending on which section I had. I looked for people who really seemed to know what they were doing, who seemed to understand why they were being interviewed. That's not a tangible thing all the time. It's not easy to grasp. I did not look for the sensational.

STAVE

It sounds like a good idea of what we were trying to find. Seems to me that you wanted to tell a good story, so that in people's own words the readers would have conveyed to them the issues that we were trying to deal with, in a manner that was interesting. I know that we weren't necessarily looking for the sensational, but some of the excerpts that we have, and there are particularly a few with husbands and wives, are fascinating stories. One particularly strong narrative involves the same family and they're telling about the breakup of the family and you get two divergent points of view, which is interesting. It's something that you can't always do. It came out of the WPA materials. But I think the reader will note that the chapters are different lengths. The segments are different lengths and what we've tried to do would be to edit, so that the commentary is brought together by some of the introductory remarks that we make in trying to tie materials together into a whole. Any surprises? John?

SUTHERLAND

This might go with why we selected the interviews that we selected. The homeland to me is an important one because we assume that as American historians we want to know about immigration because we want to know about the impact upon America. But on the other hand, we know that the impact of the immigrants upon America has to do with who they are and what their background is. Through these interviews we got some idea of the impact of immigration upon the homeland, upon the people who were left behind. Again, there are some very difficult stories there, including some of real intrafamily hostility, but one of the things that I looked for on the homeland were people who could really describe the environment in which they lived. Here is another advantage to having those WPA interviews. Those people were closer to the immigrant experience. Their discussions of their homes, of their villages, of their families, of their churches and priests, were much more graphic than we see in the later interviews. In fact, you'll find more WPA interviews in that chapter for that very reason. One of the most valuable things about that chapter is it discusses the physical environment of the villages. It describes some of them, their houses, with great care and great detail, and I think that's an advantage of the fact that these people were interviewed when they were much closer to the immigrant experience than were the most recent interviewees.

STAVE

Yes, and one thing we should keep in mind, too, and so should the readers, is that we have used material here that involves second-generation, sometimes even I think third-generation, people who are not immigrants but who are talking about the ethnic experience or the immigrant experience from what they were told or how they reacted to their parents or grandparents, who may have been immigrants. This is the dimension of generations that evolves. Particularly in the chapter on family and community, you see some of those tensions between the parents and the children.

I think all of the interviews in the book are done with people who were able to speak English. . . . I know when we did the Peoples of Connecticut project, and I think with the WPA too, these are not people who are talking in their foreign language, but are talking in English. So there is a group of people who could have been translated but were not. They're excluded. That's another dimension of the immigrant experience that is a very important one because language becomes a critical element in what happens within society. Among the people that we were studying primarily, the whole notion of bilingualism was one that's very different than it is today. While there were many attempts to maintain the language, generally they moved into English. Today you have the thrust to try to have a bilingual society, and this I think is one of the differences that we find between those we studied and people today. Any surprises with the book for us?

SALERNO

Maybe I should just say something about how I picked the interviews, since I read most of them, hundreds of them. While I was reading through them, if it jumped off the page, if it stood out, an interview was selected. That might seem like I was looking for the sensational interview, but I think what I got mostly was the people who were good describers. The thing that worried me when I was reading the Peoples of Connecticut interviews was that I was getting too rosy a view of immigration, maybe too much consensus and not enough conflict. Then when I started reading the WPA interviews, I was afraid that I was getting too much conflict and not enough consensus. So I hope we got a balance between the two of them. I think if you would ask me what was the biggest surprise I got, it was the conflict between generations, between parents and children. I came to the conclusion that it was probably stronger than I had realized, that there were often hard feelings between parents and children.

STAVE

Why would you see this as a surprise?

SALERNO

Maybe it's part of my own personal background, growing up in a close-knit Italian family. I always thought that within immigrant families the parents and the children were closer. Reading the interviews, I got the idea that the battleground was much larger between children wanting to adapt to American ways and their parents, in a sense, wanting them to hold on to traditions. Maybe in my own case now I'll have to look at my own family and ask, was there more conflict than I was willing to look at?

SUTHERLAND

That came through very clearly in the decision to immigrate. While there were mothers and fathers who encouraged and helped their children, in other cases families broke up. There was one interviewee who just left and said, in effect, "I decided I was going to be done with them all. They didn't understand or want me to leave. That's their problem, not mine." The whole village turned against one interviewee, practically, before he departed. So, yes, as you pointed out, there is a good deal of conflict in this book and it modifies the typical onward-and-upward success story, as you said before.

STAVE

And I think, just as Al has tried to empathize and to relate it to his own experience, we hope our readers would judge their own lives in terms of some of the things that they're reading about. As Franklin Roosevelt, talking to the Daughters of the American Revolution, once suggested, "We are all immigrants." All Americans who are not Native Americans trace their roots back to immigrants. It's our hope that this book will allow them to make some comparison and to have a better understanding of their own life and relationships.

Notes and References

Introduction

1. Studs Terkel, *Hard Times: An Oral History of the Great Depression* (New York: Pantheon Books, 1970), 3. For a review of the book, which considers memory and oral history, see Michael Frisch, "Oral History and Hard Times, A Review Essay," in *Red Buffalo: A Journal of American Studies* 1:2–3 (1972), 217–231, reprinted in Frisch, *A Shared Authority: Essays on the Craft and Meaning of Oral and Public History* (Albany, N.Y.: SUNY Press, 1990), 5–13.

2. Roger Daniels, *Coming to America: A History of Immigration and Ethnicity in American Life* (New York: HarperCollins Publishers, 1990), 122–123; Maldwyn Allen Jones, *American Immigration* (Chicago: University of Chicago Press, 1960), 179; Philip Taylor, *The Distant Magnet: European Emigration to the U.S.A.* (New York: Harper Torchbooks, 1971), 48.

3. See John Bodnar, *The Transplanted: A History of Immigrants in Urban America* (Bloomington, Ind.: Indiana University Press, 1985), passim.

4. Immigration for 1991 from graphic in *Willimantic* (Connecticut) *Chronicle*, 2 September 1992, based upon Immigration and Naturalization Service figures.

5. For an excellent description and evaluation of the WPA project, see Laura Anker, "Immigrant Voices from the Federal Writers Project: The Connecticut Ethnic Survey, 1937–1940," in James Gilbert et al., *The Mythmaking Frame of Mind* (Belmont, Calif.: Wadsworth Publishers, 1993), 270–302, which came to our attention after the writing of this manuscript. Anker is particularly perceptive on the role of immigrant women. For a study that also employs WPA interviews, see David Steven Cohen, ed., *America, the Dream of My Life: Selections from the Federal Writers Project's New Jersey Ethnic Survey* (New Brunswick, N.J.: Rutgers University Press, 1990). Our volume differs not only in organization but in the longer temporal span provided by the inclusion of oral history material generated during the past two decades from collections at the University of Connecticut Center for Oral History and the Institute of Local History at Manchester Community-Technical College.

6. For the public opinion poll on Italian-Americans, see John W. Jeffries, *Testing The Roosevelt Coalition: Connecticut Society and Politics in the Era of World War II* (Knoxville, Tenn.: University of Tennessee Press, 1979), 62.

7. Interview with Mr. H. by Elizabeth M. Buckingham, 16 October 1939, WPA Box 22, 109:12.

8. Interview with Stanley Dalkowski, 13 September 1991, by Bruce M. Stave. Ironically, in light of the substance under discussion, this interview was not tape-recorded but was done over the telephone. Mr. Dalkowski was not available for an oral history interview.

9. Interview with William Bradley by William J. Becker, 1 February 1940, WPA Box 22, 109:12. Interview with Leo Armstrong by P. K. Russo, 24 January 1940, WPA 22, 109:12.

10. Interview with Michael Califi by Emil A. Napolitano, 30 January 1940, WPA Box 23, 109:13.

11. *Ibid.*

12. Instructions to Field Workers for Obtaining Life History Data; Ethnic Groups in Connecticut: A Study of Their Adjustment and Acculturation—Plan of Study; Connecticut's Racial Groups and Their Characteristics: A Guide for the Collecting of Data; the quotation can be found in Report of Conference Held September 12, 1939, dated 13 September 1939, p. 2 in Report on Progress of Work on the Study, 7 December 1939. All typescripts in WPA Box 30. A significant value of the project rests in the fact that whenever possible, Koenig sought interviewers of the same immigrant and working-class background as the interviewees. Many of them, however, had struggled to become the first college graduates in their families, only to enter the world of unemployment. For a detailed discussion of this as well as the background, goals, and methodology of the project, see Anker, 272–282.

13. See Anker, 286, 290. Her tabulations indicate that 78 percent of the immigrants interviewed by the Connecticut WPA received job assistance from kinfolk or friends. Eighty-four percent found temporary housing with them.

Chapter 1

1. Victor R. Greene, *The Slavic Community on Strike: Immigrant Labor in Pennsylvania Anthracite* (Notre Dame: University of Notre Dame Press, 1968), 24.

2. Interview with Lucy Addy Richardson by John F. Sutherland, 5 June 1980, Manchester Community College, Institute of Local History.

3. John Bodnar, *The Transplanted: A History of Immigrants in Urban America* (Bloomington: Indiana University Press, 1985), Ch. 1; Philip Taylor, *The Distant Magnet: European Emigration to the U.S.A.* (New York: Harper & Row, 1971), 1–57; Greene, *The Slavic Community*, 25–27; Thomas Kessner, *The Golden Door: Italian and Jewish Immigrant Mobility in New York City, 1880–1915* (New York: Oxford University Press, 1977), 15; Kerby A. Miller, *Emigrants and Exiles: Ireland and the Irish Exodus to North America* (New York: Oxford University Press, 1985), 361–412 (see especially p. 363).

4. Bodnar, *The Transplanted*, 13.

5. *Ibid.*, 13–23; Taylor, *Distant Magnet*, 97–104.

258

6. Interview with Ignazio Ottone by John F. Sutherland, 20 July 1978, Manchester Community College, Institute of Local History.

7. Interview with Nathan Nussenbaum by Frank Nolan, 27 March 1940, WPA Box 24, 109:14.

8. Bodnar, *The Transplanted*, 38–39.

9. Interview with Anthony Tapogna by Holly Izard, 22 March 1975, Peoples of Connecticut Project.

10. For a discussion of the Polish despair at the prospect of becoming a landless peasant, see Greene, *The Slavic Community*, 17–32.

11. Interview with Mr. Michaelewski by Vincent Frazzetta, 4 January 1940, WPA Box 25, 109:19, Polish Study Series.

12. Interview with Nicholas V. by Vincent Frazzetta, 20 March 1940, WPA Box 25, 109:19, Polish Study Series.

13. Interview with John E. Heyke by Mary Bishop, 8 February 1938, WPA Box 91, 196:3.

14. Interview with Nils G. Sahlin by Mary Bishop, 2 May 1939, WPA Box 91, 196:3.

15. Interview with John Lukasavicius by Albert S. Kayeski, 13 November 1939, WPA Box 64, 158:1.

16. Interview with unidentified male Lithuanian by Margaret Brazel Brearton, 24 July 1939, WPA Box 64, 158:2.

17. Interview with Michael Daunis by Albert S. Kayeski, 24 November 1939, WPA Box 64, 158:1.

18. Interview with W. S. (male) by Rahel Mittelstein, 8 December 1939, WPA Box 92, 202:2.

19. Interview with Walter Mrozowski by Frank E. Nolen, 23 January 1940, WPA Box 25, 109:19.

Chapter 2

1. Philip A. Taylor, *The Distant Magnet: European Emigration to the U.S.A.* (New York: Harper & Row, 1971), 145–66; Alan M. Kraut, *The Huddled Masses: The Immigrant in American Society, 1880–1921* (Arlington Heights, Ill.: Harlan Davidson, 1982), 42–63; Roger Daniels, *Coming to America: A History of Immigration and Ethnicity in American Life* (New York: HarperCollins, 1990), 185–87; Thomas J. Schlereth, *Victorian America: Transformation in Everyday Life* (New York: HarperCollins, 1991), 10–11.

2. Interview with Anthony Tapogna by Holly Izard, 22 March 1975, Peoples of Connecticut Project.

3. The foregoing discussion is derived from Taylor, *The Distant Magnet*, 150–166, and Kraut, *The Huddled Masses*, 48–51.

4. Interview with Walter Mrozowski by Frank Nolan, 23 January 1940, WPA Box 25, 109:19, Polish Study Series.

5. Interview with Mary Strokonos by Margaret Brazel Bremarton, 12 May 1939, WPA Box 64, 158:2.

6. Interview with Nathan Nussenbaum by Frank Nolan, 27 March 1940, WPA Box 24, 109:14.

7. Interview with unidentified Scotch immigrant by William J. Mullane, 27 March 1940, WPA Box 26, 209:21.

8. Interview with Antonio Almeida by Andrew F. Clark, 7 February 1939, WPA Box 88, 188:2.

9. Interview with Liberato Dattolo by Vincent Frazzetta, 26 August 1939, WPA Box 23, 109:13B.

10. Interview with John Lukasavicius by Albert Kayeski, 13 November 1939, WPA Box 64, 158:1.

11. Interview with John Larson by Mary Bishop, 1 June 1938, WPA Box 91, 196:3.

12. Interview with Charles Smirnoff by Jayson Kohn, sometime in 1939 (approx.), WPA 62, 157:3.

13. Interview with unidentified Polish immigrant by Henry Coles, 1 October 1937, WPA Box 85, 187:5.

14. Interview with Morris Shapiro by Morton Tonken, 4 January 1938, WPA Box 161, 157:1C.

15. Interview with Andrew Kokas by Albert Kayeski, 19 January 1940, WPA Box 64, 158:1.

16. Interview with Harry Selmquist by Mary Bishop, 27 April 1939, WPA Box 93, 196:3.

17. Interview with Arthur Carlson by Mary Bishop, 27 April 1939, WPA Box 93, 196:3.

18. Interview with Michael Daunis by Albert Kayeski, 24 November 1939, WPA Box 64, 158:1.

19. Interview with Maxwell Lear by Matthew Magda, 14 October 1974, Peoples of Connecticut Project.

20. Interview with Anthony Ausanka by Albert S. Kayeski, 1 November 1939, WPA Box 64, 158:1.

21. Interview with Nils G. Sahlin by Mary Bishop, 3 May 1939, WPA Box 91, 196:3.

22. Interview with Morris Kavitsky by Morton Tonken, 31 January 1939, WPA.

Chapter 3

1. U.S. Bureau of the Census, *The Statistical History of the United States from Colonial Times to the Present* (New York: Basic Books, 1976), 684.

2. *Ibid.*, 666; Alfred D. Chandler, Jr., *The Visible Hand: The Managerial Revolution in American Business* (Cambridge: Harvard University Press, 1977), 240–49, 257, 266, 269–72.

3. The Cheney study and Adams quotation are from John F. Sutherland, "Of Mills and Memories: Labor-Management Interdependence in the Cheney Silk Mills," *Oral History Review* 11 (1983), 33. For several other studies, see John Bodnar, *The Transplanted: A History of Immigrants in Urban America* (Bloomington, Ind.: Indiana University Press, 1985), ch. 2. Laura Anker substantiates this conclusion in "Immigrant Voices from the Federal Writers Project: The Connecticut Ethnic Survey, 1937–1940" in James Gilbert et al., *The Mythmaking Frame of Mind* (Belmont, Calif.: Wadsworth Publishers, 1993), 286.

4. A specific study of immigrant unionization is Victor R. Greene, *The Slavic Community on Strike: Immigrant Labor in Pennsylvania Anthracite* (Notre Dame: University of Notre Dame Press, 1968). For other examples, see Bodnar, *The Transplanted*, ch. 3; Alan M. Kraut, *The Huddled Masses: The Immigrant in American Society, 1880–1921* (Arlington Heights, Ill.: Harlan Davidson, 1982), 74–95.

5. Ronald H. Bayor, *Neighbors in Conflict: The Irish, Germans, Jews, and Italians of New York City, 1929–1941* (Baltimore: Johns Hopkins University Press, 1978), 8–29.

6. Interview with Arnold Kleinschmidt by Bruce M. Stave, 23 October 1981, Connecticut Workers' Project.

7. Interview with John Kluck by Richard C. Tyo, 30 November 1980, Manchester Community College, Institute of Local History Project.

8. Interview with John Adams by Christine Schneider, 25 March 1979, Manchester Community College, Institute of Local History Project.

9. Interview with Ignazio Ottone by John F. Sutherland, 20 July 1978, Manchester Community College, Institute of Local History Project.

10. Interview with Michael Califi by Emil Napolitano, 30 January 1940, WPA Box 23, 109:13.

11. Interview with John Lukasavicius, 13 November 1939, WPA Box 64, 158:1.

12. Interview with Liberato Dattolo by Andrew F. Clark, 7 February 1939, WPA Box 88, 188:2.

13. Interview with Lucy Addy Richardson by John F. Sutherland, 5 June 1980, Manchester Community College, Institute of Local History Project.

14. Interview with Louise Gaggianesi by John F. Sutherland, 29 July 1976, Manchester Community College, Institute of Local History Project.

15. Interview with C. Guerra by Vincent Frazzetta, 16 August 1940, WPA Box 23, 109:13C.

16. Interview with Mr. Havanich by Vincent Frazzetta, 1 October 1940, WPA Box 18, 109:5a.

17. Interview with Michael Bilger by Robert Asher, 11 August 1981, Connecticut Workers' Project.

18. Interview with Lucy Addy Richardson by John F. Sutherland, 5 June 1980, Manchester Community College, Institute of Local History Project.

19. Interview with Mrs. S. by Elizabeth M. Buckingham, 22 March 1940, WPA Box 19, 109:7.

20. Interview with Frank Stamler by John F. Sutherland, 6 August 1984, Manchester Community College, Institute of Local History Project.

21. Interview with Michael Steinberg by Rosemary Talmage Nardi, 7 July 1975, Peoples of Connecticut Project.

22. Interview with Sando Bologna by Leonore Cavellero, 11 January 1975, Peoples of Connecticut Project.

23. Interview with Anthony Tapogna by Holly Izard, 22 March 1975, Peoples of Connecticut Project.

24. Interview with Mr. H. S. by William J. Burke, 20 March 1940, WPA Box 25, 109:19.

25. Interview with Miss Y. by M. G. Sayors and P. K. Russo, 13 March 1939, WPA Box 26, 109:21.

26. Interview with B. C. by M. G. Sayors, 11 September 1939, WPA Box 89, 195:1.

27. Interview with Maltilda B. by M. G. Sayors, 11 September 1939, WPA Box 89, 195:1.

Chapter 4

1. Oscar Handlin, *The Uprooted* (New York: Grosset & Dunlap, 1951), 227–229.

2. John Bodnar, *The Transplanted: A History of Immigrants in Urban America* (Bloomington, Ind.: Indiana University Press, 1985), 39, 83–84. For other examples see Virginia Yans-McLaughlin, *Family and Community: Italian Immigrants in Buffalo, 1880–1930* (Urbana, Ill.: University of Illinois Press, 1982) and Tamara K. Hareven, *Family Time and Industrial Time* (Cambridge, England: Cambridge University Press, 1982).

3. Interview with Sando Bologna by Lenore Cavallero, 11 January 1975, Peoples of Connecticut Project.

4. Interview with unidentified Italian construction worker by Vincent Frazzetta, 15 November 1939, WPA Box 22, 109:13a, Assimilation and Acculturation Series, 29.

5. Interview with Mr. Gerino by Vincent Frazzetta, 15 November 1939, WPA Box 22, 109:13a, Assimilation and Acculturation Series, 49.

6. Interview with Paul Goodwin by Holly Izard, 11 April 1975, Peoples of Connecticut Project.

7. Interview with Mr. Dugas by Vincent Frazzetta, 5 July 1939, WPA Box 18,

109:5a. Material in brackets results from available copy of interview not being clear; inserts were made to preserve continuity of the passage.

8. Interview with Mr. P. by William Spelman, 12 January 1940, WPA Box 20, 109:8b.

9. Interview with Joseph Lazzaro by Vincent Frazzetta, 14 February 1939, WPA Box 22, 109:13a.

10. Interview with unidentified Polish female by Henry Coles, 1 October 1937, WPA Box 85, 187:5. Part of this excerpt also was used in chapter 2; see note 13.

11. Interview with unidentified Italian-American by Catherine Metcalfe, 10 October 1939, WPA Box 57, 156:4.

12. Interview with Mr. D. by Frank Nolan, 3 January 1940, WPA Box 57, 156:5a.

13. Interview with Louis Goodwin by Holly Izard, 11 April 1975, Peoples of Connecticut Project.

14. Interview with Ernie Demao by Jack Goldring, 14 July 1987, Connecticut Communists Project.

15. Interview with Gennaro J. Capobianco by Leonore Cavallero, 15 January 1974, Peoples of Connecticut Project.

16. Interview with unidentified Italian-American woman by Vincent Frazzetta, 15 November 1939, WPA Box 22, 109:13a, Assimilation and Acculturation Series, 18–19.

17. Interview with Louis Goodwin by Holly Izard, 11 April 1975, Peoples of Connecticut Project.

18. Interview with Sando Bologna by Lenore Cavallero, 11 January 1975, Peoples of Connecticut Project.

19. Interview with Mr. Dugas by Vincent Frazzetta, 5 July 1939, WPA Box 18, 109:5a.

20. Interview with Mrs. R. by Vincent Frazzetta, 2 April 1940, WPA Box 25, 109:19, Polish Study Series, 109–111.

21. Interview with Mrs. W. by William J. Smallwood, 6 March 1940, WPA Box 22, 109:12.

22. Interview with Martin Brown by J. P. Driscoll, 12 January 1939, WPA Box 22, 109:12.

23. Interview with Joseph Dulka by Matthew Magda, 30 November 1974, Peoples of Connecticut Project.

24. Interview with Gennaro J. Capobianco by Lenore Cavallero, 11 January 1975, Peoples of Connecticut Project.

25. Interview with Reverend Theophil Mierzwinski by Matthew Magda, 15 January 1975, Peoples of Connecticut Project.

26. Interview with Monsignor John P. Wodarski by Matthew Magda, 29 January 1975, Peoples of Connecticut Project.

27. Interview with Mrs. R. by Vincent Frazzetta, 2 April 1940, WPA Box 25, 109:19, Polish Study Series, 112.

28. Interview with Henry Oleski by Vincent Frazzetta, 20 March 1940, WPA Box 25, 109:19, Polish Study Series, 98–100.

29. Interview with Nicholas V. by Vincent Frazzetta, 20 March 1940, WPA Box 25, 109:19, Polish Study Series, 16–19.

30. Interview with Mr. X. by P. K. Russo, (n.d.) 1940, WPA Box 25, 109:19.

31. Interview with Nathan Nussenbaum by Frank Nolan, 27 March 1940, WPA Box 24, 109:14.

32. Interview with William Bradley by William Becker, 1 February 1940, WPA Box 22, 109:19.

33. Interview with Andrew Porylo by Rahel Mittelstien, 23 June 1940, WPA Box 92, 202:2.

34. Interview with Emma Reale by Doris Matsen, n.d. but probably Fall 1939, WPA Box 57, 156:4.

35. Interview with John Capozzi by Emil Napolitano, 7 December 1939, WPA Box 23, 109:13b.

36. Interview with unidentified Italian immigrant by Vincent Frazzetta, 15 November 1939, WPA Box 22, 109:13a, Acculturation and Assimilation Series, 57–58.

37. Interview with Joseph Gursky by Vincent Frazzetta, 12 March 1940, WPA Box 25, 109:19, Polish Studies Series, 88–89.

38. Interview with Henry Masch by Frank Nolan, 28 February 1940, WPA Box 24, 109:14.

39. Interview with Ralph Pascale by Rosemary T. Nardi, 27 July 1975, Peoples of Connecticut Project.

40. Interview with Louis Goodwin by Holly Izard, 11 April 1975, Peoples of Connecticut Project.

Chapter 5

1. *Historical Statistics of the United States: Colonial Times to 1970. Part I* (U.S. Department of Commerce: Bureau of the Census, Washington, D.C., 1975), Series D 49–62, 133.1.

2. Roger Biles, *A New Deal for the American People.* (DeKalb, Ill., 1991), ch. 10, especially 194, 202–203.

3. Sydney Stahl Weinberg, *The World of Our Mothers: The Lives of Jewish Immigrant Women* (Chapel Hill, N.C.: University of North Carolina Press, 1988), 133. The complex relationships between men and women as revealed in the Connecticut WPA project are also explored in Laura Anker, "Immigrant Voices from the Federal Writers Project: The Connecticut Ethnic Survey, 1937–1940" in James Gilbert et al.,

The Mythmaking Frame of Mind (Belmont, Calif.: Wadsworth Publishers, 1993), 270–302.

4. Interview with 68-year-old Italian housewife by Vincent Frazzetta, 15 November 1939, WPA Box 22, 109:13a.

5. Interview with unidentified interviewee by Vincent Frazzetta, 15 November 1939, WPA Box 22, 109:13a.

6. Interview with Joseph Lazzaro by Vincent Frazzetta, 14 February 1939, pp. 7–10, WPA Box 22, 109:13a.

7. Interview with John Burns by John P. Driscoll, 19 March 1940, WPA Box 22, 109:12.

8. Interview with Mr. P. S., of 85 Fifth Street, Bridgeport, by M. Finnell, 16 November 1939, WPA Box 22, 109:12.

9. Interview with Mr. M. by Elizabeth M. Buckingham, 30 October 1939, WPA Box 22, 109:12.

10. Interview with Mr. R., of Bassick Avenue, Bridgeport, by M. Finnell, 1 December 1939, WPA Box 22, 109:12.

11. Interview with Mr. J. Hayes by Elizabeth M. Buckingham, 20 November 1939, WPA Box 22, 109:12.

12. Interview with Nancy M. by Elizabeth M. Buckingham, 31 October 1939, WPA Box 22, 109:12.

13. Interview with Mr. D. by Elizabeth Buckingham, 26 October 1939, WPA Box 22, 109:12.

14. Interview with Sean Ginty by Elizabeth Buckingham, 16 November 1939, WPA Box 22, 109:12.

15. Interview with Louis Goodwin by Holly Izard, 11 April 1975, Peoples of Connecticut Project.

16. Interview with Teresa Falcigno by Holly Izard, 20 March 1975, Peoples of Connecticut Project.

17. Interview with Andrew Porylo by Rahel Mittelstein, 23 June 1939, WPA Box 92, 202:2.

18. Interview with Marie Esposito by William J. Becker, 16 February 1940, WPA Box 22, 109:13a.

19. Interview with Mrs. M. by Vincent Frazzetta, 13 February 1940, WPA Box 25, 109:19.

20. Interview with Mr. M. by Vincent Frazzetta, 12 December 1940, WPA Box 25, 109:19. Because of the nature of the subject matter, Mr. and Mrs. M. will be kept anonymous, although they are identified in the WPA collection. To avoid confusion with the previous interview, they are identified as Mr. and Mrs. N.

21. Interview with Mrs. M. by Vincent Frazzetta, 12 December 1939, WPA Box 25, 109:19.

22. Interview with Mrs. S. by Vincent Frazzetta, 4 February 1941, transcribed 11 February 1941, WPA Box 26, 109:22, Swede Interview No. 3, pp. 1–81/2.

23. Interview with Ernest Demao by Jack Goldring, 14 July 1987, Connecticut Communists Project.

24. Interview with Mrs. W., of Park Avenue, Bridgeport, by William J. Smallwood, 19 March 1940, WPA Box 22, 109:12.

25. Interview with Eva Hudak by Matthew Magda, 12 April 1975, Peoples of Connecticut Project.

Chapter 6

1. Definitions of nativism, xenophobia, and racism from *Webster's Seventh New Collegiate Dictionary* (Springfield, Mass.: G. & C. Merriam Company, 1963).

2. Roger Daniels, *Coming to America: A History of Immigration and Ethnicity in American Life* (New York: HarperCollins Publishers, 1990), 109 and *passim*. Also see Alan M. Kraut, *The Huddled Masses: The Immigrant in American Society, 1880–1921* (Arlington Heights, Ill.: Harlan Davidson, 1982), ch. 5.

3. *Ibid.*; *The Kiplinger Washington Letter*, 27 December 1991; *The New Yorker*, 8 June 1992.

4. David S. Wyman, *The Abandonment of the Jews: America and the Holocaust, 1941–1945* (New York: Pantheon Books, 1984), 9.

5. Studs Terkel, *Race: How Blacks and Whites Think and Feel About the American Obsession* (New York: The New Press, 1992).

6. Interview with Louis Gerson by Dana Klein, 24 February 1982, Holocaust Survivors Project, 18–19.

7. Interview with Adeline Capucci by William D'Antonio, part of a group interview, 18 January 1975, Peoples of Connecticut Project.

8. Interview with anonymous Scotsman by William J. Mullane, n.d., edited 27 March 1940, WPA Box 26, 109:21.

9. Interview with Gennaro J. Capobianco by Leonore Cavallero, 15 January 1974, Peoples of Connecticut Project.

10. Interview with Carl Malmberg by Holly Izard, 4 May 1975, Peoples of Connecticut Project.

11. Interview with Alexander Karlonas by Albert S. Kayeski, 11 December 1939, WPA Box 64, 158:1.

12. Interview with Maxwell Lear by Matthew Magda, 14 October 1974, Peoples of Connecticut Project, 36–37.

13. Interview with Mr. M. by Elizabeth M. Buckingham, 30 October 1939, WPA Box 22, 109:12.

14. Interview with Edmond J. G. by M. V. Rourke, 3 June 1939, WPA Box 22, 109:12.

15. Interview with Emma Reale by Doris Matsen, n.d. but probably fall 1939, WPA Box 57, 156:4.

16. Interview with Mrs. G. by Elizabeth Buckingham, 6 October 1939, WPA Box 22, 109:12.

17. Interview with Harold H. by Francis Donovan, n.d. but probably December 1939, WPA Box 92, 210:5.

18. Interview with Mrs. O. by Elizabeth Buckingham, n.d. but probably 1939, WPA Box 22, 109:12.

19. Interview with Sean Ginty by Elizabeth Buckingham, 16 November 1939, WPA Box 22, 109:12.

20. Interview with Mr. Hayes by Elizbeth Buckingham, 20 November 1939, WPA 22, 109:12.

21. Interview with Mrs. Murphy, of Jones Avenue, Bridgeport, by Elizabeth Buckingham, 4 December 1939, WPA Box 22, 109:12.

22. Interview with John Burns by John P. Driscoll, edited 19 March 1940, WPA Box 22, 109:12.

23. Interview with Housewife #2 by Vincent Frazzetta, 15 November 1939, WPA Box 22, 109:13a.

24. Interview with Mr. Paumi by Vincent Frazzetta, 15 November 1939, WPA Box 22, 109:13a.

25. Interview with Mrs. John Schread by M. V. Rourke, received 31 December 1939, WPA Box 22, 109:12.

26. Interview with George (no last name) by M. V. Rourke, 7 April 1939, WPA Box 22, 109:12.

27. Interview with James Osochowsky by R. Mittelstein, 22 June 1939, WPA Box 92, 202:2. Quote taken from paper "Miscellaneous Ukrainians of New Haven," 6–7.

28. Interview with Frank Kovalauskas by Albert S. Kayeski, 13 November 1939, WPA Box 64, 158:1.

29. Interview with Monsignor John P. Wodarski by Matthew Magda, 29 January 1975, Peoples of Connecticut Project.

30. Interview with Joseph Gursky by Vincent Frazzetta, 12 March 1940, WPA Box 25, 109:19, Polish Study, 89–90.

31. Interview with Martin Brown by John P. Driscoll, 12 January 1939, WPA Box 22, 109:12.

32. Interview with Mary Knott by M. V. Rourke, 1 June 1939, WPA Box 22, 109:12.

33. Interview with Mr. D. by Henry R. Coles, 28 September 1939, WPA Box 89, 195:1.

34. Interview with William Winter by Edward Reich, 8 June 1939, WPA Box 24, 109:14.

35. Interview with John Havas by unidentified interviewer, n.d., WPA Box 24, 109:16.

36. Interview with Stephen Kovath by unidentified interviewer, n.d., WPA Box 24, 109:16.

37. Interview with Murray Braverman by Morton Tonken, 4 March 1938, WPA Box 61, 157:1c. The Jews of Hartford, Second Generation, Informant #IV.

38. Interview with unidentified Jewish housewife, Informant #10, by Rahel Mittelstein, n.d., 1939, WPA Box 62, 157:3.

39. Interview with Mr. N. by Marjorie Earle, 3 March 1940, WPA Box 93, 210:6B.

40. Interview with Louis Sachs by Matthew Magda, 25 October 1974, Peoples of Connecticut Project.

41. Interview with Mr. K. by Marjorie Earle, 27 March 1940, WPA Box 93, 210:6B.

42. Interview with Miss K. by Marjorie Earle, 2 April 1940, WPA Box 93, 210:6B.

43. Interview with Calvin R. by Marjorie Earle, 15 July 1940, WPA Box 93, 210:6B.

44. Interview with Dr. S. by Marjorie Earle, 26 February 1940, WPA Box 93, 210:66.

45. Interview with C. W. by Marjorie Earle, 30 July 1940, WPA Box 93, 210:66.

46. Interview with R. W. by Marjorie Earle, 5 August 1940, WPA Box 93, 210:66.

47. Interview with Grenville Griswold by John Kilgore, 10 July 1940, WPA Box 93, 210:6A.

48. Interview with Liberato Dattolo by Vincent Frazetta, 26 August 1939, WPA Box 23, 109:13B.

49. Interview with Edna Mary Purtell by Carole Nichols, 18 June and 8 July 1980, Political Activities of Fully Enfranchised Connecticut Women Project.

50. Interview with William Winter by Edward Reich, 18 June 1939, WPA Box 24, 109:14.

51. Interview with unidentified third-generation Irish saloonkeeper by George Fisher, 22 June 1939, WPA Box 25, 109:17.

52. Interview with Clyde Trudeau by Jack Goldring, 30 April 1987, Connecticut Communists Project.

53. Interview with Michael Califi by Emil Napolitano, n.d. 1940, WPA Box 23, 109:13B.

54. Interview with Mr. Dugas by Vincent Frazzetta, 5 July 1939, WPA Box 18, 109:5a.

55. Interview with Gennaro J. Capobianco by Leonore Cavallero, 15 January 1974, Peoples of Connecticut Project.

56. Interview with Joseph Dulka by Matthew Magda, 30 November 1974, Peoples of Connecticut Project.

57. Interview with Mrs. E. by Rhoda Cameron, 28 April 1939, WPA Box 89, 195:1.

58. Interview with Anthony Tapogna by Holly Izard, 22 March 1975, Peoples of Connecticut Project.

Bibliography

Manuscript Collections

Connecticut Works Progress Administration Ethnic Group Survey—Historical Manuscripts and Archives, The University of Connecticut Homer Babbidge Library

The box listing is offered as a guide to readers and researchers. Not all the WPA boxes were used for this study; asterisks indicate those that were cited.

Box 18
*Folder   109:5A Czechoslovaks in Bridgeport
Box 19
 Folder   109:6B Yankees and British-American Interviews
 Folder   109:7 French-Canadians in Bridgeport
Box 20
*Folder   109:8B, C, and D Germans in Bridgeport
Box 21
 Folder   109:9 Greeks in Bridgeport
 Folder   109:11 Hungarians in Bridgeport
Box 22
*Folder   109:12 Irish in Bridgeport
*Folder   109:13A Italians in Bridgeport
Box 23
*Folders 109:13A, B, and C Italians in Bridgeport
Box 24
*Folder   109:14 Jews in Bridgeport
*Folder   109:16 Magyar Hungarians and Hungarians in Norwalk (Bridgeport District)
Box 25
*Folder   109:17 Negroes in Bridgeport
*Folder   109:19 Polish in Bridgeport
Box 26
 Folder   109:20 Russians in Bridgeport and Stratford
*Folder   109:21 Scotch in Bridgeport
*Folder   109:22 Swedish in Bridgeport

Box 44
Folder 145:1 Germans in New Britain
Box 57
Folder 156:3 Italians in Hartford
*Folder 156:4 Italians in New Britain
Box 61
*Folder 157:1C and E Jews in Hartford
Box 62
Folder 157:2 Jews in New Britain
*Folder 157:3 Jews in New Haven
Box 64
*Folder 158:1 Lithuanians in New Britain
Folder 158:2 Lithuanians in Waterbury
Box 85
Folder 187:3 Polish in New Haven
Folder 187:4 Polish in Stamford
Box 87
Folder 187:7B Polish in New Britain
Box 88
*Folder 188:2 Portuguese in Hartford
Folder 190 Russians in Hartford
Box 89
*Folder 195 Stamford: Racial Element Survey
Box 90
Folder 196:1A Swedish in Hartford
Box 91
*Folder 196:3 Swedish in New Haven
Box 92
Folder 202:1 Ukrainians in New Britain
*Folder 202:2 Ukrainians in New Haven
*Folder 210:5 Yankees of Thomaston
Box 93
*Folder 210:6A and B Yankees in New Haven

Oral History Collections

Connecticut Communists Project, The University of Connecticut Center for Oral History

Connecticut Workers Project, The University of Connecticut Center for Oral History

Holocaust Survivors Project, The University of Connecticut Center for Oral History

Institute of Local History Project, Manchester (Connecticut) Community-Technical College

Peoples of Connecticut Project, The University of Connecticut Center for Oral History

Political Activities of Fully Enfranchised Connecticut Women Project, University of Connecticut Center for Oral History

Secondary Sources

While not all of these works have been cited in this study, the list represents the scholarship that has influenced our thinking on immigration. Asterisks indicate those books that have been cited.

Altschuler, Glenn C. *Race, Ethnicity, and Class in American Social Thought, 1865–1919.* Arlington Heights, Ill., 1982.

Anker Schwartz, Laura. "Immigrant Voices from the Federal Writers Project: The Connecticut Ethnic Survey, 1947–1940," in James Gilbert et al., *The Mythmaking Frame of Mind.* Belmont, Calif., 1993.

——. "Women and Migration: Southern Italian and Eastern European Immigrant Families in Urban Connecticut," *Polish American Studies* (Winter 1988), 23–49.

——. "Immigrant Voices From Home, Work, & Community: Women and Family in the Migration Process, 1890–1938." Ph.D. Dissertation, Department of History, State University of New York at Stony Brook," 1983.

Archdeacon, Thomas. *Becoming American: An Ethnic History.* New York, 1983.

Asher, Robert. *Connecticut Workers and Technological Change.* Storrs, Conn., 1983.

Banks, Ann. *First Person America.* New York, 1980.

Baum, Willa K. *Oral History for the Local Historical Society.* Nashville, Tenn., 1987.

*Bayor, Ronald. H. *Neighbors in Conflict: The Irish, Germans, Jews, and Italians of New York City, 1929–1941.* Baltimore, 1978.

*Biles, Roger. *A New Deal for the American People.* DeKalb, Ill., 1991.

Blewett, Mary H. *The Last Generation: Work and Life in the Textile Mills of Lowell, Massachusetts.* Amherst, Mass., 1990.

*Bodnar, John. *The Transplanted: A History of Immigrants in Urban America.* Bloomington, Ind., 1985.

——. *Workers' World.* Baltimore, 1982.

—— et al. *Lives of Their Own: Blacks, Italians, and Poles in Pittsburgh.* Urbana, Ill., 1982.

Brecher, Jeremy, et al. *Brass Valley: The Story of Working People's Lives and Struggles in an American Industrial Region.* Philadelphia, 1982.

*Chandler, Alfred D., Jr. *The Visible Hand: The Managerial Revolution in American Business.* Cambridge, 1977.

273

*Cohen, David, S., ed. *America, the Dream of My Life: Selections from the Federal Writers Project's New Jersey Ethnic Survey.* New Brunswick, N.J., 1990.

*Daniels, Roger. *Coming to America: A History of Immigration and Ethnicity in American Life.* New York, 1990.

Dinnerstein, Leonard and David M. Reimers. *Ethnic Americans: A History of Immigration and Assimilation.* New York, 1988.

Doty, C. Stewart, ed. *The First Franco-Americans: New England Life Histories from the Federal Writers' Project, 1938–1939.* Orono, Me., 1985.

Dunaway, David K. and Willa K. Baum. *Oral History: An Interdisciplinary Anthology.* Nashville, Tenn., 1984.

Fishman, Joshua, et al. *Language Loyalty in the United States.* London, England, 1966.

*Frisch, Michael. *A Shared Authority: Essays on the Craft and Meaning of Oral and Public History.* Albany, 1990.

Glazer, Nathan and Daniel P. Moynihan. *Beyond the Melting Pot.* Rev. ed. Cambridge, 1970.

*Greene, Victor R. *The Slavic Community on Strike: Immigrant Labor in Pennsylvania Anthracite.* South Bend, Ind., 1968.

Grele, Ronald. *Envelopes of Sound: The Art of Oral History.* Chicago, 1985.

Halbwachs, Maurice. *The Collective Memory.* New York, 1980.

Hall, Jacquelyn D., et al. *Like a Family.* Chapel Hill, N.C., 1987.

*Handlin, Oscar. *The Uprooted: The Epic Story of the Great Migration That Made the American People.* 2nd ed. Boston, 1973.

*Hareven, Tamara. *Family Time and Industrial Time.* Cambridge, England, 1982.

———. "The Search for Generational Memory: Tribal Rites in Industrial Society." *Daedalus* 137 (Fall 1978).

Hareven, Tamara and Randolph Langenbach. *Amoskeag: Life and Work in an American Factory City.* New York, 1978.

Higham, John. *Send These to Me: Immigrants in Urban America.* Baltimore, 1984.

———. *Strangers in the Land: Patterns of American Nativism, 1860–1925.* 2d ed. New Brunswick, N.J., 1988.

*Ibson, John Duffy. *Will the World Break Your Heart?: Dimensions and Consequences of Irish-American Assimilation.* New York, 1990.

*Jeffries, John W. *Testing the Roosevelt Coalition: Connecticut Society and Politics in the Era of World War II.* Knoxville, Tenn., 1979.

*Jones, Maldwyn, A. *American Immigration.* Chicago, 1960.

*Kessner, Thomas. *The Golden Door: Italian and Jewish Immigrant Mobility in New York City, 1880–1915.* 2nd ed. New York, 1977.

——— and Betty B. Caroli. *Today's Immigrants: Their Stories.* New York, 1981.

Koenig, Samuel. *Immigrant Settlements in Connecticut.* Hartford, 1938.

*Kraut, Alan. *The Huddled Masses: The Immigrant in American Society, 1880–1920.* Arlington Heights, Ill., 1982.

Lewin, Rhoda G., ed. *Witnesses to the Holocaust: An Oral History.* Boston, 1990.

Liptak, Dolores A. *European Immigrants and the Catholic Church in Connecticut, 1870–1920.* Staten Island, N.Y., 1987.

*Miller, Kerby A. *Emigrants and Exiles: Ireland and the Irish Exodus to North America.* New York, 1985.

Olson, James. *The Ethnic Dimension in American History.* New York, 1979.

Portelli, Alessandro. *The Death of Luigi Trastulli and Other Stories: Form and Meaning in Oral History.* Albany, 1991.

Rothchild, Sylvia. *Voices from the Holocaust.* New York, 1981.

Santoli, Al. *New Americans: An Oral History.* New York, 1990.

Schach, Paul. *Languages in Conflict.* Lincoln, Neb., 1980.

*Schlereth, Thomas J. *Victorian America: Transformation in Everyday Life.* New York, 1991.

Seller, Maxine. *To Seek America: A History of Ethnic Life in America.* Englewood, N.J., 1977.

Skolnick, Arlene. *Embattled Paradise: The American Family in an Age of Uncertainty.* New York, 1991.

Stave, Bruce M. and John F. Sutherland, eds. *Talking about Connecticut: Oral History in the Nutmeg State.* Rev. ed. Connecticut, 1990.

*Sutherland, John F. "Of Mills and Memories: Labor-Management Interdependence in the Cheney Silk Mills." *Oral History Review* 11 (1983).

*Taylor, Philip. *The Distant Magnet: European Emigration to the United States.* New York, 1971.

*Terkel, Studs. *Hard Times: An Oral History of the Great Depression.* New York, 1970.

*———. *Race: How Blacks and Whites Think and Feel About the American Obsession.* New York, 1992.

Thelen, David, ed. "Memory and American History: A Special Issue." *The Journal of American History* 75 (March 1989).

Thernstrom, Stephan, ed. *Harvard Encyclopedia of American Ethnic Groups.* Cambridge, Mass., 1980.

Thompson, Paul. *The Voice of the Past.* 2nd ed. Oxford, England, 1988.

*U.S. Bureau of the Census. *Historical Statistics of the United States: Colonial Times to 1970, Part 1.* Washington, D. C., 1975.

*U.S. Bureau of the Census. *The Statistical History of the United States from Colonial Times to the Present.* New York, 1976.

*Weinberg, Sydney S. *The World of Our Mothers: The Lives of Jewish Immigrant Women.* Chapel Hill, N.C., 1988.

Weisser, Michael R. *A Brotherhood of Memory*. Ithaca, N.Y., 1989.

*Wyman, David. S. *The Abandonment of the Jews: America and the Holocaust, 1941–1945*. New York, 1984.

*Yans-McLaughlin, Virginia. *Family and Community: Italian Immigrants in Buffalo, 1880–1930*. Urbana, Ill., 1982.

Index

Adams, John, 52, 53
African-Americans, 43, 46, 176–77,
    221–31, 233; and police brutality, 230;
    prejudice against, xv; referred to as
    "coon," 153, 223; referred to as
    "nigger," 177, 190, 198, 199, 210, 221,
    223, 225–28. *See also* Racism
Almeida, Antonio, 34
American Protective Association, 175
Anti-Catholicism, 191, 207, 215, 216
Anti-Semitism, xx, 176, 177, 186,
    196–200, 207, 213, 242; in the
    Depression, 192–93; and educated Jews,
    210, 215, 219–20; and oppression,
    217. *See also* Jewish war refugees
Apprenticeship programs, 63–64, 66, 78
Ausanka, Anthony, 47
Austria, 3
Authority, respect for, 93, 96, 97, 99, 108

B. C., 86
Bayor, Ronald H., 52
Bilger, Michael, 63
Bilingualism, 253
Bodnar, John, 2, 93; *The Transplanted*, 239
Bojnowski, Msgr. Lucian, 122–23
Bologna, Sando, 75, 94, 112
Bradley, William, 130
Braverman, Murray, 199
Bridgeport, Connecticut, 33–34, 35, 55,
    161
Brown, Martin, 118, 193
Burns, John, 142, 187

C. W., 212
Califi, Michael, xvii–xviii, 54, 225

Calvin R., 210
Capitalism, xiii, 2, 93, 197, 199; and the
    Great Depression, xv
Capobianco, Gennaro, 119
Capozzi, John, 132
Capucci, Adeline, 178
Carlson, Arthur, 44
Castle Gardens, 56
Catholics, 130, 155, 170, 183, 189, 198;
    prejudice against (*see* Anti-Catholicism);
    priests, 120–24, 131, 189, 207
Catholic, church, 120–28, 130–31, 156,
    209, 216; and divorce, 19, 130; parish
    programs, 123–24. *See also* Catholics;
    Polish National Church
Chain migration, 38
Cheney silk mills (Manchester, Conn.),
    51–54, 61, 72, 239
Child labor, 76, 102
Community. *See* Neighborhoods
Community colleges, 78
Congregational Immigrant Home, 37
Connecticut Yankees, 208, 211, 213, 214,
    215, 216, 245
Coughlin, F. Charles E., 175, 176, 193,
    202
Cousins, Norman, 139
Crane Valve Company, 55

Daniels, Roger, 175, 239
Dattolo, Liberato, 35, 58, 218
Daunis, Michael, 18, 45
Demao, Ernie, 108, 140, 172
Depression. *See* Great Depression
Discipline, of children, 94, 98, 99–107
Dr. S., 212

Drunkenness, 140, 165, 167, 168, 170, 249
Dulka, Joseph, 230

Edmond, J. G., 182
Education, xix, 77, 80, 94, 107–9, 155;
adult, 28, 64; compulsory, 47; for girls,
15, 21, 103–4, 147, 169; higher, 78,
80–81; in the homeland, 12, 15, 16,
21, 22; for immigrant children, 46, 94,
107, 176, 177–80, 181; lack of
opportunity for, 4, 5, 7, 8, 10, 20, 69; and
language problems, 177–80; parochial,
121–22, 156, 180, 181; through reading,
8, 11, 18, 151
Ellis Island, 44, 48, 102
Emergency Quota Act (1921), 176
English immigrants, 208, 211, 214, 215
Esposito, Marie, 140, 148
Ethnic clubs, 94, 118–19. See also Mutual
aid societies
Ethnic tensions, xx, 59, 176, 177, 190–93,
217–18, 232, 237; among children, 181,
199, 220, 231; and economic hardship, xx,
192–93, 245, 250–51; in marriage, 140,
167; and politics, xix, 94, 134

Factory jobs, 51–55, 56–60, 68–70, 76,
83–91, 93
Falcigno, Teresa, 146
Fall River, Massachusetts, 45
Family, 16–17, 93–109, 236, 247; abuse in,
xix, 140, 162–66, 167, 171; and Asian
immigrants, 247; breakdown, 237, 238,
249, 252; as collective economic unit,
xix, 4, 67, 68–70, 73, 76, 80, 93; Eastern
European, 99, 197–8, 114; and
employment in America, xix, 51–52, 54,
56, 58, 61, 102, 240; father as head of,
16, 19, 21, 96, 97, 140, 150; generational
differences in, xix, 93, 95, 96–108, 253,
254; Italian, 97, 101, 142, 147; Swedish,
169–70
Family businesses, 75, 79, 81, 82, 146
Family farms, 3, 4, 18, 37, 72–73, 95
Farm consolidation, 2
Food: in America, 38, 43, 44, 45, 46, 48,
58, 74, 110, 115; at the Automat, 48;
on the crossing, 39; in the homeland, 10,
12, 14, 73; regional differences in,
187–88, 200, 202

Franklin, Benjamin, 175
French-Canadians, 208, 210

Gaggianesi, Louise, 61
Galicia, 20–21
German immigrants, xiii, 53, 100–101, 183,
208, 211, 213, 215
Gerson, Louis, 177
Ginty, Sean, 145, 185
Goodwin, Louis, 146
Goodwin, Paul, 97
Great Depression, xv, 52, 135, 138, 239,
240, 244; and ethnic tensions, 192–93,
245; food relief in, 157, 223; layoffs in,
85, 156; and women's role, 139. See
also New Deal programs
Greene, Victor R., 1
Griswold, Grenville, 216
Guerra, C., 61
Gursky, Joseph, 135

H. S., 82
Handcrafts, 60–67; and technology, 61–63,
65–66, 249
Handlin, Oscar: The Uprooted, 93, 238, 239
Harold H., 184
Havas, John, 197
Hayes, J., 144
Health conditions, 49
Heyke, John E., 7
Housing: in America, 45, 48, 73, 79, 102,
111, 112, 150; discrimination in, 222,
228; in the homeland, 1, 8, 10, 12, 14,
18
Hudak, Eva, 141, 173

Ibson, John: Will the World Break Your
Heart?, 249
Immigration laws, 2, 176, 246
Intermarriage, 170, 184–87, 190, 196,
215
Ireland, 1–2, 60
Irish immigrants, xii, 117–18, 144–45, 183,
188, 203, 209, 212, 213–14, 221–24,
245–46, 249; and the Church, 130; and
intermarriage, 185–87, 190; in politics,
192, 203, 210; prejudice against,
215; referred to as "Harp," 192; referred
to as "Paddies," 189
Italy, 3–5, 62, 97, 206, 219

Italian immigrants, xiii, xv, 35, 95–97, 101, 104–7, 108–9, 178–79, 186–88, 200, 212, 217–21, 224–27; in the neighborhoods, 110–11, 112–13, 119–20; and padrone system, 52; in politics, 134, 192, 232–33; prejudice against, 188, 207, 209, 210, 213, 217, 232; referred to as "dago," 198; referred to as "Guinea," 59; referred to as "Wop," 59, 86, 153, 186, 187, 194, 199, 210; women, 141–42, 146–47, 172; and work experience, 54–55, 58–63, 75–82, 86–90

Jews, xiii, 137, 149–55, 183, 196, 197–98, 203, 204–5, 207, 210–11, 212, 215; Austrian, 3, 29–32, 128–29; communities, 112; and education, 38, 107, 186, 202; and Gentiles, 201–3, 209; and intermarriage, 140, 182, 196; Polish, 48–50, 177–78, 200; prejudice against, xv, 90, 182, 190, 219–20, (see also Anti-Semitism); and religious observance, 128–29; Russian, 38–40, 41–42, 46–47, 73–75, 97–99, 107–8, 146, 181, 200, 248, war refugees, 138, 176, 177

Karlonas, Alexander, 180
Kavitsky, Morris, 48
Kleinschmidt, Ike, 53
Kluck, John, 53
Knott, Mary, 194
Know Nothing party, 175
Koenig, Samuel, xvi, xviii
Kokas, Andres, 42
Kovalauskas, Frank, 190–91
Kovath, Stephen, 198

Labor unions, 52, 57, 69, 83–91, 158, 173
Larson, John, 36
Lateral migration, 60
Lazzaro, Joseph, 101, 142
Lear, Maxwell, 46, 181
Leisure activities, 113–15, 170–71
Letters, importance of, 5, 19–20, 71
Lithuania, 11–20, 36; farming in, 12, 18; and Russia, 19, 36
Lukasavicius, John, 11, 36, 55–56

Marriage arrangements, 19, 152
Masch, Henry, 135
Matilda B., 86, 88
Mierzwinski, F. Theophil, 120
Mining, 56, 57; and "Molly Maguires," 191
Miss K., 209–10
Miss Y., 83
Movies, 114, 142
Mr. D., 145, 194
Mr. Dugas, 99, 113
Mr. Havanich, 63
Mr. K., 206–208
Mr. M., 143, 182
Mr. Michaelewski, 5
Mr. N., 160, 161
Mr. P., 100
Mr. P. S., 143
Mr. Paumi, 188
Mr. R., 144
Mrozowski, Walter, 22, 26
Mrs. E., 231
Mrs. G., 184
Mrs. M., 140, 148, 156
Mrs. Murphy, 186
Mrs. N., 140, 161, 162
Mrs. O., 185
Mrs. R., 116
Mrs. S., 68, 140, 167, 168
Mrs. Schread, 188–90
Mrs. W., 117, 141, 172
Mussolini, Benito, 106, 219–21
Mutual aid societies, 119–20. See also Ethnic clubs

Nancy M., 144
National Organization for Women (NOW), 141, 174
National Origins Act (1924), 176
Nativism, 175–76, 177, 189, 194–95, 206–17, 237; and stereotypes, 206–17
Neighborhoods, xix, 94–138, 224; and the automobile, 114; boardinghouses in, 111; changes in, 114, 115, 117; "Little Italy" 's, 110, 112–13; mixed, 111, 113, 117, 180–84
New Deal programs, 78, 87, 136, 137
New Haven, Connecticut, 38, 45; Jewish community in, 111–12
New York, xix, 42, 49; gangs in, 150–51; Jewish immigrants in, 31–32, 39–40, 150; Lower East Side, 40, 49, 150–51

Nicholas V., 5–7
Night school. *See* Education, adult
Nineteenth Amendment, 140
Nussenbaum, Nathan, 3, 29, 128

Osochowsky, James, 190
Ottone, Ignazio, 2, 54

Padrone system, 52
Pelley, William Dudley, 176
Pennsylvania, colonial, 175
Peoples of Connecticut Project, 239–40, 243
Philadelphia, 37
Pilsudski, Joseph, 7
Poland, 5–7, 20–22, 104, 190, 200
Polish immigrants, xiii, 26–28, 40–41, 57, 102–4, 116–17, 118–19, 156–66, 192, 204, 207–8, 212; prejudice against, 206, 209, 218; referred to as "Polack," 59, 135, 156, 161, 177, 181, 185, 192, 194, 196, 210, 218, 219, 220; and work experience, 57–58, 82–83, 173–74
Polish language, 7, 126, 127
Polish National Church, 124–26, 127
Politics, xix, 94, 134–38; women in, 172–74
Porylo, Andrew, 130, 147–48
Postindustrial immigration, xiv, 246, 247
Poverty, in America, 47, 48, 136, 140, 163; in the Depression, 157, 159
Prejudice, xv, xix; wartime, 175, 176. *See also* Anti-Catholicism; Anti-Semitism; Ethnic tensions; Nativism; Racism
Primogeniture, 18
Providence, Rhode Island, as immigration center, 42
Purtell, Edna Mary, 221

R. W., 214
Racism, xx, 175, 176–77, 218, 220–21, 225, 250
Reale, Emma, 131, 183
Religion, 7, 9, 49, 120–31, 155, 192; and authority, 115; commercialism in, 129–31; and divorce, 16, 19, 21, 130; feeling against, 126–28, 130–31, 184–85; and intermarriage, 170, 184–85; and women's suffrage, 172
Richardson, Lucy, 1, 60, 68
Rodriguez, Richard, 246

Roosevelt, Franklin D., 94, 135–38, 255; death of, 136–37
Russia, 197; emigration from, xiv, 246

Sachs, Louis, 205
Sahlin, Nils G., 9, 47
Scandinavians, stereotypes of, 208, 209, 211, 213, 217. *See also* Sweden
School. *See* Education
Selmquist, Harry, 43
Shapiro, Morris, 41
Sit-down strike, 84–85
Smirnoff, Charles, 38
Socioeconomic conditions, America vs. homeland, 49–50
Sons of Italy, 119–20
Soviet Union. *See* Russia
Springfield, Massachusetts, 73–74
Stamford, Connecticut, 86
Stamler, Frank, 72
Statue of Liberty, 25, 39, 176
Steamships, 25; improvements in, 26; steerage conditions in, xix, 26, 29, 39, 44
Steinberg, Michael, 73, 94
Strokonos, Mary, 28
Superstition, 131–33
Sweden, 7, 9, 37; divorce in, 9, 11; music in, 8, 171; socioeconomic conditions in, 8, 9–10

Tapogna, Anthony, 4, 25, 78, 232
Tariff policies, 2
Terkel, Studs, 177; *Hard Times*, xiii
Trudeau, Clyde, 224
Truman, Harry, 137

Ukraine, 20–22

W. S., 20
Wales, 2, 217
Wartime prejudice, 175, 176
Waterbury, Connecticut, 112
Weinberg, Sydney Stahl, 140
Winrod, Gerald B., 176
Winter, William, 196, 197, 222
Wodarski, Msgr. John P., 121
Women, 242; in domestic service, 139, 164; in the home vs. on the job, xix, 139–40, 142, 143–48, 156, 158, 169; and

"homework," 76, 93, 139, 146; public role of, xix, 140–41, 172–74
Women's suffrage, 140, 172
Work ethic, 76, 79–80
WPA Ethnic Group Survey, xv, 239–44

Wyman, David S., 176

Xenophobia. *See* Nativism

YMCA, 119

The Authors

Bruce M. Stave is a professor of history and director of the Center for Oral History at the University of Connecticut. He has served as editor of the *Oral History Review* and is a past president of the New England Historical Association and the New England Association of Oral History, from which he was the recipient of the first Harvey Kantor Memorial Award for Significant Work in Oral History. He is the author of nine other books, the most recent being *Witnesses to Nuremberg: An Oral History of American Participants at the War Crimes Trials*. With John F. Sutherland he co-edited *Talking About Connecticut: Oral History in the Nutmeg State*. He has lectured abroad extensively and has been a Fulbright Professor in India, New Zealand, Australia, the Philippines, and the People's Republic of China. He lives with his wife, Sondra Astor Stave, in Coventry, Connecticut.

John F. Sutherland is emeritus professor of history and the former director of the Institute of Local History at Manchester Community-Technical College in Connecticut. He is a past president of the New England Association of Oral History. His articles on immigration and housing reform in Philadelphia and on labor history in Connecticut have appeared in the *Oral History Review*, the *American Jewish Historical Quarterly*, the *Pennsylvania Magazine of History and Biography*, *Connecticut History*, and in the book *The Peoples of Philadelphia*. With Bruce M. Stave he co-edited *Talking About Connecticut: Oral History in the Nutmeg State*. He lives in Vernon, Connecticut.

Aldo E. Salerno holds a doctoral degree from the University of Connecticut where he wrote his dissertation, "Defining the American Dream: The Children of Immigrants as Social Reformers, 1900–1929." A graduate of Rutgers University in Newark, he was a member of the United States Coast Guard for ten years.

UNIVERSITY PRESS OF NEW ENGLAND
publishes books under its own imprint and is the publisher for
Brandeis University Press, Dartmouth College, Middlebury College Press,
University of New Hampshire, Tufts University, and Wesleyan University Press.

Library of Congress Cataloging-in-Publication Data
Stave, Bruce M.
    From the old country : an oral history of European migration to
America / Bruce M. Stave, John F. Sutherland, with Aldo Salerno.
      p.   cm.
    Originally published: New York : Twayne, © 1994.
    Includes bibliographical references and index.
    ISBN 0–87451–908–X (alk. paper)
    1. European Americans—History. 2. Immigrants—United States—
Interviews. 3. United States—Emigration and immigration—History.
4. Europe—Emigration and immigration—History. 5. United States—
Ethnic relations. I. Sutherland, John F. (John Fulton), 1938– .
II. Salerno, Aldo. III. Title.
E184.E95S73 1999
973'.04034—dc21   98–42361